# THE SEMIOTIC CHALLENGE

# THE SEMIOTIC CHALLENGE

## Roland Barthes

TRANSLATED BY RICHARD HOWARD

UNIVERSITY OF CALIFORNIA PRESS
Berkeley · Los Angeles

University of California Press
Berkeley and Los Angeles, California

First California Paperback Printing 1994

Translation copyright © 1988 by Farrar, Straus and Giroux, Inc.
Originally published in French as *L'aventure sémiologique*
Copyright © 1985 by Éditions du Seuil
Printed in the United States of America
Designed by Mina Greenstein

"The Sequences of Actions" first published in English in *Patterns of Literary Style*, edited by Joseph Strelka, © 1971 by the Pennsylvania State University Press. "Semiology and Medicine" first published in *Les Sciences de la Folie*, edited by Roger Bastide, © 1972 by Éditions Mouton. "Wrestling with the Angel: Textual Analysis of Genesis 32.23–33" first published in *Analyse Structurale et Exégèse Biblique*, © 1972 by Labor et Fides (Geneva). "Textual Analysis of a Tale by Edgar Allen Poe" first published in *Sémiotique Narrative et Textuelle*, © 1973 by Éditions Larousse

The French edition of *L'aventure sémiologique* includes the essay "Éléments de sémiologie," published separately in English as *Elements of Semiology* by Hill and Wang

Library of Congress Cataloging-in-Publication Data

Barthes, Roland.
    [Aventure sémiologique. English]
    The semiotic challenge / Roland Barthes ; translated by Richard Howard.
      p.  cm.
    Translation of: L'aventure sémiologique.
    Originally published: New York : Hill and Wang, 1988.
    Includes bibliographical references.
    ISBN 0-520-08784-4
    1. Semiotics.  2. Discourse analysis.  I. Title.
P99.B28613  1994
302.2—dc20                             94-7124
                                            CIP

1  2  3  4  5  6  7  8  9

# Contents

---

## THREE
# ANALYSES

# THE SEMIOTIC CHALLENGE

# Introduction:
# The Semiological
# Adventure

Several days ago, a student came to see me; she wanted to prepare
a third-cycle doctorate on the following subject, which she proposed
quite ironically, though without a trace of hostility: An *Ideological
Critique of Semiology*.

I find in this little "scene" all the elements by which one might
characterize the situation of semiology and its recent history:

—first of all, the ideological, *i.e.*, political complaint so frequently made of semiology, that it is a reactionary science, or at
the very least a science indifferent to ideological commitment: was
not structuralism, too, and before structuralism the *Nouveau Roman*—right here in Italy, if memory serves—accused of being a
science in complicity with technocracy, even with Gaullism?

—then, the notion that my student's interlocutor was a *representative* of that semiology which was, precisely, to be dismantled
(in the double sense of analyzed and confounded, taken to pieces
and taken apart)—whence her touch of irony: by proposing her
subject, she was *provoking* me (I spare you the psychoanalytic interpretation of this scene);

—lastly, the intuition that, in the role of quasi-official semiologist
she was attributing to me, there subsisted a certain ambiguity, a

certain duplicity, a certain semiological *infidelity* which might rather parodically make this student's interlocutor someone who was both *in* semiology and outside it: whence the touch of camaraderie (but I may have got this wrong) which this scene so full of intellectual coquetry has left in my memory.

Before taking up the questions on which this little psychodrama was propped, I must say that I do not *represent* semiology (or structuralism): no one in the world can *represent* an idea, a belief, a method, *a fortiori* no one who *writes*, whose chosen practice is neither speech nor reportage, but writing.

Intellectual society can make of you what it likes, what it needs: this is never anything but a form of the social *game*; but I cannot experience myself as an image, the *imago* of semiology. With regard to that *imago*, I am in a double state: of availability and of evasion:

—on the one hand, I ask nothing better than to be associated with the corps of semiologists, nothing better than to reply with them to their attackers: spiritualists, vitalists, historicists, spontaneists, anti-formalists, archeo-Marxists, etc. That sentiment of solidarity comes all the more easily to me in that I experience no divisive impulse: it does not interest me to oppose, as is obligatory in splinter groups, those whom I am close to (a narcissistic pulsion well analyzed by Freud apropos of the myth of the Warring Brothers);

—but on the other hand, Semiology is not a Cause for me; it is not a science, a discipline, a school, a movement with which I identify my own person (it is already a good deal to grant it a name: in any case, for me it is a name that is constantly revocable).

Then what is Semiology for me? It is an adventure—it is what *advenes*: what comes to me from the Signifier.

This adventure—personal but not subjective, since it is precisely the subject's displacement which is staged here, and not his expression—this adventure is articulated, for me, in three moments:

1.   The first moment has been one of amazement. Language, or to be more precise, *discourse* has been the constant object of my work, since my first book, *Writing Degree Zero*. In 1956, I had

collected a kind of mythic ore of consumer society, published in Nadeau's journal *Les Lettres nouvelles*, under the name *Mythologies*; it was then that I first read Saussure; and having read Saussure, I was dazzled by this hope: to give my denunciation of the self-proclaimed petit-bourgeois myths the means of developing scientifically; this means was semiology or the close analysis of the processes of meaning by which the bourgeoisie converts its historical class-culture into universal nature; semiology appeared to me, then, in its program and its tasks, as the fundamental method of an ideological critique. I expressed this amazement and this hope in the postface to *Mythologies*, a text that may show its age scientifically, but a euphoric text, since it *reassured* intellectual commitment by giving it an instrument of analysis, and *responsibilized* the study of meaning by giving it a political range.

Semiology has evolved since 1956, its history has, in some sense, been a *runaway*; but I remain convinced that any ideological critique, if it would escape an obsessive preoccupation with its own necessity, must be semiological: to analyze semiology's ideological content, as my student sought to do the other day, could nonetheless be done only by semiological means.

2.   The second moment was that of science, or at least of scientificity. Between 1957 and 1963, I was making a semiological analysis of a crucially signifying object, the garment of Fashion; the goal of this work was quite personal, ascetic, if I may say so: to reconstitute the grammar of a known language which had not yet been analyzed; it mattered little to me that the articulation of this task risked being tedious—what counted for my pleasure was to work it out, to *operate*.

At the same time, I was trying to conceive a certain way of teaching semiology (in *Elements of Semiology*).

All around me, semiological science was being elaborated according to the origins, movement, and independence proper to each investigator (I am thinking above all of my friends and companions Greimas and Eco); certain junctures were made with the great elders, such as Jakobson and Benveniste, and younger investigators such as Bremond and Metz; an Association and a *Revue internationale de sémiologie* were created.

For me, what dominates this period of my work, I think, is less the project of instituting semiology as a science than the pleasure of exercising a *Systematics:* there is, in the activity of classification, a kind of creative intoxication known to such great classifiers as Sade and Fourier; in its scientific phase, semiology was this kind of an intoxication for me: I reconstituted, I went in—giving a lofty sense to the expression—for a *bricolage* of systems, of games; I have never written books except *for pleasure:* the pleasure of System now replaced the superego of Science: this was already a preparation for the third phase of this adventure: finally indifferent to an indifferent science (an *adiaphoric science,* as Nietzsche had said), I entered by "pleasure" into the Signifier, into the Text.

3.   The third moment is, in fact, that of the Text.

Discourses were being woven around me, which were displacing prejudices, questioning the "obvious," proposing new concepts:

Propp, discovered through Lévi-Strauss, made it possible to apply semiology with some rigor to a literary object, narrative;

Julia Kristeva, profoundly transforming the semiological landscape, gave me personally and principally the new concepts of *paragrammatism* and *intertextuality;*

Derrida vigorously displaced the very notion of sign, postulating the retreat of signifieds, the decentering of structures;

Foucault accentuated the problematics of the sign by assigning it a historical niche in the past.

Lacan gave us a complete theory of the scission of the subject, without which science is doomed to remain blind and mute as to the place from which it speaks;

*Tel Quel,* finally, initiated the attempt, unique even today, to relocate all these mutations within the Marxist field of dialectical materialism.

For me, this period is inscribed between the *Introduction to the*

*Structural Analysis of Narratives* (1966) and *S/Z* (1970), the latter work in some sense denying the former by abandoning the structural model and resorting to the practice of the infinitely different Text.

And what is the Text? I shall not answer by a definition, which would be to fall back into the signified.

The Text, in the modern, current sense which we are trying to give this word, is fundamentally to be distinguished from the literary work:

it is not an esthetic product, it is a signifying practice;

it is not a structure, it is a structuration;

it is not an object, it is a work and a game;

it is not a group of closed signs, endowed with a meaning to be rediscovered, it is a volume of traces in displacement;

the instance of the Text is not signification but the Signifier, in the semiotic and psychoanalytic acceptation of that term;

the Text exceeds the old literary work; there is, for example, a Text of Life, one I tried to enter by writing apropos of Japan.

And these three semiological experiences—hope, Science, Text—how are they present in me today?

It is said that Louis XVIII, a royal gourmet, had his chef prepare several cutlets piled one upon the other, and ate only the one on the bottom, which had received the juices trickling into it from all the others. In the same fashion, I should like the present moment of my semiological adventure to receive the juices of the earlier ones—for the sieve to be, as in the case of the royal cutlets, woven of the very substance that it strains, for the filtering medium to be the filter itself, as the signified is the signifier—so that consequently you will find in my present work the pulsions which have animated the whole past of this semiological adventure: the will to unite myself with a community of rigorous investigators, and loyalty to the tenacious alliance of the political and the semiological.

Yet I can acknowledge these two legacies today only by saying what modifications I bring to them:

—concerning the first point, the scientificity of Semiology, I no longer believe—nor do I desire—that Semiology should be a simple science, a positivist science, and this for a primordial reason: it is the responsibility of semiology, and perhaps of Semiology alone of all the human sciences today, to question its own discourse: as a science of language, of languages, it cannot accept its own language as a datum, a transparency, a tool, in short as a metalanguage; strong with the powers of psychoanalysis, it interrogates itself as to *the place from which it speaks,* an interrogation without which any science and any ideological criticism are ridiculous: for Semiology, at least so I hope, there exists no *extraterritoriality* for the subject, even if he is a scientist, with regard to his discourse; in other words, finally, science knows no site of security, and in this it must acknowledge itself as *writing;*

—concerning the second point, the ideological commitment of Semiology, I believe the stake has grown considerably larger: what Semiology must attack is not only, as in the days of *Mythologies,* the petit-bourgeois good conscience, but the symbolic and semantic system of our entire civilization; it is not enough to seek to change contents, we must above all aim at *fissuring* the meaning-system itself: we must emerge from the Occidental enclosure, as I postulated it in my text on Japan.

And in conclusion, one remark about this introduction: it is spoken by an *I.* It is understood that this first person is *imaginary* (in the psychoanalytic sense of the term): if it were not so, if sincerity were not a misapprehension, it would no longer be worthwhile writing, it would suffice to speak. Writing is precisely that space in which the persons of grammar and the origins of discourse mingle, combine, and lose each other until they are unidentifiable: writing is the truth not of the person (of the author), but of language. This is why writing always goes farther than speech. To consent to *speak* of one's writing, as has been done here, is merely to tell the other that one needs his speech.

A lecture given in Italy and reprinted in *Le Monde,* 1974

# ONE

# ELEMENTS

# The Old Rhetoric:
# an aide-mémoire

What follows is the transcription of a seminar given at the École pratique
des hautes études in 1964–1965. At the source—or on the horizon—of
this seminar, as always, there was the modern text, i.e., the text which
does not yet exist. One way to approach this new text is to find out
from what point of departure, and in opposition to what, it seeks to come
into being, and in this way to confront the new semiotics of writing with
the classical practice of literary language, which for centuries was known
as Rhetoric. Whence the notion of a seminar on the old Rhetoric: old
does not mean that there is a new Rhetoric today; rather old Rhetoric
is set in opposition to that new which may not yet have come into being:
the world is incredibly full of old Rhetoric.

  Nor would these working notes have been published if there existed a
book, a manual, a memorandum of some sort which might present a
chronological and systematic panorama of that classical Rhetoric. Unfortunately, so far as I know, there is nothing of the kind (at least in
French). I have therefore been obliged to construct my knowledge myself,
and it is the result of this personal propaedeutics which is offered here:
this is the manual I should have liked to find ready-made when I began
to inquire into the death of Rhetoric. Nothing more, then, than an
elementary system of information, an introduction to a certain number

*of terms and classifications—which does not mean that in the course of
this study I have not often been moved to admiration and excitement by
the power and subtlety of that old rhetorical system, and the modernity
of certain of its propositions.*

*Unfortunately, I can no longer (for practical reasons) authenticate
the references for this "scholarly text": I must write this manual in part
from memory. My excuse is that it deals with a commonplace learning:
Rhetoric is inadequately known, yet knowledge of it implies no task of
erudition; hence anyone can readily avail himself of the bibliographic
references which are lacking here. What is collected (sometimes, perhaps,
in the form of involuntary quotations) derives essentially: 1. from several
treatises on rhetoric from classical antiquity; 2. from the scholarly intro-
ductions to the Guillaume Budé series; 3. from two fundamental books
by Curtius and Baldwin; 4. from several specialized articles, notably
with regard to the Middle Ages; 5. from several reference books, including
Morier's* Dictionnaire de rhétorique, *F. Brunot's* Histoire de la
langue française, *and R. Bray's* La Formation de la doctrine classique
en France; *6. from several related readings, themselves incomplete and
contingent (Kojève, Jaeger).* [1]

## 0.1.  Rhetorical practices

The rhetoric under discussion here is that metalanguage (whose
language-object was "discourse") prevalent in the West from the
fifth century B.C. to the nineteenth century A.D. We shall not deal
with more remote efforts (India, Islam), and with regard to the

[1] Ernst R. Curtius, *European Literature and the Latin Middle Ages*, trans. Willard R. Trask,
New York: Bollingen Foundation, 1953.

Charles S. Baldwin, *Ancient Rhetoric and Poetic Interpreted from Representative Works*,
Gloucester, Mass.: Peter Smith, 1959; *Medieval Rhetoric and Poetic (to 1400) Interpreted from
Representative Works*, Gloucester, Mass.: Peter Smith, 1959.

Ferdinand Brunot, *Histoire de la langue française*, Paris: Colin, 1923.

René Bray, *La Formation de la doctrine classique en France*, Paris: Nizet, 1951.

Henri Morier, *Dictionnaire de poétique et de rhétorique*, Paris: PUF, 1961.

Werner W. Jaeger, *Paideia: The Ideals of Greek Culture*, trans. Gilbert Highet, 3 vols.,
New York: Oxford University Press, 1943–1945.

Alexandre Kojève, *Essai d'une histoire raisonnée de la philosophie païenne*, 3 vols., Paris:
Gallimard, 1968.

West itself, we shall limit ourselves to Athens, Rome, and France. This metalanguage (discourse on discourse) has involved several practices, simultaneously or successively present, according to periods, within "Rhetoric":

1. A *technique*, *i.e.*, an "art," in the classical sense of the word; the art of persuasion, a body of rules and recipes whose implementation makes it possible to convince the hearer of the discourse (and later the reader of the work), even if what he is to be convinced of is "false."

2. A *teaching*: the art of rhetoric, initially transmitted by personal means (a rhetor and his disciples, his clients), was soon introduced into institutions of learning; in schools, it formed the essential matter of what would today be called higher education; it was transformed into material for examination (exercises, lessons, tests).

3. A *science*, or in any case a proto-science, *i.e.*, *a.* a field of autonomous observation delimiting certain homogeneous phenomena, to wit the "effects" of language; *b.* a classification of these phenomena (whose best-known trace is the list of rhetorical "figures"; *c.* an "operation" in the Hjelmslevian sense, *i.e.*, a metalanguage, a body of rhetorical treatises whose substance—or signified—is a language-object (argumentative language and "figured" language).

4. An *ethic*: as a system of "rules," rhetoric is imbued with the ambiguity of that word: it is at once a manual of recipes, inspired by a practical goal, and a Code, a body of ethical prescriptions whose role is to supervise (*i.e.*, to permit and to limit) the "deviations" of emotive language.

5. A *social practice*: Rhetoric is that privileged technique (since one must pay in order to acquire it) which permits the ruling classes

to gain *ownership of speech*. Language being a power, selective rules of access to this power have been decreed, constituting it as a pseudo-science, closed to "those who do not know how to speak" and requiring an expensive initiation: born 2500 years ago in legal cases concerning property, rhetoric was exhausted and died in the "rhetoric" class, the initiatory ratification of bourgeois culture.

6.   A *ludic practice*: since all these practices constituted a formidable ("repressive," we now say) institutional system, it was only natural that a mockery of rhetoric should develop, a "black" rhetoric (suspicions, contempt, ironies): games, parodies, erotic or obscene allusions,[2] classroom jokes, a whole schoolboy practice (which still remains to be explored, moreover, and to be constituted as a cultural code).

## 0.2.  The rhetorical empire

All these practices attest the breadth of the rhetorical phenomenon—a phenomenon, however, which has not yet produced any important synthesis, any historical interpretation. Perhaps this is because rhetoric (aside from the taboo which weighs upon language), a veritable empire, greater and more tenacious than any political empire in its dimensions and its duration, flouts the very

---

[2] Numerous obscene jokes on *casus* and *conjunctio* (actually grammatical terms), of which this extended metaphor, borrowed from the *Arabian Nights*, gives some notion: "Then he spent the rest of the night with her in embracing and clipping, plying the particle of copulation in concert and joining the conjunctive with the conjoined, whilst her husband was as a cast-out nunnation of construction." [Burton translation, *The Book of The Thousand Nights and a Night*, New York: Heritage Press, 1962, vol.4, p. 3484]. More nobly, Alain de Lille explains that humanity commits *barbarisms* in the union of the sexes, *metaplasms* (licenses) which contravene the rules of Venus; man falls into *anastrophes* (inversions of construction); in his folly, he even commits *tmesis* (Curtius, *op. cit.*, pp. 414–416); similarly Calderon, commenting on the situation of a lady observed while visiting her suitor: "It is a great barbarism of love to venture to see and to be seen, for, as a bad grammarian, a passive person may be made into an active person." We know in what anatomical sense Pierre Klossowski lately revived the terms of scholasticism (*utrumsit, sed contra, vacuum, quidest*: "The Inspectress's *quidest*"). It follows that the collusion of grammar (of rhetoric or of scholasticism) and the erotic is not only "funny"; it marks out with precision and seriousness a transgressive site where two taboos are lifted: that of language and that of sex.

concepts of science and historical reflection, to the point of calling into question history itself, at least as we are accustomed to imagine and employ history, and of compelling us to conceive what we might elsewhere have called a *monumental history*; the scientific scorn attached to rhetoric would then participate in this general refusal to recognize multiplicity, overdetermination. Yet if we consider that rhetoric—whatever the system's internal variations may have been—has prevailed in the West for two and a half millennia, from Gorgias to Napoleon III; if we consider all that it has seen—watching immutable, impassive, and virtually immortal—come to life, pass, and vanish without itself being moved or changed: Athenian democracy, Egyptian kingdoms, the Roman Republic, the Roman Empire, the great invasions, feudalism, the Renaissance, the monarchy, the French Revolution; it has digested regimes, religions, civilizations; moribund since the Renaissance, it has taken three centuries to die; and it is not dead for sure even now. Rhetoric grants access to what must be called a super-civilization: that of the historical and geographical West: it has been the only practice (with grammar, born subsequently) through which our society has recognized language's sovereignty (*kurôsis*, as Gorgias says), which was also, socially, a "lordship"; the classification it has imposed is the only feature really shared by successive and various historical groups, as if there existed, superior to ideologies of content and to direct determinations of history, an ideology of form; as if—a principle anticipated by Durkheim and Mauss, affirmed by Lévi-Strauss—there existed for each society a *taxonomic identity*, a sociologic in whose name it is possible to define another history, another sociality, without destroying those recognized at other levels.

## 0.3. The journey and the network

This vast territory will be explored here (in the loose and hasty sense of the verb) in two directions: a diachronic direction and a systematic direction. We shall certainly not reconstruct a history of rhetoric; we shall confine ourselves to isolating a few significant moments, we shall traverse Rhetoric's two thousand years by making a few stopovers which will be something like the "days" of our journey (these "days" may be of very unequal length). In all, this long diachrony will comprise seven moments, seven "days" whose value will be essentially didactic. Then we shall collect the rhetors' classifications in order to form a single network, a kind of artifact which will permit us to conceive of the art of rhetoric as a kind of subtly articulated machine, a tree of operations, a "program" destined to produce discourse.

# A. THE JOURNEY

## A.1. Birth of rhetoric

### A.1.1. Rhetoric and property

Rhetoric (as a metalanguage) was born in the legal actions concerning property. Around 485 B.C., two Sicilian tyrants, Gelon and Hieron, effected deportations, transfers of population, and expropriations in order to populate Syracuse and pay the mercenaries; when they were deposed by a democratic uprising and an attempt was made to return to the *ante quo*, there was endless litigation, for property rights had been obscured. Such litigation was of a new type: it mobilized large people's juries that had to be convinced by the "eloquence" of those who appeared before them. Such eloquence, partly democratic and partly demagogic, partly judiciary and partly political (which was subsequently known as *deliberative*), was rapidly constituted into an object of instruction. The first teachers of this new discipline were Empedocles of Agrigento; Corax, his pupil from Syracuse (the first to be paid for his instruction); and Tisias. Such teaching passed no less rapidly to Attica (after the Persian wars), thanks to the litigation of merchants, who pleaded both in Syracuse and in Athens: by the middle of the fifth century, rhetoric was already partly Athenian.

### A.1.2. A great syntagmatics

What was this proto-rhetoric, this Coracian rhetoric? A rhetoric of the syntagm, of discourse, and not of the feature, of the figure. Corax already posited the five major parts of *oratio* which for centuries would form the "plan" of oratorical discourse: 1. exordium; 2. narration or action (the relating of facts); 3. argument or proof; 4. digression; 5. epilogue. It is easy to see that in shifting from legal discourse to academic dissertation, this plan has kept its main organization: an introduction, a demonstrative body, a conclusion. This first rhetoric is by and large a great syntagmatics.

### A.1.3. Feigned speech

It is entertaining to note that the art of speech is originally linked to a claim of ownership, as if language, as object of a transformation, condition of a practice, had been determined not from a subtle ideological mediation (as may have been the case in so many forms of art), but from the baldest sociality, affirmed in its fundamental brutality, that of earthly possession: we began to reflect upon language in order to defend our own. It is on the level of social conflict that was born a first theoretical sketch of *feigned speech* (different from fictive speech, that of the poets: poetry was then the only literature, prose not acceding to this status until later).

## A.2. Gorgias, or prose as literature

Gorgias of Leontium (today Lentini, north of Syracuse) came to Athens in 427; he was the teacher of Thucydides, and the Sophist interlocutor of Socrates in the *Gorgias*.

### A.2.1. Codification of prose

Gorgias's role (for us) is to have brought prose under the rhetorical code, accrediting it as a learned discourse, an esthetic object, "sovereign language," ancestor of "literature." How? The funeral panegyrics (threnodies), initially composed in verse, shift to prose, they are entrusted to statesmen; they are, if not written (in the modern sense of the word), at least memorized, *i.e.*, in a certain fashion, *set*; thus is born a third genre (after the legal and the deliberative), the *epideictic*: this is the advent of a decorative prose, a prose-as-spectacle. In this transition from verse to prose, meter and music are lost. Gorgias seeks to replace them by a code immanent to prose (though borrowed from poetry): words of similar consonance, symmetrical sentences, antitheses reinforced by assonance, alliteration, metaphor.

### A.2.2.  Advent of elocutio

Why does Gorgias constitute a stopover on our journey? There are, by and large, in a complete art of rhetoric (that of Quintilian, for instance) two poles: a syntagmatic pole (the order of the parts of the discourse, *taxis* or *dispositio*) and a paradigmatic pole (the "figures" of rhetoric, *lexis* or *elocutio*). We have seen that Corax had initiated a purely syntagmatic rhetoric. Gorgias, requiring the elaboration of "figures," gives rhetoric a paradigmatic perspective: he opens prose to rhetoric, and rhetoric to "stylistics."

## A.3.  Plato

Plato's dialogues which deal directly with Rhetoric are the *Gorgias* and the *Phaedrus*.

### A.3.1.  The two rhetorics

Plato deals with two rhetorics, one bad, the other good: 1. the rhetoric of fact is constituted by *logography*, an activity which consists in writing any discourse whatever (no longer a question of legal rhetoric alone; the totalization of the notion is important); its object is verisimilitude, illusion; this is the rhetoric of the rhetors, of the schools, of Gorgias, of the Sophists; 2. the rhetoric of law is the true rhetoric, a philosophic or even dialectical rhetoric; its object is the truth; Plato calls it a *psychagogy* (formation of souls by speech). —The opposition of good to bad rhetoric, of Platonic to Sophistic rhetoric, belongs to a larger paradigm: on one side, flatteries, servile occupations, falsehoods; on the other, austerity, the rejection of all complacency; on one side, empiricism and routine, on the other the arts: the industries of pleasure are a despicable imitation of the arts of the Good: rhetoric is the counterfeit of Justice, sophistry of legislation, cookery of medicine, toiletry of gymnastics: rhetoric (that of the logographers, of the rhetors, of the sophists) is therefore not an art.

### A.3.2.  Eroticized rhetoric

True rhetoric is a psychagogy; it requires a total, disinterested, general knowledge (this will become a *topos* in Cicero and Quintilian, but the notion will be made insipid: what will be asked of the orator is a good "general culture"). The object of this "synoptic" knowledge is the correspondence or the interaction which unites types of souls to types of discourse. Platonic rhetoric sets writing aside and seeks out personal interlocution, *adhominatio*; the basic mode of discourse is the dialogue between teacher and pupil, united by an inspired love. *Thinking in common* might be the motto of the dialectic. Rhetoric is a dialogue of love.

### A.3.3.  Division and mark

Dialecticians (those who live this eroticized rhetoric) undertake two allied enterprises: on the one hand, an impulse of union, of ascent toward an unconditional goal (Socrates, reproving Lysias in the *Phaedrus*, defines love in its *total unity*); on the other, an impulse of descent, a division of unity according to natural articulations, according to its types, down to indivisible species. This "descent" proceeds in steps: at each stage, on each step, there are two terms; one must be chosen over the other in order to take the next step down and accede to a new binary opposition, from which the descent will continue; such is the gradual definition of the sophist:

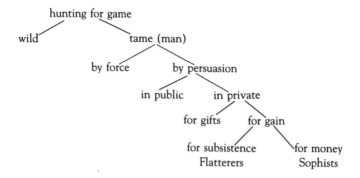

This divisional rhetoric—as opposed to Aristotle's syllogistic rhetoric—closely resembles a cybernetic, digital program: each choice determines the next alternative; or again, it resembles the paradigmatic structure of language, whose binary oppositions involve a marked and an unmarked term: here the marked term sets up a new alternation. But where does the mark come from? Here we return to Plato's eroticized rhetoric: in the Platonic dialogue, the mark is effected *by an acknowledgment of the respondent* (the pupil). Plato's rhetoric implies two interlocutors, one of whom offers an acknowledgment or a concession: this is the condition of movement. Hence all those particles of agreement which we encounter in Plato's dialogues and which often make us smile (when we do not find them tedious) by their silliness and their apparent banality, are actually structural "marks," rhetorical acts.

## A.4.   Aristotelian rhetoric

### A.4.1.   Rhetoric and Poetics

Isn't all rhetoric (if we except Plato) Aristotelian? No doubt it is: all the didactic elements which feed the classical manuals come from Aristotle. Yet a system is not defined only by its elements—it is also and especially defined by the opposition in which it is set. Aristotle wrote two treatises which concern the phenomena of discourse, but they are quite distinct: the *Technè rhétorikè* deals with an art of everyday communication, with public discourse; the *Technè poiétikè* deals with an art of imaginary evocation; in the first case, we are concerned to order the progress of the discourse from idea to idea; in the second, the progress of the work from image to image: these are, for Aristotle, two specific ways of proceeding, two autonomous "*technai*"; and it is the opposition of these two systems, one rhetorical, the other poetic, which in fact defines Aristotelian rhetoric. All the authors who acknowledge this opposition can be situated within Aristotelian rhetoric; that rhetoric will cease when the opposition is neutralized, when Rhetoric and Poetics unite, when rhetoric becomes a poetic *technè* (of "creation"): this occurs, approximately, in the age of Augustus (with Ovid and Horace) and a little later (with Plutarch and Tacitus)—though Quintilian still practices an Aristotelian rhetoric. The fusion of Rhetoric and Poetics is consecrated by the vocabulary of the Middle Ages, when the poetic arts are rhetorical arts, when the great rhetoricians are poets. This fusion is crucial, for it is at the very source of the notion of literature: Aristotelian rhetoric emphasizes reasoning; *elocutio* (or the distribution of figures) is only a part of it (a minor part in Aristotle himself); subsequently, it is the contrary which is the case: rhetoric is identified with problems, not of "proof" but of composition and of style: literature (the total act of writing) is defined by *fine writing*. Hence we must constitute as a stopover of our journey, under the general name of Aristotelian rhetoric, all the rhetorics anterior to poetic totalization. This Aristotelian rhetoric is theorized for us by Aristotle himself, is practiced by Cicero, is taught by Quintilian, and is transformed (generalized) by Dionysius of Halicarnassus, Plutarch, and the anonymous author of the treatise *On the Sublime*.

### A.4.2.  *Aristotle's* **Rhetoric**

Aristotle defines rhetoric as "the art of extracting from every subject the proper degree of persuasion it allows," or as "the faculty of speculatively discovering what in each case are the available means of persuasion." What is perhaps more important than these definitions is the fact that rhetoric is a *technè* (not an empiric practice), *i.e.*: *the means of producing a thing which may equally be or not be*, whose origin is in the creating agent, not in the object created: there is no *technè* of natural or necessary things: thus discourse belongs to neither the one nor the other. —Aristotle conceives of discourse (*oratio*) as a message and subjects it to a division of the cybernetic type. Book I of his *Rhetoric* is the book of the message-emitter, the book of the orator: it deals chiefly with the conception of arguments, insofar as they depend on the orator, on his adaptation to the public, according to the three recognized kinds of discourse (legal, deliberative, epideictic). Book II is the book of the message-receiver, the book of the public: it deals with the emotions (the passions), and once again with arguments, but this time insofar as they are *received* (and no longer, as before, *conceived*). Book III is the book of the message itself: it deals with *lexis* or *elocutio*, *i.e.*, with "figures," and with *taxis* or *dispositio*, *i.e.*, with the order of the parts of discourse.

### A.4.3. Probability

Aristotle's Rhetoric is above all a rhetoric of proof, of reasoning, of the approximative syllogism (enthymeme); it is a deliberately diminished logic, one adapted to the level of the "public," *i.e.*, of common sense, of ordinary opinion. Extended to literary productions (which was not its original intention), it would imply an esthetic of the public, more than an esthetic of the work. This is why, *mutatis mutandis* and making all (historical) allowances, it would be well suited to the products of our so-called mass culture, in which an Aristotelian "probability" prevails, *i.e.*, "what the public believes possible." How many films, pulp novels, commercial articles might take as their motto the Aristotelian rule: "better an impossible probability than an improbable possibility": better tell what the public believes possible, even if it is scientifically impossible, than tell what is really possible, if such possibility is rejected by the collective censorship of *public opinion*. It is obviously tempting to conflate this mass rhetoric with Aristotle's politics; which was, as we know, a politics of the happy medium, favoring a balanced democracy, centered on the middle classes, and responsible for reducing antagonisms between rich and poor, majority and minority; whence a rhetoric of good sense, deliberately subordinate to the "psychology" of the public.

### A.4.4. *Cicero's* Rhetorica

In the second century B.C., Greek rhetors abounded in Rome; schools of rhetoric were founded which functioned in classes determined by age; here two exercises were current: the *suasoriae*, a kind of "persuasive" composition (especially in the deliberative genre) for children, and the *controverses* (legal genre) for older students. The earliest Latin treatise is the *Rhetorica ad Herennium*, sometimes attributed to Cornificius, sometimes to Cicero. In the Middle Ages, which ceaselessly reproduced this manual, it became the fundamental text on the art of writing, along with Cicero's *De inventione.* —Cicero is an orator who speaks of the art of oratory; whence a certain pragmatization of Aristotelian theory (and therefore nothing really new in relation to this theory). Cicero's *Rhetorica* comprise: 1. the *Rhetorica ad Herennium* (assuming it is his), which is a sort of digest of Aristotelian rhetoric; however, the classification of "questions" replaces in importance the theory of the enthymeme: rhetoric is professionalized. The theory of the three styles (low, high, middle) also appears here. 2. *De inventione oratoria*: this is an (incomplete) work of the author's youth, purely legal, chiefly devoted to the *epicheireme*, a developed syllogism in which one or two premises are followed by their proofs: this is the "good argument." 3. *De oratore*, a work highly regarded up to the nineteenth century ("a masterpiece of good sense," "of healthy and right reason," "of generous and lofty thought," "the most original of rhetorical treatises"): as if he had Plato in mind, Cicero moralizes rhetoric and reacts against the teaching of the schools: this is the cultured man turning against specialization; the work takes the form of a dialogue (Crassus, Antonius, Mucius Scaevola, Rufus, Cotta): it defines the orator (who must have a general culture) and reviews the traditional divisions of rhetoric (*inventio, dispositio, elocutio*). 4. *Brutus*, a history

of the art of oratory in Rome. 5. *Orator*, an ideal portrait of the
Orator; the second part is more didactic (it will receive lengthy
commentaries by Pierre Ramus): here is specified the theory of the
oratorical "number," repeated by Quintilian. 6. The *Topica*: a digest
of Aristotle's *Topics* written from memory in eight days on the ship
taking Cicero to Greece after Mark Antony had seized power; the
most interesting thing about it for us is the structural network of
the *quaestio* (cf. *infra*, B.1.25). 7. The *Partitiones*: this little manual
of questions and answers, in the form of a dialogue between Cicero
and his son, is the driest and least ethical of Cicero's treatises (and
consequently the one I prefer): it is a complete elementary rhetoric,
a kind of catechism which has the advantage of giving the entire
scope of rhetorical classification (this is the meaning of *partitio*:
systematic segmentation).

### A.4.5.  Ciceronian rhetoric

Ciceronian rhetoric can be characterized by the following features: *a.* fear of "system"; Cicero owes everything to Aristotle, but
de-intellectualizes him, seeking to penetrate the speculation on
"taste," on the "natural"; the apex of this destructuring will be
reached in Augustine's *Rhetorica sacra* (Book IV of the *Christian
Doctrine*): no rules for eloquence, which is nonetheless necessary
for the Christian orator: one need only be clear (this is an act of
charity), and more concerned with truth than with terms: such
rhetorical pseudo-naturalism still prevails in academic conceptions
of style; *b.* nationalization of rhetoric: Cicero tries to romanize it
(the meaning of the *Brutus*), and *romanitas* appears; *c.* mythic collusion of professional empiricism (Cicero is a lawyer immersed in
political life) with an appeal to high culture; this collusion will
have a great future: culture becomes the backdrop for politics;
*d.* assumption of style: Ciceronian rhetoric heralds a development
of *elocutio*.

### A.4.6. *Quintilian's work*

There is a certain pleasure in reading Quintilian; he is a good teacher, not too prolix, not too moralistic; a mind at once classifying and sensitive (a combination which always seems astounding to the world at large); we might assign him the epitaph M. Teste dreamed of for himself: *Transiit classificando*. He was an official rhetor, appointed by the State; his fame was very great in his lifetime, suffered an eclipse upon his death, but was revived in the fourth century; Luther preferred him to all others; Erasmus, Bayle, La Fontaine, Racine, Rollin thought highly of him. His *De institutione oratoria* traces in twelve books the orator's education from childhood on; it is a complete plan of pedagogical formation (the meaning of *institutio*). Book I deals with elementary education (studies with the grammarian, then with the rhetor); Book II defines rhetoric, its utility; Books III to VII discuss *Inventio* and *Dispositio*; Books VIII to X discuss *Elocutio* (Book X gives practical advice on how to "write"); Book XI discusses minor aspects of rhetoric: Action (preparation of the discourse) and Memory; Book XII discusses the ethical qualities necessary to be an orator and posits the requirement of a general culture.

### A.4.7. *The rhetorical course of study*

Education consists of three phases (in France today, we speak of three cycles): 1. apprenticeship to language; nurses and tutors must have no language defects (Chrysippus wanted them to be trained in philosophy); parents should be as educated as possible; the student must begin with Greek, then learn to read and write; students are not to be hit; 2. studies with the *grammaticus* (a more extended meaning than our word "grammarian": one might say it means *master of grammar*); the child works with the *grammaticus* from the age of seven; he listens to lectures on poetry and reads aloud (*lectio*); he writes themes (retells fables, paraphrases poems, expands on maxims); he takes lessons from an actor (animated recitation); 3. studies with the *rhetor*: the student must begin rhetoric quite early, probably at fourteen, or at puberty; the teacher must constantly provide examples himself (but the students are not to stand up and applaud him); the two main exercises are: *a. narrations*, summaries and analyses of narrative arguments, of historical events, elementary panegyrics, parallels, amplifications of commonplaces (themes), speeches following an outline (*preformata materia*); *b. declamations*, discourses on hypothetical cases; an exercise, so to speak, in *fictive rationality* (hence *declamatio* is already very close to the finished work). We can see how far such pedagogy *forces* speech: speech is beset on all sides, expelled from the student's body, as if there were a native inhibition to speak and it required a whole technique, a whole education to draw it out of silence, and as if this speech, learned at last, conquered at last, represented a good "object relation" with the world, a real mastery of the world and of men.

### A.4.8.  *Writing*

In dealing with tropes and figures (Books VIII to X), Quintilian establishes a first theory of "writing." Book X is addressed to *those who wish to write.* How to obtain this "well-founded facility" (*firma facilitas*), *i.e.*, how to conquer native sterility, terror of the blank page (*facilitas*), and yet how to say something, not to be carried away by garrulity, verbiage, logorrhea (*firma*)? Quintilian sketches a propaedeutics for the writer: one must read and write frequently, imitate models (make pastiches), revise constantly, but only after having let the matter "rest," and know how to end. Quintilian notes that the hand is slow, "thought" and writing have two different speeds (the surrealists' problem: how to achieve writing as rapid . . . as itself?); here the hand's deliberation is beneficial: no dictation, writing must remain attached not to the voice but to the hand, to the muscles: to remain with the hand's slowness: no quick drafts.

### A.4.9.  *Generalized rhetoric*

The last stage of Aristotelian rhetoric: its dilution by syncretism: Rhetoric ceases to be set in opposition to Poetics but becomes a transcendent notion which we should today call "Literature"; it is no longer exclusively constituted as an object of instruction but becomes an art, in the modern sense of the word; it is henceforth both a theory of writing and a thesaurus of literary forms. We can observe this transition at five points: 1. Ovid is often cited in the Middle Ages as having postulated the relationship of poetry to the art of oratory; this comparison is also affirmed by Horace in his *Ars Poetica*, whose substance is frequently rhetorical (theory of *styles*); 2. Dionysius of Halicarnassus, a Greek contemporary of Augustus, in his *De compositione verborum*, abandons an important element of Aristotelian rhetoric (the enthymeme) for an exclusive concern with a new value: the movement of sentences; here appears an autonomous notion of style: style is no longer based on logic (subject before predicate, substance before accidence), word order is variable, guided only by rhythmic values; 3. in Plutarch's *Moralia* we find a tract "*Quomodo adulescens poetas audire debeat*" (how the young should study poetry), which thoroughly moralizes the literary esthetic; a Platonist, Plutarch tries to lift Plato's ban on the poets; how? precisely by uniting Poetics to Rhetoric; rhetoric is the means by which to "detach" the imitated action (often a reprehensible one) from the (frequently admirable) art which imitates it; from the moment one can read the poets esthetically, one can read them morally; 4. *On the Sublime* (*Peri Hypsous*) is an anonymous treatise of the first century A.D. (mistakenly attributed to Longinus and translated by Boileau): it is a sort of "transcendental" Rhetoric; *sublimitas* is actually the "elevation" of style; it is style itself (in the expression "to have style"); it is *literariness*, defended in a heated, inspired tone: the myth of "creativity" begins to dawn; 5. in the *Dialogue of the Orators* (whose authenticity is sometimes contested), Tacitus politicizes the reasons for the decadence of eloquence: these reasons are not the "bad taste" of the times, but Domitian's tyranny which imposes silence on the Forum and shifts poetry toward a non-engaged art; but thereby eloquence emigrates to "Literature," penetrates it, and constitutes it (*eloquentia* comes to signify *literature*).

## A.5.  Neo-rhetoric

### A.5.1.  A literary esthetic

We call *neo-rhetoric* or *second sophistic* the literary esthetic (Rhetoric, Poetics, and Criticism) which prevailed in the united Greco-Roman world from the second to fourth centuries A.D. This was a period of peace, of commerce, of exchanges favorable to leisure societies, above all in the Middle East. Neo-rhetoric was truly ecumenical: the same figures were learned by Saint Augustine in Latin Africa, by the pagan Libanius, by Saint Gregory Nazianzen in eastern Greece. This literary empire was built on a double reference: 1. sophistic: the orators of Asia Minor, without political allegiance, seek to revive the name of Sophists, whom they suppose they are imitating (Gorgias), with no pejorative connotation; these entirely decorative orators enjoy widespread celebrity; 2. rhetoric: it encompasses everything, no longer counters any neighboring idea, absorbs all speech; it is no longer a (specialized) *technè*, but a general culture, and even more: a national education (at the level of the schools in Asia Minor); the *sophistès* is the director of a school, appointed by the emperor or by a city; the teacher serving under him is the *rhetor*. In this collective institution, no name can be cited: there is a dust of authors, a movement known only through Philostratus's *Lives of the Sophists*. What did this educaton of speech consist of? Once again we must distinguish syntagmatic rhetoric (parts) from paradigmatic rhetoric (figures).

### A.5.2.  declamatio *and* ekphrasis

On the syntagmatic level, one exercise is preponderant: *declamatio* (*mêlêtê*); this is a regulated improvisation on a theme; for example: Xenophon refuses to survive Socrates; the Cretans claim they possess Zeus's tomb; the man in love with a statue, etc. Improvisation shifts the order of the parts (*dispositio*) to the background; discourse, having no persuasive goal but being purely decorative, is destructured, atomized into a loose series of brilliant fragments, juxtaposed according to a rhapsodic model. The principal fragment (which was highly prized) was *descriptio* or *ekphrasis*. *Ekphrasis* is an anthology piece, transferable from one discourse to another: it is a regulated description of places or persons (origin of certain medieval *topoi*). Here first appeared a new syntagmatic unit, the *piece*: less extensive than the traditional parts of the discourse, longer than the period; this unit (landscape or portrait) abandons oratorical (legal, political) discourse and readily unites with narration, with a *story line*: once again, the rhetorical "eats into" the literary.

### A.5.3.  Atticism / asianism

On the paradigmatic level, neo-rhetoric consecrates the assumption of "style"; it assigns an ultimate value to the following ornaments: archaism, extended metaphor, antithesis, rhythmic phrase. Since this tendency toward the baroque produces its reaction, a struggle begins between two schools: 1. *Atticism*, chiefly defended by grammarians, guardians of a pure vocabulary (the castrating ethic of "purity," which still exists today); 2. *Asianism* refers, in Asia Minor, to the development of an exuberant style tending toward the strange, based, like mannerism, on the effect of surprise; here the "figures" play an essential role. Asianism was obviously condemned (and continues to be by the classicizing esthetic which is the heir of atticism).[3]

## A.6.  The Trivium

### A.6.1.  Agonistic structure of instruction

In Antiquity, the mainstays of culture were essentially oral instruction and the transcriptions to which it might give rise (acroa-

---

[3] *Atticism*: This ethnocentrism obviously invokes what might be called a class racism: it must not be forgotten that the expression "classical" ("classicism") originates in the opposition proposed by Aulus Gellius (second century A.D.) between the *classicus* author and the *proletarius*: allusion to the constitution of Servius Tullius, which divided citizens according to wealth into five classes, the first of which formed the *classici* (the *proletarii* were outside these classes); hence *classic* etymologically means: belonging to the social "upper crust" (wealth and power).

matic treatises and the *technai* of the logographers). After the eighth century, instruction takes an agonistic turn, reflecting a situation of sharp rivalries. Free schools (alongside the monastic or episcopal schools) are left to the initiative of any master, often a very young one (in his twenties); everything depends on success: Abelard, a gifted student, "defeats" his teacher, takes away his paying audience, and founds a school of his own; financial rivalry is closely linked to the rivalry of ideas: the same Abelard forces his teacher Guillaume de Champeaux to renounce realism: he *liquidates* it, from every point of view; the agonistic structure coincides with the commercial structure: the *scholasticos* (teacher, student, or former student) is a combatant of ideas and a professional rival. There are two school exercises: 1. the *lesson*, reading and explication of a set text (Aristotle, the Bible), which includes: *a. expositio*, interpretation of the text according to a subdividing method (a kind of analytic delirium); *b. quaestiones*, propositions of the text which can have a *pro* or a *con*: these are discussed and determined by refutation; each reasoning must be presented in the form of a complete syllogism; the *lesson* was gradually neglected because of its tedium; 2. the *dispute*, a ceremony, a dialectical duel, conducted with the teacher presiding; after several days, the teacher determines the result. What is involved here is by and large a game culture: athletes of speech are trained: speech is the object of a certain glamor and of a regulated power, aggression is coded.

### A.6.2.   The written text

As for the written text, it was not subject, as it is today, to a judgment of originality; what we call the *author* did not exist; around the ancient text, the only text used and in a sense *managed*, like reinvested capital, there were various functions: 1. the *scriptor* who purely and simply copies; 2. the *compilator* who adds to what he copies, but nothing that comes from himself; 3. the *commentator* who introduces himself into the copied text, but only to make it intelligible; 4. the *auctor*, finally, who presents his own ideas but always by depending on other authorities. These functions are not clearly hierarchized: the *commentator*, for example, can have the prestige a great writer would have today (this was the case, in the twelfth century, of one Pierre Hélie, nicknamed "the Commentator"). What we might anachronistically call the *writer* is therefore essentially, in the Middle Ages: 1. a *transmitter*: he passes on an absolute substance which is the treasure of antiquity, the source of authority; 2. a *combiner*: he is entitled to "break" works of the past, by a limitless analysis, and to recompose them ("creation," a modern value, had it occurred to the Middle Ages, would have been desacralized into a structuration).

### A.6.3.  *The* Septennium

In the Middle Ages, "culture" is a taxonomy, a functional network of "arts," *i.e.*, of languages subject to rules (the etymology of the period relates *art* to *arctus*, which means *articulated*), and these "arts" are called "liberal" because they do not serve to earn money (in opposition to the *artes mechanicae*, manual activities): these are general, sumptuous languages. Such liberal arts take the place of that "general culture" which Plato rejected in the name and behalf of philosophy alone, but which was subsequently reclaimed (Isocrates, Seneca) as propaedeutic to philosophy. In the Middle Ages, philosophy itself is reduced and passes into the general culture as one art among the others (*Dialectica*). It is no longer for philosophy that a liberal culture prepares, but for theology, which remains sovereignly outside the Seven Arts (the *Septennium*). Why seven? As early as Varro, we find a theory of the liberal arts: they are then nine (ours, with the addition of medicine and architecture); this structure is repeated and codified in the fifth and sixth centuries by Martianus Capella (a pagan African) who institutes the hierarchy of the *Septennium* in an allegory, *The Marriage of Mercury and Philology* (*Philology* here designates total knowledge): Philology, the learned virgin, is promised to Mercury; she receives as a wedding present the seven liberal arts, each being presented with its symbols, its costume, its language; for example, *Grammatica* is an old woman, she has lived in Attica and wears Roman garments; in a little ivory casket, she carries a knife and a file to correct the children's mistakes; *Rhetorica* is a beautiful woman, her garments are embellished with all the figures, she carries the weapons intended to wound her adversaries (coexistence of persuasive rhetoric and ornamental rhetoric). These allegories of Martianus Capella were widely known, we find statues of them on the facade of Notre-Dame in Paris, at Chartres, and drawn in the works of Botticelli. Boethius and Cassiodorus (sixth century) specify the theory of the *Septennium*, the first by shifting Aristotle's *Organon* into *Dialectica*, the second by postulating that the liberal arts are inscribed for all eternity in divine wisdom and in Scripture (the Psalms are full of "figures"): rhetoric receives the guarantee of Christianity, it can legally emigrate from Antiquity into the Christian West (and hence into modern times); this right will be confirmed by Bede, in Charlemagne's time. —What constitutes the *Septennium*? First we must recall to what it is opposed: on the one hand, to techniques (the "sciences," as disinterested languages, belong to the *Septennium*) and, on the other, to theology (the *Septennium* organizes human nature *in its humanity*; this nature can be subverted only by the Incarnation which, if it is applied to a classification, takes the form of a subversion of language: the Creator becomes creature, the Virgin conceives, etc.: *in hac verbi copula stupet omnis regula*). The Seven Arts are divided into two unequal groups, which correspond to the two paths (*viae*) of wisdom: the *Trivium* includes *Grammatica*, *Dialectica*, and *Rhetorica*; the *Quadrivium* includes *Musica*, *Arithmetica*, *Geometria*, *Astronomia* (Medicine will be added later). The opposition of the Trivium and of the Quadrivium is no longer that of Letters and Sciences; it is rather the opposition of the secrets of speech and the secrets of nature.[4]

[4] There existed a mnemonic list of the seven arts: *Gram*(matica) loquitur. *Dia*(lectica) vera docet. *Rhe*(torica) verba colorat. *Mu*(sica) canit. *Ar*(ithmetica) numerat. *Ge*(ometria) ponderat. *As*(tronomia) colit astra.

An allegory by Alain de Lille (twelfth century) accounts for the system in all its complexity: the Seven Arts are summoned to provide a chariot for *Prudentia*, who wishes to guide mankind: *Grammatica* provides the pole, *Logica* (or *Dialectica*) the axle, which Rhetorica embellishes with jewels; the quadrivium furnishes the four wheels, the horses are the five senses, harnessed by *Ratio*; the equipage goes toward the saints, Mary, God; when the limit of human powers is reached, *Theologia* relieves *Prudentia* (Education is a redemption).

### A.6.4.  The diachronic play of the Trivium

The *Trivium* (which alone concerns us here) is a taxonomy of speech; it attests to the persistent effort of the Middle Ages to establish the place of speech within man, within nature, within the creation. Speech is not in this period, as it will be subsequently, a vehicle, an instrument, the meditation of *something else* (soul, thought, passion); it absorbs the entirety of the mental: no experience, no psychology: speech is not expression but immediate construction. What is interesting about the *Trivium* is therefore less the content of each discipline than the play of these three disciplines among themselves, down through ten centuries: from the fifth to the fifteenth centuries, leadership emigrated from one art to another, so that each period of the Middle Ages comes under the dominance of one art: in turn, it is *Rhetorica* (from the fifth to the seventh century), then *Grammatica* (from the eighth to the tenth century), then *Logica* (from the eleventh to the fifteenth century) which dominates her sisters, who are consigned to the rank of poor relations.

## Rhetorica

### A.6.5. Rhetorica *as supplement*

Ancient Rhetoric had survived in the traditions of several Roman schools in Gaul and among certain Gallic rhetors, such as Ausonius (310–393), *grammaticus* and *rhetor* in Bordeaux, and Sidonius Apollinaris (430–484), Bishop of Auvergne. Charlemagne entered the figures of rhetoric in his academic reforms, after the Venerable Bede (673–735) had entirely Christianized rhetoric (a task begun by Saint Augustine and Cassiodorus), showing that the Bible itself is full of "figures." Rhetoric does not prevail for long; it is soon "squeezed" between *Grammatica* and *Logica*: it is the poor relation of the *Trivium*, destined to have a splendid resurrection only when it can revive as "Poetry" and more generally as "Belles Lettres." This weakness of Rhetoric, diminished by the triumph of the castrating languages, grammar (we recall the file and the knife of Martianus

Capella) and logic, results perhaps from the fact that it is entirely shoved toward *ornament, i.e.,* toward what is regarded as inessential—in relation to truth and to fact (first appearance of the referential ghost[5]): it then appears as *what comes afterwards.*[6] This medieval rhetoric is supplied essentially by Cicero's treatises (*Rhetorica ad Herennium* and *De inventione*) and Quintilian's (better known to teachers than to students), but it did produce treatises chiefly relative to ornaments, to figures, to "colors" (*colores rhetorici*), or later arts of poetry (*artes versificatoriae*); *dispositio* is approached only from the angle of the "beginning" of the discourse (*ordo artificialis, ordo naturalis*); the figures identified are chiefly of amplification and abbreviation; style is related to the three genres of Virgil's wheel[7]: *gravis, humilis, mediocrus,* and to two ornaments: *facile* and *difficile.*

### A.6.6.  *Sermons,* dictamen, *arts of poetry*

The domain of *Rhetorica* encompasses three canons of rules, three *artes.* 1. *Artes sermocinandi:* these are the oratorical arts in general (the object of rhetoric, strictly speaking), *i.e.,* essentially, sermons or paraenetic discourses (exhorting to virtue); sermons can be writ-

---

[5] This ghost still walks. Outside of France today, in certain countries where it is necessary, in opposition to a colonial past, to reduce French to the status of a foreign language, it is declared that what must be taught is only the French language, and not French literature: as if there were a threshold between language and literature, as if language were *here* and not *there,* as if it could be halted somewhere, beyond which there would be inessential supplements, literature among them.

[6] "*Suprema manus apponit, opusque sororum / Perficit atque semel factum perfectius ornat.*" "[Rhetoric] affords the final touch, completes the work of her sisters, and embellishes the fact in a more accomplished fashion."

[7] Virgil's wheel is a figured classification of the three "styles"; each of the three sectors of the wheel assembles a homogeneous group of terms and symbols:

| *Aeneid* | *Eclogues* | *Georgics* |
|---|---|---|
| *gravis stylus* | *humilis stylus* | *mediocrus stylus* |
| *miles dominans* | *pastor otiosus* | *agricola* |
| Hector, Ajax | Tityrus, Meliboeus | Triptolemus |
| *equus* | *ovis* | *bos* |
| *gladius* | *baculus* | *aratrum* |
| urbs, castrum | *pascua* | *ager* |
| laurus, cedrus | *fagus* | *pomus* |

ten in two languages: *sermones ad populum* (for the people of the parish), written in the vernacular language, and *sermones ad clerum* (for the synods, the schools, the monasteries), written in Latin; however, everything is prepared in Latin; the vernacular is only a translation; 2. *Artes dictandi, ars dictaminis*, epistolary art: the growth of administration, after Charlemagne, involves a theory of admin‑ istrative correspondence: the *dictamen* (concerned with dictating letters); the *dictator* is an acknowledged profession, which is taught; the model is the *dictamen* of the papal chancellery: the *stylus romanus* takes precedence over all; a stylistic notion appears, the *cursus*, the quality of the text's fluency, apprehended through criteria of rhythm and accentuation; 3. *Artes poeticae*: poetry initially belongs to the *dictamen* (the *prose/poetry* opposition is for a long time extremely vague); then the *artes poeticae* take over *rythmicum*, borrow Latin verse from *Grammatica*, and begin to aim at imaginative "litera‑ ture." A structural reworking appears, which will set in opposition, at the end of the fifteenth century, the *First Rhetoric* (or general rhetoric) to the *Second Rhetoric*, from which emerge the Arts of Poetry, such as Ronsard's.

## Grammatica

### A.6.7.  *Donatus and Priscian*

After the Invasions, the leaders of the culture are Celts, English‑ men, and Franks; they must learn Latin grammar; the Carolingians consecrate the importance of grammar by the famous Schools of Fulda, Saint Gall, and Tours; grammar leads to general education, to poetry, to the liturgy, to Scripture; it includes, alongside grammar strictly speaking, poetry, metrics, and certain figures. —The two great grammatical authorities of the Middle Ages are Donatus and Priscian. 1. Donatus (*circa* 350) produces an abridged grammar (*ars minor*) which deals with the eight parts of the sentence, in the form of questions and answers, and an extended grammar (*ars major*). Donatus enjoyed an enormous fame; Dante puts him in heaven (as opposed to Priscian); several pages by him are among the first printed

work, on a footing with Scripture; he has given his name to elementary grammatical treatises, the *donats*. 2. Priscian (end of the
fifth century, beginning of the sixth) was a Mauritanian, a Latin
teacher in Byzantium, educated on Greek theories, notably the
grammatical doctrine of the Stoics. His *Institutio grammatica* is a
normative grammar (*grammatica regulans*), neither philosophical nor
"scientific"; it survives in two abridgments: the *Priscianus minor*
deals with construction, the *Priscianus major* deals with morphology.
Priscian offers many examples borrowed from the Greek Pantheon:
man is Christian, but the rhetor can be pagan (we know the fortunes
of this dichotomy). Dante sends Priscian to the Seventh Circle of
the Inferno, that of the Sodomites: an apostate, a drunkard, a
madman, but known as a great scholar. Donatus and Priscian represent absolute law—except when they do not agree with the Vulgate: grammar can then be only normative, since it is believed that
the "rules" of locution were invented by the grammarians; they
were widely circulated by *Commentatores* (such as Pierre Hélie) and
by versified grammars (enjoying a great vogue). Until the twelfth
century, *Grammatica* includes grammar and poetry, and deals with
"precision" as well as with "imagination"; with letters, syllables,
the sentence, the period, figures, metrics; it yields very little to
*Rhetorica*: certain figures. It is a fundamental science, linked to an
*Ethica* (part of human wisdom, articulated in the texts outside of
theology): "science of speaking well and writing well," "the cradle
of all philosophy," "the first nurse of all literary study."

### A.6.8.  *The* Modistae

In the twelfth century, *Grammatica* becomes speculative once
again (as it had been with the Stoics). What is called *Speculative
Grammar* is the work of a group of grammarians known as *Modistae*
because they wrote treatises entitled *De modis significandi*; many
were from the monastic province of Scandinavia then known as
*Dacia*, and more specifically from Denmark. The Modists were de-

nounced by Erasmus for their barbarous Latin, for the chaos of their definitions, for the excessive subtlety of their distinctions; as a matter of fact they provided the basis for grammar during two centuries, and we are still in their debt for certain speculative terms (for example: *instance*). the Modists' treatises take two forms: the *modi minores*, whose substance is presented *modo positivo*, *i.e.*, without critical discussion, in a brief, clear, very didactic fashion, and the *modi majores*, given in the form of *quaestio disputata*, *i.e.*, with the *pro* and the *con*, by increasingly specialized questions. Each treatise includes two parts, in Priscian's manner: *Ethymologia* (morphology)—poor spelling was a period matter and corresponds to a false etymology of the word *Etymologia*—and *Diasynthetica* (syntax), but it is preceded by a theoretical introduction concerning the relations of the *modi essendi* (being and its properties), the *modi intelligendi* (taking possession of being under its aspects) and the *modi significandi* (level of language). The *modi significandi* themselves include two strata: 1. *designation* corresponds to the *modi signandi*; their elements are: *voice*, the phonic signifier, and *dictio*, the concept-word, a generic semanteme (in *dolor*, *doleo*, this is the notion of suffering, the *dolorous*); the *modi signandi* do not yet belong to the grammarian: *vox*, the phonic signifier, depends on the *philosophus naturalis* (we should say the phonetician), and *dictio*, referring to an inert state of the word, which is not yet animated by any relation, escapes the logician of language (it would derive from what we should call lexicography); 2. the level of the *modi significandi* is reached when we add to *designation* an intentional sense; on this level, the word, neutral in *dictio*, is endowed with a relation, it is apprehended as "*constructible*": it appears in the higher unit of the sentence; it then pertains to the speculative grammarian, to the logician of language. Thus, far from blaming the Modists, as has sometimes been the case, for having reduced language to a nomenclature, we must congratulate them for having done just the opposite: for them language begins not at *dictio* and at the *significatum*, *i.e.*, at the word-sign, but at the *consignificatum* or *construc-*

*tibile*, *i.e.*, at the relation, at the inter-sign: a founding privilege is granted to syntax, to flexion, to rection, and not to the semanteme, in a word, to *structuration*, which would perhaps be the best way of translating *modus significandi*. Hence there is a certain relationship between the Modists and certain modern structuralists (Hjelmslev and glossematics, Chomsky and competence): language is a structure, and this structure is in a sense "guaranteed" by the structure of being (*modi essendi*) and by that of mind (*modi intelligendi*): there is a *grammatica universalis*; this was new, for it was commonly believed that there were as many grammars as languages: *Grammatica una et eadem est secundum substantiam in omnibus linguis, licet accidentaliter varietur. Non ergo grammaticus sed philosophus proprias naturas rerum diligenter considerans . . . grammaticam invenit.* (Grammar is one and the same as regards substance in all languages although it can vary by accidents. Hence it is not the grammarian, it is the philosopher who, by the examination of the nature of things, discovers grammar.)

## Logica (*or* Dialectica)

### A.6.9.   studium *and* sacerdotium

*Logica* dominates in the twelfth and thirteenth centuries: it pushes aside *Rhetorica* and absorbs *Grammatica*. This struggle takes the form of a conflict of schools. In the first half of the twelfth century, the schools of Chartres in particular develop the teaching of *Grammatica* (in the extended sense we have discussed): this is *studium*, with a literary orientation; contrary to it, the school of Paris develops theological philosophy: this is *sacerdotium*. There is a victory of Paris over Chartres, of *sacerdotium* over *studium*: *Grammatica* is absorbed by *Logica*; this is accompanied by a retreat of pagan literature, by an intensified enthusiasm for the vernacular, by a withdrawal of humanism, by an impulse toward the lucrative disciplines (medicine, law). *Dialectica* is initially sustained by Cicero's *Topics* and by the work of Boethius, who first introduced Aristotle; then, in the twelfth and thirteenth centuries, after the (massive) second entrance of Aristotle, by the whole of Aristotelian logic which dealt with the dialectical syllogism.[8]

### A.6.10. *Disputatio*

*Dialectica* is an art of living discourse, of dialogue. There is nothing Platonic about such dialogue, there is no question of a subjection on principle of the beloved to the master; dialogue here is aggressive, its stake is a victory which is not predetermined: it is a battle of syllogisms, Aristotle staged by two partners. Hence *Dialectica* is finally identified with an exercise, a mode of exposition, a ceremony, a game, *disputatio* (which might be called: a colloquy of opponents). The procedure (or the protocol) is that of *Sic et Non*: contradictory testimonies are collected on a question; the exercise confronts an opponent and a respondent; the respondent is usually the candidate: he responds to the objections presented by the opponent; as in Conservatory competitions, the opponent is on the staff: he is a friend or is appointed *ex officio*; the thesis is posited, the opponent counters it (*sed contra*), the candidate responds (*respondeo*): the conclusion is given by the master, who presides.

---

[8] In citing certain ancient sources for the Middle Ages, it must be remembered that the unrivaled intertextual *matter* is always Aristotle, and even, in a sense, Aristotle *against* Plato. Plato was partially transmitted by Saint Augustine and sustains, in the twelfth century, the school of Chartres (a "literary" school as opposed to the school of Paris, which was "logical" and Aristotelian) and the Abbey of Saint Victor; however, in the thirteenth century the only real translations are those of the *Phaedo* and *Meno*, and even these are little known. In the fifteenth and sixteenth centuries, an intense struggle is engaged against Aristotle in Plato's name (Marsilio Ficino and Giordano Bruno). —As for Aristotle, he enters the Middle Ages in two stages: the first time, in the sixth and seventh centuries, and partially, through Martianus Capellus, Porphyry's *Categories*, and Boethius; the second time, in force, in the twelfth and thirteenth centuries: in the ninth century, all of Aristotle was translated into Arabic; in the twelfth century, translations of all of Aristotle were available, made either from the Greek or from the Arabic: this is the massive influx of the *Posterior Analytics*, the *Topics*, the *Sophistical Refutations*, the *Physics* and *Metaphysics*; Aristotle was Christianized (Saint Thomas). Aristotle's third appearance will be that of his *Poetics* in the sixteenth century in Italy, in the seventeenth century in France.

*Disputatio* is invasive;[9] it is a sport: the masters dispute among themselves in the students' presence once a week; the students dispute on the occasion of the examinations. The argument proceeded upon permission granted by a gesture from the presiding master (there is a parodic echo of these gestures in Rabelais). All this is codified, ritualized in a treatise which minutely regulates *disputatio*, to keep the discussion from digressing: the *Ars obligatoria* (fifteenth century). The thematic material of the *disputatio* comes from the argumentative part of Aristotelian Rhetoric (through the *Topics*); it includes *insolubilia*, propositions extremely difficult to prove, *impossibilia*, theses which seem impossible to everyone, *sophismata*, clichés and paralogisms, which serve by and large for the *disputationes*.

### A.6.11.  Neurotic meaning of the disputatio

If we wanted to evaluate the neurotic meaning of such an exercise, we should doubtless go back to the Greek *machê*, that kind of agonistic sensibility which made intolerable to the Greeks (then to the West) *all expressions in which the subject is in contradiction with*

---

[9] Even Christ's death on the Cross is made part of the scenario of *Disputatio* (some people today would find this reduction of the Passion to a school exercise sacrilegious; others on the contrary would admire the medieval freedom of mind which laid no taboo upon the "drama" of the intellect): *Circa tertiam vel sextam ascendunt magistri [in theologia] cathedram suam ad disputandum et querunt unam questionem. Cui questioni respondet unus assistentium. Post cujus responsionem magister determinat questionem, et quando vult ei defferre et honorem facere, nihil aliud determinat quam quod dixerat respondens. Sic fecit hodie Christus in cruce, uni ascendit ad disputandum; et proposuit unam questionem Deo Patri: Eli, Eli lamma sabachtani, Deus, Deus meus, quid medereliquisti? Et Pater respondit: Ha, Fili mi, opera manuum tuarum ne dispicias: non enim Pater redemit genus humanum sine te. Et ille respondens ait: Ha, Pater, bene determinasti questionem meam. Non determinabo eam post responsionem tuam. Non sicut ego volo, sed sicut tu vis. Fiat voluntas tua.* (Toward the third or the sixth hour, the masters [in theology] mount the pulpit to dispute and ask a question. One of those attending answers this question. After that response, the master concludes the question and when he wishes to bestow on him an honor, he does not conclude in any other way than by what the respondent had said. This is what Christ did on the Cross one day, when he mounted for the disputation. He posed a question to God the Father: *Eli, Eli, lamma sabachtani*, God, my God, why have you forsaken me? And the Father answered: My Son, do not despise the works of your hands, for the Father could not redeem the human race without you. And Christ responded: My Father, you have concluded my question well. I could not conclude it otherwise after your response, etc.)

*itself*: it sufficed to force an adversary to contradict himself to *reduce* him, eliminate him, cancel him out: Callicles (in the *Gorgias*) refuses to answer rather than to contradict himself. The syllogism is the very weapon which permits this *liquidation*, it is the invincible knife which delivers victory: the two disputants are two executioners who try to castrate each other (whence the mythic episode of Abelard, the castrator castrated). So intense did it become that the neurotic explosion had to be codified, the narcissistic wound limited: logic was turned to sport (as today the agonistic feelings of so many peoples, chiefly underdeveloped or oppressed, are turned "into soccer"): this is the *eristic*. Pascal saw this problem: he seeks to avoid setting the other in radical contradiction with himself; he wants to "correct" the other without wounding him to death, to show him that one need merely "complete" (and not deny). The *disputatio* has disappeared, but the problem of the (ludic, ceremonial) rules of the verbal game remains: how do we dispute, nowadays, in our writings, in our colloquies, in our meetings, in our conversations, and even in the "scenes" of private life? Have we settled our accounts with the syllogism (even when it is disguised)? Only an analysis of our intellectual discourse will some day be able to answer with any degree of precision.[10]

### A.6.12.   *Restructuration of the* Trivium

We have seen that the three liberal arts fought a battle among themselves for precedence (to the final advantage of *Logica*): it is actually the system of the Trivium in its fluctuations which is significant. Its contemporaries were aware of this: some tried to restructure the whole of spoken culture. Hugh of St. Victor (1096–1141) set in opposition to the theoretical, practical, and mechanical sciences, the logical sciences: *Logica* took over the *Trivium* in its entirety: it is the whole science of language. Saint Bon-

---

[10] Charles Perelman and L. Olbrechts-Tyteca, *The New Rhetoric: A Treatise on Argumentation*, trans. John Wilkinson and Purcell Weaver, Notre Dame: University of Notre Dame Press, 1969.

aventure (1221–1274) tried to discipline all forms of knowledge by subjecting them to Theology; in particular, *Logica*, or the science of interpretation, comprehends *Grammatica* (expression), *Dialectica* (education), and *Rhetorica* (persuasion); once again, as if to set the mental in opposition to nature and to grace, language absorbs it entirely. But above all (for this heralds the future), since the twelfth century, something which we must certainly call *Letters* is separated out from philosophy; for John of Salisbury, *Dialectica* functions in all the disciplines where the result is abstract; *Rhetorica* on the contrary collects what *Dialectica* rejects: it is the field of the *hypothesis* (in ancient rhetoric, the hypothesis is set in opposition to the thesis, like the contingent to the general [cf. *infra*, B.1.25]), that is to say, everything which implicates concrete circumstances (who? what? why? how?); thus appears an opposition which will have a great mythic success (it still survives): that of the concrete and the abstract: Letters (deriving from *Rhetorica*) will be concrete, Philosophy (deriving from *Dialectica*) will be abstract.

## A.7. Death of rhetoric

### A.7.1. *Aristotle's third entrance: the* Poetics

We have seen that Aristotle had appeared twice in the West: once in the sixth century with Boethius, once in the twelfth century with the Arabs. He makes a third entrance: through his *Poetics*. This *Poetics* is very little known in the Middle Ages, except in the form of some distorting abridgments; but in 1498 there appears in Venice the first Latin translation made from the original; in 1503, the first edition in Greek; in 1550, Aristotle's *Poetics* is translated with a commentary by a group of Italian scholars (Castelvetro, Scaliger—of Italian origin—and Bishop Veda). In France, the text itself is little known; it is through Italian influence that it makes its impact in seventeenth-century France; the generation of 1630 included numerous devotees of Aristotle; the *Poetics* supplies French Classicism with its chief element: a theory of verisimilitude; it is the code of literary "creation," whose theoreticians are authors, critics. Rhetoric, whose chief object is "fine writing," style, is limited to instruction, where moreover it triumphs: this is the realm of the teachers (Jesuits).

### A.7.2. Triumphant and moribund

Rhetoric is triumphant: it rules over instruction. Rhetoric is moribund: limited to this sector, it falls gradually into great intellectual discredit. This discredit is occasioned by the promotion of a new value, *evidence* (of facts, of ideas, of sentiments), which is self-sufficient and does without language (or imagines it does so), or at least claims no longer to use language except as an *instrument*, as a mediation, as an expression. This "evidence" takes, from the sixteenth century on, three directions: a personal evidence (in Protestantism), a rational evidence (in Cartesianism), a sensory evidence (in empiricism). Rhetoric, if it is tolerated (in Jesuit instruction), is no longer a logic at all, but only a *color*, an ornament, closely supervised in the name of the "natural." No doubt there was in Pascal some postulation of this new spirit, since it is to him that we owe the Anti-Rhetoric of modern humanism; what Pascal demands is a mentalist rhetoric (an "art of persuasion"), sensitive as though by instinct to the complexity of things (to *"finesse"*); eloquence consists not in applying an external code to discourse, but in becoming aware of the thought nascent within us, so that we can reproduce this movement when we speak to the other, thus sweeping him into truth, as if he himself, by himself, were discovering it; the *order* of discourse has no intrinsic characteristic (clarity or symmetry); it depends on the nature of thought, to which, in order to be "correct," language must conform.

### A.7.3. Jesuit instruction in rhetoric

At the end of the Middle Ages, as we have seen, the teaching of rhetoric was losing ground; it nonetheless subsisted in certain colleges, in England and in Germany. In the sixteenth century, this heritage was organized, assumed a stable form, at first in the Gymnase Saint-Jérôme, located in Liège and run by Jesuits. This college was imitated in Strasbourg and in Nîmes: the form of instruction in France for three centuries was set. Very quickly some forty colleges followed the Jesuit model. The instruction given here was codified in 1586 by a group of six Jesuits: this is the *Ratio Studiorum*, adopted in 1600 by the University of Paris. This *Ratio* sanctions the preponderance of the "humanities" and of Latin rhetoric; it invades all of Europe, but its greatest success is in France; the power of this new *Ratio* no doubt derives from the fact that there is, in the ideology it legalizes, an identity of an academic discipline, of a discipline of thought, and of a discipline of language. In this humanist instruction, Rhetoric itself is the noble substance, it dominates everything. The only academic prizes are the prizes for Rhetoric, for translation, and for memory, but the prize for Rhetoric, awarded at the conclusion of a special contest, designates the first pupil, who is henceforth called (and the titles are significant) *imperator* or *tribune* (let us not forget that speech is a power—and even a political power). Until around 1750, outside the sciences, eloquence constitutes the only prestige; in this period of Jesuit decline, rhetoric receives a certain amount of new life from Freemasonry.

### A.7.4.  *Treatises and manuals*

The codes of rhetoric are innumerable, at least until the end of the eighteenth century. Many (in the sixteenth and seventeenth centuries) are written in Latin; these are the academic manuals written by Jesuits, notably those of Fathers Nuñez, Susius, and Soarez. The "Institution" of Father Nuñuz, for example, consists of five books: preparatory exercises, the three main parts of rhetoric (invention, arrangement, and style) and an ethical part ("wisdom"). Yet rhetorics in the vernacular proliferate (we shall cite here only those in French). At the end of the fifteenth century, rhetorics are primarily poetics (art of making verses, or arts of the second Rhetoric); we must cite: Pierre Fabri, *Grand et Vrai Art de Pleine Rhétorique* (six editions from 1521 to 1544) and Antoine Foclin (Fouquelin), *Rhéthorique française* (1555), which includes a clear and complete classification of figures. In the seventeenth and eighteenth centuries, until about 1830 in fact, the Treatises of Rhetoric prevail; these treatises generally offer: 1. paradigmatic rhetoric ("figures"); 2. syntagmatic rhetoric ("oratorical construction"); these two categories are felt to be necessary and complementary, so that a commercial digest of 1806 can combine the two most famous rhetoricians: the Figures, by Dumarsais, and oratorical construction, by Du Batteux. Let us cite the best known of these treatises. For the eighteenth century, it is no doubt the *Rhétorique* by Père Bernard Lamy (1675): this is a complete treatise of speech, useful "not only in schools, but also in all of life, *in buying and selling*"; it is based, obviously, on the principle of the exteriority of language and of thought: one has a "picture" in the mind and one seeks to "render" it with words. For the eighteenth century, the most famous treatise (and moreover the most intelligent) is that of Dumarsais (*Traité des Tropes*, 1730): Dumarsais, a poor man, unsuccessful in his lifetime, frequented D'Holbach's irreligious circle and was an Encyclopedist; his work, more than a rhetoric, is a linguistics of the changes of meaning. At the end of the eighteenth century and at the beginning of the nineteenth, many classical treatises were still published, absolutely indifferent to the shock of the Revolution and the changes which followed (Blair, 1783; Gaillard, 1807; *La Rhétorique des demoiselles*; Fontanier, 1827—recently republished and introduced by Gérard Genette). In the nineteenth century, rhetoric survives only artificially, under the protection of official regulations; the very title of the manuals and treatises changes in a significant fashion: 1881, F. de Caussade, *Rhétorique et Genres littéraires*; 1889, Prat, *Eléments de Rhétorique et de Littérature*: Literature still stands warrant for rhetoric, before smothering it completely; but the old rhetoric, in its death throes, is rivaled by "psychologies of style."

### A.7.5. End of Rhetoric

However, to say in a categorical way that Rhetoric is dead would mean we could specify what has replaced it, for, as we have sufficiently remarked in this diachronic journey, Rhetoric must always be read in the structural interplay with its neighbors (Grammar, Logic, Poetics, Philosophy): it is the play of the system, not each of its parts in itself, which is historically significant. On this problem we shall note, to conclude, several orientations of the inquiry. 1. It would be necessary to make a contemporary lexicology of the word: Where does it still find acceptance? It still sometimes receives original contents, personal interpretations, from writers not from rhetors (Baudelaire and "deep rhetoric," Valéry, Paulhan); but above all, we should have to reorganize the contemporary field of its connotations: here pejorative,[11] there analytic,[12] and in yet another place revalidated,[13] so as to draw up an ideological case history of the old rhetoric. 2. In education, the end of treatises of rhetoric is, as always in this case, difficult to date; in 1926, a Jesuit in Beirut wrote another manual of rhetoric in Arabic; in 1938, a Belgian, M. J. Vuillaume, published still another; and classes in Rhetoric and in Advanced Rhetoric have only lately vanished. 3. To what degree and with what reservations has the science of language taken over the field of the old rhetoric? First of all, there has been a shift to psycho-stylistics (or stylistics of expressivity[14]); but today, when linguistic mentalism is hunted down and harried? Out of all rhetoric, Jakobson has retained only two figures, metaphor and metonymy, making them into an emblem of the two axes of language; for some, the formidable labor of classification performed by the old rhetoric

[11] (The mystics' sophistic-of-negation: "to be all, make yourself nothing.") "By an easily explained paradox, this destructive logic delights the conservative: it is harmless; abolishing *all*, it disturbs *nothing*. Without efficacity, it is ultimately nothing but a rhetoric. A few faked moods, a few operations performed on language, this is not going to change the course of the world" (Sartre, *Saint Genet, Actor & Martyr*, trans. Frechtman, New York: George Braziller, 1963, p. 202).

[12] Julia Kristeva, *Sèméiotikè*, Paris: Éd. du Seuil, 1969.

[13] Group µ, *A General Rhetoric*, trans. Burrell and Slotkin, Baltimore: Johns Hopkins University Press, 1980.

[14] "The disappearance of traditional rhetoric has created a gap in the humanities, and stylistics has already gone a long way to fill this gap. In fact it would not be altogether wrong to describe stylistics as a 'new rhetoric' adapted to the standards and requirements of contemporary scholarship in the linguistic as well as the literary field" (Stephen Ullman, *Language and Style*, New York: Barnes & Noble, 1964, p. 130).

seems still usable, especially if applied to the marginal fields of communication or signification, such as the advertising image,[15] where it is not yet worn out. In any case, these contradictory evaluations show clearly the present ambiguity of the rhetorical phenomenon: glamorous object of intelligence and penetration, grandiose system which a whole civilization, in its extreme breadth, perfected in order to classify, *i.e.*, in order to think its language, instrument of power, locus of historical conflicts whose reading is utterly absorbing precisely if we restore this object to the diverse history in which it developed; but also an ideological object, falling into ideology at the advance of that "other thing" which has replaced it, and today compelling us to take an indispensable critical distance.

## B. THE NETWORK

### B.O.1.  *The demand for classification*

All the treatises of Antiquity, especially the post-Aristotelian ones, show an obsession with classification (the very term of *partitio* in oratory is an example): rhetoric openly offers itself as a classification (of materials, of rules, of parts, of genres, of styles). Classification itself is the object of a discourse: announcement of the plan of the treatise, discussion of the classification proposed by predecessors. The passion for classification always seems Byzantine to those who do not participate in it: why discuss so bitterly the place of the *propositio*, sometimes put at the end of the *exordium*, sometimes at the beginning of the *narratio*? Yet in most cases, as is natural, the taxonomic option implies an ideological one: there is always a *stake* in where things are placed: *tell me how you classify and I'll tell you who you are.* Hence we cannot adopt—as we shall do here, for didactic purposes—a single, canonical classification

---

[15] See notably Jacques Durand, "Rhétorique et image publicitaire," *Communications*, #15 (1970), pp. 70–95.

which will deliberately "forget" the many variations of which the plan of the *technè rhétorikè* has been the object, without first saying a word about these variations.

### B.O.2. *Starting points for classification*

The account of Rhetoric has been made, essentially, from three different starting points (to simplify matters). 1. For Aristotle, what comes first is *technè* (speculative institution of a power to produce what may or may not exist); the *technè* (*rhétorikè*) engenders four types of operations, which are the parts of the rhetorical *art* (and not the parts of discourse, of *oratio*): *a. Pisteis*, establishment of "proofs" (*inventio*); *b. Taxis*, arrangement of these proofs throughout the discourse, according to a certain order (*dispositio*); *c. Lexis*, verbal formulation (at the level of the sentence) of the arguments (*elocutio*); *d. Hyprocrisis*, staging of the total discourse by an orator who must become a performer (*actio*). These four operations are examined three times (at least with regard to the *inventio*): from the point of view of the emitter of the message, from the point of view of its receiver, from the point of view of the message itself (cf. *supra*, A.4.2.). In accord with the notion of *technè* (which is a power), the Aristotelian starting point foregrounds the *structuration* of discourse (active operation) and relegates to the background its *structure* (discourse as product). 2. For Cicero, it is *doctrina dicendi* which comes first, *i.e.*, no longer a speculative *technè*, but a body of knowledge taught for practical ends; the *doctrina dicendi*, from a taxonomic point of view, engenders: *a.* an energy, a force, *vis oratoris*, on which depend the operations called for by Aristotle; *b.* a product, or one might say, a form, the *oratio*, to which are attached the extended parts of which it is composed; *c.* a subject or, one might say, a content (a type of content), the *quaestio*, on which the genres of discourse depend. Thus appears a certain autonomy of the work in relation to the labor which has produced it. 3. A synthesizer and pedagogue, Quintilian combines Aristotle and Cicero; his starting point is certainly *technè*, but it is a practical and pedagogical *technè*, not speculative; it aligns: *a.* the operations (*de arte*)—which are those of Aristotle and Cicero; *b.* the operator (*de artifice*); *c.* the work itself (*de opere*) (these last two themes are discussed but not subdivided).

### B.O.3. The stake of the classification: the place of the plan

We can situate precisely the stake of these taxonomic variations (even if they seem minimal): it is the place of place, of *dispositio*, of the order of the parts of the discourse; to what is this *dispositio* to be connected? Two choices are possible: either we regard the "plan" as an "ordering" (and not just as an order), as a creative act of the distribution of the materials, in a word a labor, a structuration, and then we connect it to the preparation of discourse; or else we take the plan as a product, as a fixed structure, and we then connect it to the work, to *oratio*; either it is a dispatching of materials, a distribution, or else it is a grid, a stereotyped form. In short, is order active and creative, or passive and created? Each option has had its representatives, who have taken it to its limit: some connect *dispositio* to *probatio* (discovery of proofs); others connect it to *elocutio*: it is a simple verbal form. We know the breadth this problem assumed on the threshold of modern times: in the sixteenth century, Ramus, violently anti-Aristotelian (*technè* is a sophistication contrary to nature), radically separates *dispositio* from *inventio*: order is independent of the discovery of arguments: *first* the search for arguments, *then* their grouping, called *method*. In the seventeenth century, the decisive blows against a decadent rhetoric were struck precisely against the reification of the plan of *dispositio*, as it had ultimately been conceived by a rhetoric of the product (and not of production): Descartes discovers the coincidence of invention and of order, no longer with the rhetors but with the mathematicians; and for Pascal, order has a creative value, it suffices to found the new (it cannot be a ready-made grid, external and prior): "Let it not be said that I have said nothing new: the arrangement (*disposition*) of the materials is new." The relation between the *order of invention* (*dispositio*) and the *order* of presentation (*ordo*), and notably the gap in the orientation (contradiction, inversion) of the two parallel orders, always has a theoretical bearing: it is a whole conception of literature which is at stake each time, as is evidenced by Poe's exemplary analysis of his own poem "The Raven": starting, in order to write the work, from the *last thing apparently received* by the reader (received as "ornament"), *i.e.*, the melancholy effect of the word *nevermore* (*e/o*), then tracing back from this to the invention of the story and of the metrical form.

### B.O.4   The rhetorical machine

If, forgetting this stake or at least resolutely opting for the Aristotelian starting point, we manage to superimpose the sub-classifications of Classical Rhetoric, we get a canonical distribution of the different parts of the *technè*, a network, a tree, or rather a great liana descending from stage to stage, sometimes splitting a generic element, sometimes collecting scattered parts. This network is a *montage*. One thinks of Diderot and his machine for making stockings: "It can be seen as a single and unique reasoning whose conclusion is the fabrication of the object . . ." In Diderot's machine, textile material is fed in at the beginning, and at the end, it is stockings which emerge. In the rhetorical machine, what one puts in at the beginning, barely emerging from a native aphasia, are the raw materials of reasoning, facts, a "subject"; what comes out at the end is a complete, structured discourse, fully armed for persuasion.

### B.O.5.   The five parts of the technè rhétorikè

Our point of departure will therefore be constituted by the different mother-operations of *technè* (it will be understood from the preceding that we shall connect the order of the parts, the *dispositio*, to the *technè* and not to *oratio*: this is what Aristotle did). In its greatest extension, the *technè rhétorikè* includes five principal *operations*; we must insist on the *active, transitive, programmatic, operational* nature of these divisions: it is not a question of the elements of a structure, but of the actions of a gradual structuration, as is clearly shown by the verbal form (verbs) of these definitions:

1. INVENTIO

     Euresis          *invenire quid dicas*     finding what to say

2. DISPOSITIO

     Taxis            *inventa disponere*       ordering what is found

3. ELOCUTIO

     Lexis            *ornare verbis*           adding the ornament of words, of figures

4. ACTIO

     Hypocrisis       *agere et pronuntiare*    performing the discourse like an actor: gestures and diction

5. MEMORIA

     Mnémè            memoriae mandare          committing to memory

The first three operations are the most important (*Inventio, Dispositio, Elocutio*); each supports a broad and subtle network of notions, and all three have fed rhetoric beyond Antiquity (above all *Elocutio*). The last two (*Actio* and *Memoria*) were rapidly sacrificed, as soon as rhetoric no longer concerned the spoken (declaimed) discourses of lawyers or statesmen, or of "lecturers" (epideictic genre), but also, and then almost exclusively, (written) "works." No doubt, though, that these two parts are of great interest: the first (*Actio*) because it refers to a dramaturgy of speech (*i.e.*, to a hysteria and to a ritual); the second because it postulates a level of stereotypes, a fixed intertextuality, transmitted mechanically. But, since these two last operations are absent from the work (as opposed to *oratio*), and since, even among the Ancients, they have given rise to no classification (but only to brief commentaries), we shall eliminate them here from the rhetorical machine. Our tree will therefore include only three branches: 1. *Inventio*; 2. *Dispositio*; 3. *Elocutio*. Yet we may note that between the concept of *technè* and these three starting points there is interposed one more level: that of the "substantial" materials of discourse: *Res* and *Verba*. I do not think this is to be translated merely as Things and Words. *Res*, Quintilian says, are *quae significantur*, and *Verba: quae significant*; in short, on the level of the discourse, the signifieds and the signifiers. *Res* is what is already promised to meaning, constituted from the outset as the raw material of signification; *Verbum* is the form which already seeks out meaning to fulfill it. It is the paradigm *res/verba* which counts, the relation of complementarity, the exchange, not the definition of each term. —Since *Dispositio* bears at once on the materials (*res*) and on the discursive forms (*verba*), the first starting point of our tree, the first working-drawing of our machine, will look like this:

### B.1. Inventio

#### B.1.1. Discovery and not invention

*Inventio* refers less to an invention (of arguments) than to a discovery: everything already exists, one must merely recognize it: this is more an "extractive" notion than a "creative" one. This is corroborated by the designation of a "place" (the Topic), from which the arguments can be extracted and from which they must be brought: *inventio* is a progress (*via argumentorum*). This notion of *inventio* implies two sentiments: on one hand, a complete confidence in the power of a method, of a path: if the net of argumentative forms is cast over the raw material with a good technique, one is certain to draw up the content of an excellent discourse; on the other, the conviction that the spontaneous, the unmethodical brings nothing in return: to the power of final speech corresponds a nothingness of original speech; man cannot speak without having given birth to his speech, and for this delivery there is a special *technè, inventio*.

#### B.1.2. To convince/to move

Two wide paths start from *inventio*, one logical, the other psychological: *to convince* and *to move*. To convince (*fidem facere*) demands a logical or pseudo-logical apparatus which is called, by and large, *Probatio* (domain of "Proofs"): by reasoning, we must do actual violence to the mind of the hearer, whose character and whose psychological dispositions do not then concern us: the proofs have their own power. *To move* (*animos impellere*) consists, on the contrary, in thinking the probative message not in itself but according to its destination, the mood of its audience, in mobilizing subjective, ethical proofs. We shall first proceed down the long path of *probatio* (*to convince*), and then return to the second term of the initial dichotomy (*to move*).

### B.1.3. Proofs within-techné and proofs outside-techné

*Pisteis*, the proofs? We shall keep the word out of habit, but for us it has a scientific connotation whose very absence defines the rhetorical *pisteis*. It would be better to say: convincing reasons, ways of persuasion, means of credit, mediators of confidence (*fides*). The binary division of *pisteis* is famous: there are the reasons which are outside *techné* (*pisteis atechnoi*) and the reasons which belong to *techné* (*pisteis entechnoi*), in Latin: *probationes inartificiales/artificiales*; in French (B. Lamy): *extrinsèques/intrinsèques*. This opposition is not difficult to understand if we recall what a *techné* is: a speculative institution of the means of producing what may or may not exist, *i.e.*, which is neither scientific (necessary) nor natural. Proofs outside-*techné* are therefore those which escape to the freedom of creating the contingent object; they are to be found outside the orator (the operator of the *techné*); they are reasons inherent in the nature of the object. Proofs within-*techné* depend, on the contrary, on the orator's reasoning power.

### B.1.4. Proofs outside-techné

What can the orator do with proofs outside-*techné*? He cannot *conduct* them (induce nor deduce); he can only, because they are "inert" in themselves, arrange them, show them to advantage by a methodical disposition. What are they? They are fragments of reality which pass directly into the *dispositio*, by a simple *showing* and not by transformation; or again: they are elements of the "dossier" which one cannot invent (deduce) and which are furnished by the case itself, by the client (for the moment we are in the purely judicial realm). These *pisteis atechnoi* are classified in the following way: 1. *praejudicia*, the earlier decrees, jurisprudence (the problem is to destroy them without attacking them directly); 2. *rumores*, public testimony, the *consensus* of an entire city; 3. confessions obtained under torture (*tormenta, quaesita*): no ethical sentiment, but a social sentiment with regard to torture: Antiquity recognized the right to torture slaves, but not free men; 4. evidence (*tabulae*): contracts, agreements, transactions between individuals, even forced relations (theft, murder, armed robbery, assault); 5. oath (*jusjurandum*): this is the element of a tactic and of a language: one can agree or refuse to swear, one accepts or rejects another's oath, etc.; 6. testimony (*testimonia*): this is essentially, at least for Aristotle, noble testimony, either from the ancient poets (Solon citing Homer to support the claims of Athens against Salamis), or proverbs, or famous contemporaries; hence they are more like "citations."

### B.1.5.   Meaning of the atechnoi

The "extrinsic" proofs are acceptable to the judicial (*rumores* and *testimonia* can serve for the deliberative and the epideictic); but we can imagine that they serve in private life to judge an action, to discern when to praise, etc. This is what Lamy has done. Hence these extrinsic proofs can sustain fictional representations (novel, play); yet we must realize that they are not *indices*, which belong to reasoning; they are simply the elements of a dossier which comes from the outside world, from an already institutionalized reality; in literature such proofs would serve to compose *dossier-novels* (there are such), which would abandon any attempt at consistent writing, any organized representation, and would present only fragments of reality already constituted as language by society. This is the real meaning of the *atechnoi*: *constituted* elements of the social language, which pass directly into the discourse, without being *transformed* by any technical operation on the part of the orator, of the author.

### B.1.6   Proofs within-technè

Set in opposition to these fragments of the social language given directly, in a raw state (except for the advantage of arrangement), are the *reasonings* which depend entirely on the power of the orator (*pisteis entechnoi*). *Entechnos* really means here: deriving from a *practice* of the orator, for the material is *transformed* into persuasive force by a logical operation. This operation, strictly speaking, is a double one: induction and deduction. The *pisteis entechnoi* are therefore divided into two types: 1. the *exemplum* (induction); 2. the *enthymeme* (deduction); these are obviously a non-scientific induction and deduction, simply "public" (for the public). These two paths are obligatory: all orators, in order to produce persuasion, demonstrate by examples or by enthymemes; there are no other means (Aristotle). Yet a kind of quasi-esthetic difference, a difference of style, has been introduced between the example and the enthymeme: the *exemplum* produces a gentler persuasion, more highly prized by common people; it is a luminous force that charms through the pleasure inherent in any comparison; the enthymeme, more powerful, more vigorous, produces a violent, disturbing force, it enjoys the energy of the syllogism; it performs a veritable seizure, it is proof in all the force of its purity, of its essence.

### B.1.7.   Exemplum

*Exemplum* (*paradeigma*) is rhetorical induction: we proceed from one particular to another by the implicit link of the general: from an object we infer the class, then from this class, a new object.[16] The *exemplum* can have any dimension, it can be a word, a fact, a group of facts, and the account of these facts. It is a persuasive

---

[16] An example of *exemplum* given by Quintilian: "Some flute-players who had left Rome were recalled by a decree of the Senate; with all the more reason ought we recall great citizens who had deserved well of the Republic and whom bad times had forced into exile": the general link of the inductive chain: the class of useful people, driven away and recalled.

similitude, an argument by analogy: one finds good *exempla* if one
has the gift of seeing analogies—and also, of course, contraries;[17]
as its Greek name indicates, it is in the realm of the paradigmatic,
of the metaphorical. Since Aristotle, the *exemplum* has been subdivided into real and fictive; the fictive subdivided into *parable* and
*fable*; the *real* covers historical, but also mythological examples, in
opposition not to the imaginary but to what one invents oneself;
the *parable* is a short comparison,[18] the *fable* (*logos*) a group of
actions. This indicates the narrative nature of the *exemplum*, which
will flourish.

### B.1.8.  The exemplary figure: imago

At the beginning of the first century B.C., a new form of *exemplum*
appears: the exemplary character (*eikôn*, *imago*) designates the incarnation of a virtue in a figure: *Cato illa virtutum viva imago* (Cicero). An *imago*-repertoire is established for use by the rhetorical
schools (Valerius Maximus, under Tiberius: *Factorum ac dictorum
memorabilium libri novem*), followed later by a versified version. This
collection of figures enjoys vast popularity in the Middle Ages; a
learned poetry proposes the definitive canon of these characters, a
veritable Olympus of archetypes whom God has placed in the course
of history; the *imago virtutis* sometimes apprehends quite secondary
characters, who will enjoy a great celebrity, such as Amyclas, the
boatman who carried "Caesar and his fortune" from Epirus to Brin-
disi during a storm ( = poverty and sobriety); there are many such
in Dante. The very fact that a repertoire of *exempla* could be constituted emphasizes what might be called the structural vocation of
the *exemplum*: it is a detachable fragment, which specifically involves a meaning (heroic portrait, hagiographic narrative); it is easy
to understand that it can be traced in writing, both discontinuous
and allegorical, down to the popular press of our own day: Churchill,

---

[17] *Exemplum a contrario*: "Those pictures and statues which Marcellus restored to his
enemies, Verres took from his allies." (Cicero)

[18] Example of a parable from a speech of Socrates: magistrates must not be chosen by lot,
any more than athletes and pilots.

John XXIII are each an *imago*, examples intended to persuade us that we must be courageous, that we must be good.

### B.1.9. Argumenta

Parallel to the *exemplum*, a mode that is persuasive by induction, there is the group of modes of deduction, the *argumenta*. The ambiguity of the word *argumentum* is significant here. The usual sense in ancient times is: object of a stage fable (the *argument* of a comedy by Plautus), or again: articulated action (as opposed to *muthos*, a group of actions). For Cicero, this is both a "fictive thing which might have happened" (the plausible) and "a probable idea used to convince," whose logical bearing Quintilian clarifies: "manner of proving one thing by another, of confirming what is dubious by what is not." Thus appears an important duplicity: that of a "reasoning" ("any form of public reasoning" says one rhetor) which is impure, easily dramatizable, which participates both in the intellectual and in the fictional, in the logical and in the narrative (do we not find this same ambiguity in many modern "essays"?). The apparatus of the *argumenta* which begins here and which will not end until the end of the *probatio* starts with a powerful device, a tabernacle of deductive proof, the *enthymeme*, which is sometimes called *commentum*, *commentatio*, a literal translation of the Greek *enthumema* (any reflection one has in the mind), but most often, by a significant synecdoche: *argumentum*.

### B.1.10 The enthymeme

The enthymeme has received two successive significations (which are not contradictory). 1. For Aristotelians, it is a syllogism based on probability or signs, and not on the true and the immediate (as is the case for the scientific syllogism); the enthymeme is a *rhetorical syllogism*, developed solely *on the level of the public* (as we say: to put ourselves on someone's level), starting from the *probable*, *i.e.*, starting from what the public thinks; it is a deduction whose value is concrete, posited in view of a *presentation* (a sort of acceptable spectacle), as opposed to an abstract deduction made uniquely for analysis; it is a public reasoning, easily employed by ignorant men. By virtue of this origin, the enthymeme affords persuasion, not demonstration; for Aristotle, the enthymeme is sufficiently defined by the *probable* character of its premises (the probable admits of contraries); whence the necessity of defining and classifying the premises of the enthymeme (cf. *infra*, B.1.13,14,15,16). 2. After Quintilian, and triumphing entirely in the Middle Ages (since Boethius), a new definition prevails: the enthymeme is defined not by the content of its premises, but by the elliptical character of its articulation: it is an incomplete syllogism, an abbreviated syllogism: it has "neither as many parts nor as distinct parts as the philosophical syllogism": One of the two premises or the conclusion can be suppressed: hence it is a syllogism truncated by the suppression (in utterance) of a proposition whose reality seems incontestable and which is, for this reason, simply "kept in mind" (*en thumo*). If we apply this definition to that master syllogism of our culture (with its odd insistence on our mortality)—and though its premise is not simply probable, which keeps it from being an enthymeme in the first sense—we arrive at the following enthymemes: *man is mortal, hence Socrates is mortal; Socrates is mortal because men are; Socrates is a man, hence mortal*, etc. We may prefer to this funereal model the more current one proposed by Port-Royal: "Any body reflecting light from all sides is uneven; the moon reflects light from all sides; hence the moon is an uneven body," and all the enthymematic forms which can be derived from it (the moon is uneven because it reflects light from all sides, etc.). This second definition of the enthymeme is in fact chiefly that of the *Logic* of Port-Royal, and we see clearly why (or how): man in the classical period believes that the syllogism is entirely made within the mind ("the number of three propositions is quite proportional with the extent of our mind"); if the enthymeme is an imperfect syllogism, this can only be *on the level of language* (which is not the level of the "mind"): it is a perfect syllogism in the mind, but imperfect in expression; in short, it is an accident of language, a deviation.

### B.1.11. Metamorphoses of the enthymeme

Here are some varieties of rhetorical syllogisms: 1. the *prosyllo-gism*, a chain of syllogisms in which the conclusion of one becomes the premise of the next; 2. the *sorites* (*soros*, a heap), an accumulation of premises or a sequence of truncated syllogisms; 3. the *epicheirema* (often discussed in Antiquity), or developed syllogism, each premise being accompanied by its proof; the epicheirematic structure can be extended to an entire discourse in five parts: proposition, reason for the major premise, assumption or minor premise, proof of the minor, complexion or conclusion: A . . . because . . . Now, B . . . because . . . Therefore C;[19] 4. the *apparent enthymeme*, or reasoning based on a trick or play on words; 5. the *maxim* (*gnômè*, *sententia*): a very elliptical, monodic form, it is a fragment of an enthymeme whose remainder is virtual: "Never overeducate your children (for they reap the envy of their fellow citizens)."[20] A significant development, the *sententia* shifts from *inventio* (of reasoning, of syntagmatic rhetoric) to *elocutio*, to style (figures of amplification or diminution); in the Middle Ages, it flourishes, contributing to a thesaurus of citations on all subjects of wisdom: sentences, gnomic verses learned by heart, collected and classified in alphabetical order.

### B.1.12. Pleasures of the enthymeme

Since the rhetorical syllogism is made for the public (and not under the auspices of science), psychological considerations are

---

[19] An extended epicheirema: Cicero's *Pro Milone*: 1. it is permissible to kill those who set ambushes for us; 2. proofs drawn from natural law and the right of peoples, from *exempla*; 3. now, Clodius has set ambushes for Milon; 4. proofs drawn from facts; 5. hence it is permissible for Milon to kill Clodius.

[20] The maxim (*gnômè*, *sententia*) is a formula expressing generality, but only a generality whose object is actions (that can be chosen or avoided); for Aristotle, the basis of the *gnômè* is always the *eikos*, according to his definition of the enthymeme by the *content* of its premises; but, for the classical rhetoricians who define the enthymeme by its "truncation," the *maxim* is essentially a "contraction": "it also happens occasionally that two propositions are enclosed in a single proposition: the enthymematic *sententia* (example: "Mortal, do not harbor an immortal hatred").

pertinent, and Aristotle insists upon them. The enthymeme has
the pleasures of a progress, of a journey: one sets out from a point
which has no need to be proved and from there one proceeds toward
another point which does need to be proved; one has the agreeable
feeling (even if under duress) of discovering something new by a
kind of natural contagion, of capillarity which extends the known
(the opinable) toward the unknown. However, to produce all its
pleasure, this progress must be supervised: the reasoning must not
be carried too far, and one must not pass through all the stages in
order to reach a conclusion: that would be tiresome (the epicheirema must be used only on grand occasions); for one must contend
with the ignorance of the listeners (ignorance is precisely that
incapacity to infer by many steps and to follow a reasoning at
length); or rather: such ignorance must be exploited by giving the
listener the feeling that he has brought it to an end himself, by his
own mental power: the enthymeme is not a syllogism truncated by
defect or corruption, but because the listener must be granted the
pleasure of contributing to the construction of the argument; it is
something like the pleasure of completing a given pattern or grid
(cryptograms, crossword puzzles). Port-Royal, though always re-
garding language as defective in relation to the mind—and the
enthymeme is a syllogism of language—recognizes this pleasure of
incomplete reasoning: "Such suppression [of a part of the syllogism]
flatters the vanity of those to whom one is speaking, by leaving
something to their intelligence; and by shortening the discourse,
it makes it stronger and livelier";[21] yet we see the ethical change
(in relation to Aristotle): the pleasure of the enthymeme is assigned
less to a creative autonomy on the part of the listener than to an
excellence of *concision*, triumphantly given as the sign of a *surplus*
of thought over language (thought triumphs by length over language): "one of the chief beauties of a discourse is to be full of

---

[21] An example of felicitous contraction: a verse from Ovid's *Medea* "which contains a
very elegant enthymeme": *Servare potui, perdere an possim rogas?* I was able to save you, then
can I not destroy you? (He who can save can destroy, now, I have been able to save you,
hence I could destroy you.)

meaning and to *give occasion to the mind to form a thought of greater extent than its expression . . .*"

### B.1.13.   The enthymematic premises

The place we start from in order to follow the pleasant path of the enthymeme is its premises. This is a known place, and certain, but not with scientific certainty: with our human certainty. And what is it we regard as certain? 1. what falls within the realm of the senses, what we see and hear: the sure indices, *tekmeria*; 2. what falls within the realm of meaning, that on which men have generally reached agreement, what is established by laws, what has passed into usage ("the gods exist," "honor thy parents," etc.): these are the probabilities, *eikota*, or, generically, the probable (*eikos*); 3. between these two types of human "certainty," Aristotle posits a more fluid category: the *semeia*, the signs (a thing which serves to make another understood, *per quod alias res intelligitur*).

### B.1.14.   The *tekmerion, the sure index*

The *tekmerion* is the sure index, the necessary sign, or even "the indestructible sign," the one which is what it is and cannot be otherwise. A woman has given birth: this is the sure index (*tekmerion*) that she has had intercourse with a man. This premise is closely related to the one which inaugurates the scientific syllogism, though it is based only on universality of experience. As always when we exhume this old logical (or rhetorical) material, we are struck by seeing it function so readily among the works of so-called mass culture—to the point where we may wonder if Aristotle is not the philosopher of that culture and consequently does not establish the criticism which can have some grasp of it; these works, in fact, mobilize current examples of physical "evidence" which may serve as points of departure for implicit reasoning, for a certain rational perception of the unfolding of the anecdote. In *Goldfinger*, there is an electrocution by water: this is a known phenomenon, has no need to be proved, it is a "natural" premise, a *tekmerion*; elsewhere (in the same film) a woman dies because her body has been gold-

plated; here, we have to know that being painted with gold keeps
the skin from breathing and therefore provokes asphyxia: this, being
rare, needs to be established (by an explanation); hence it is not
a *tekmerion*, or at least it is "suspended" until an antecedent certainty
is established (asphyxia causes death). It follows that the *tekmeria*
do not have, historically, the fine stability which Aristotle attributes
to them: what is public "certainty" depends on public "knowledge"
and this varies with periods and societies; to return to Quintilian's
example (and belie it), I am told that certain populations make no
connection between giving birth and the sexual relation (the child
sleeps in the mother, God wakens it).

### B.1.15. *Eikos,* the probable

The second type of (human, not scientific) "certainty" which
can serve as a premise for the enthymeme is the probable, a crucial
notion in Aristotle's eyes. This is a general notion based on the
judgment which men have made by imperfect experiments and
inductions (Perelman proposes calling it the *preferable*). In Aristotelian probability, there are two nuclei: 1. the notion of *general*,
as distinct from the notion of *universal*: the universal is necessary
(it is the attribute of science), the general is not; it is a human
"generality," ultimately determined statistically by the opinion of
the greatest number; 2. the possibility of the contrary; of course
the enthymeme is received by the public as a sure syllogism, it seems
to start from an opinion believed to be "as hard as rock"; but in
relation to science, the probable admits of its contrary: within the
limits of human experience and of ethical life, which are those of
*eikos*, the contrary is never impossible: one cannot foresee with any
(scientific) certainty the resolutions of a free being: "a man in good
health will see the sun tomorrow," "a father loves his children,"
"a theft committed without breaking in must have been an inside
job," etc.; very likely, but the contrary is still possible; the analyst,
the rhetorician perceives the force of these opinions, but in all
honesty he keeps them at a distance by introducing them with an

*esto* (*so be it*), which clears him in the eyes of science, where the contrary is never possible.

### B.1.16.   Semeion, *the sign*

The *semeion*, third possible point of departure for the enthymeme, is a more ambiguous index, less certain than the *tekmerion*. Traces of blood suggest a murder, but this is not a certainty: such blood can result from a nosebleed or a sacrifice. For the sign to be convincing, there must be other concomitant signs; or again: for the sign to cease to be polysemic (the *semeion* is in fact the polysemic sign), a context must be resorted to. Atalanta was not a virgin, since she would run through the woods with boys: for Quintilian, this remains to be proved; the proposition is in fact so uncertain that he rejects the *semeion* outside the orator's *technè*: the orator cannot apprehend the *semeion* in order to transform it, by an enthymematic conclusion, into a certainty.

### B.1.17.   *Practice of the enthymeme*

Insofar as the enthymeme is a "public" reasoning, it was licit to extend its practice outside the judicial, and it is possible to meet with it outside rhetoric (and outside Antiquity). Aristotle himself studied the *practical syllogism*, or enthymeme, whose conclusion is a decisional act; the major premise is occupied by a current maxim (*eikos*); in the minor premise, the agent (myself, for instance) notes that he finds himself in the situation covered by the major premise; he concludes by a decision of conduct. How does it happen, then, that the conclusion so often contradicts the major premise, and that the action resists knowledge? It is because, very often, there is a deviation from the major to the minor premise: the minor premise surreptitiously implies another major premise: "drinking alcohol is harmful to man; now, I am a man; hence I must not drink" and yet, despite this fine enthymeme, I drink; this is because I "secretly" refer to another major premise: the sparkling and the ice-cold quench my thirst, quenching my thirst is a good thing (a major premise familiar to advertising and to barroom conversations). Another possible extension of the enthymeme: into the "cold" and rational languages, at once distant and public, such as institutional languages (public diplomacy, for example): Chinese students having staged a demonstration in front of the American embassy in Moscow (March 1965), the demonstration having been suppressed by the Russian police, and the Chinese government having protested against this suppression, a Soviet note answers the Chinese protest by a splendid epicheirema, worthy of Cicero (cf. *supra*, B.1.11): 1. major premise: *eikos*, general opinion: *there exist diplomatic norms, respected by all countries*; 2. proof of the major premise: *the Chinese themselves respect, in their own country, these norms of reception*; 3. minor premise: *now, the Chinese students, in Moscow, have violated these norms*; 4. proof of the minor premise: the account of the demonstration (*insults, street fighting, and other actions mentioned in the criminal code*); 5. the conclusion is not uttered (it is an enthymeme), but it is clear: it is the note itself as a rejection of the Chinese protest: the adversary has been shown in contradiction with the *eikos* and with himself.

### B.1.18.   Place, topos, locus

The classes of enthymematic premises have been articulated, but we must still fill these classes, find premises: we have the main forms, but how to invent the contents? This is the agonizing question always posed by Rhetoric and which it seeks to answer: *what is to be said?* Whence the importance of the answer, attested to by the breadth and the success of that part of the *Inventio* which is responsible for supplying reasoning with its contents and which begins here: the *Topics*. Indeed the premises can be derived from certain *places*. What is a place? It is, says Aristotle, that in which a plurality of oratorical reasonings coincide. Places, says Port-Royal, are "certain general heads to which can be attached all the proofs used in the various matters treated"; or again (Lamy): "general opinions which remind those who consult them of all the sides by which a subject can be considered." Yet the metaphoric approach to place is more significant than its abstract definition. Many metaphors have been used to identify place. First of all, why *place?* Because, says Aristotle, in order to remember things, it suffices to recognize the place where they happen to be (place is therefore the element of an association of ideas, of a conditioning, of a training, of a mnemonics); places then are not the arguments themselves but the compartments in which they are arranged. Hence every image conjoining the notion of a space with that of storage, of a localization with an extraction: a region (where one can find arguments), a *vein of some mineral*, a *circle*, a *sphere*, a *spring*, a *well*, an *arsenal*, a *treasury*, and even a *pigeon-hole* (W. D. Ross); "Places," says Dumarsais, "are the cells where everyone can find, so to speak, the substance of a discourse and arguments on all sorts of subjects." A scholastic logician, exploiting the domestic nature of place, compares it to a label which indicates the content of a receptacle (*pyxidum indices*); for Cicero, the arguments, deriving from places, will present themselves for the case to be argued "like the letters for the word to be written": hence places form that very special storehouse constituted by the alphabet: a *corpus* of forms without meaning in themselves, but determining meaning by selection, arrangement, actualization. In relation to place, what is the *Topics?* It appears that we can distinguish three successive definitions, or at least three orientations of the word. The Topics is—or has been: 1. a method; 2. a grid of empty forms; 3. a storehouse of filled forms.

### B.1.19.  The Topics: a method
Originally (following Aristotle's *Topica*, anterior to his Rhetoric), the Topics was a collection of commonplaces of dialectic, *i.e.* of the syllogism based on probability (intermediary between certain and probable knowledge), then Aristotle makes a method of it, more practical than dialectic: a method which "enables us, on any subject proposed, to supply conclusions drawn from probable rea-

sons." This meaning—of the Topics as a method—was able to persist or at least to reappear at intervals throughout rhetoric's history: in time the method became the art (an organized knowledge with a view to instruction: *disciplina*) of finding arguments (Isidore), or further: a group of "brief and easy means for finding the substance of discoursing even on subjects which are entirely unknown" (Lamy)— we can understand philosophy's suspicions with regard to such a method.

### B.1.20.   The Topics: a grid

The second meaning is that of a network of forms, of a quasi-cybernetic process to which we subject the material we want to transform into a persuasive discourse. Matters must be represented thus: a *subject* (*quaestio*) is given to the orator; in order to find arguments, the orator "passes" his subject over a grid of empty forms: from the contact between the subject and each compartment (each "place") of the grid (of the Topics) appears a possible idea, an enthymematic premise. There existed in Antiquity a pedagogic version of this procedure: the *chréia* or "useful" exercise was a test of virtuosity given to students which consisted in "passing" a theme through a series of places: *quis? quid? ubi? quibus auxiliis? cur? quomodo? quando?* Taking his inspiration from ancient Topics, Lamy, in the seventeenth century, proposes the following grid: genre, difference, definition, enumeration of parts, etymology, conjugations (this is the associative field of the verbal root), comparison, repugnance, effects, causes, etc. Let us suppose that we must produce a discourse on literature: we "dry up" (with good reason), but fortunately we possess Lamy's Topics: we can then, at least, ask ourselves questions and try to answer them: to what "genre" will we attach literature? art? discourse? cultural production? If it is an "art," how does it differ from the other arts? How many parts are we to assign to it, and which ones? What does the etymology of the word suggest to us? its relation to its morphological neighbors (*literary*, *literal*, *letters*, etc.)? With what does literature sustain a relation of repugnance? Money? Truth? etc.[22] The conjunction of the grid and the *quaestio* resembles that of the theme and its predicates, the subject and its attributes: the "attributive Topics" achieves its apogee in the tables of the Lullists (*ars brevis*): the general attributes are kinds of places. —We see the range of the topical grid: the metaphors which aim at place (*topos*) suggest it quite clearly: the arguments are *hidden*, they *lurk* in regions, depths from which they must be drawn, wakened, etc.: the Topics is the midwife of the *latent*: it is a form which articulates contents and thereby produces fragments of meaning, intelligible units.

### B.1.21.   The Topics: a storehouse

The *places* are in principle empty forms; but these forms quickly tended to be filled, always in the same way, to require certain contents, at first contingent, then repeated, reified. The Topics became a storehouse of stereotypes, of consecrated themes, of full "pieces" which are almost obligatorily employed in the treatment of any subject. Whence the historical ambiguity of the expression *commonplaces* (*topoi koinoi, loci communi*): 1. they are empty forms common to all arguments (the emptier they are, the more common, cf. *infra* B.1.23); 2. they are stereotypes, hackneyed propositions. The Topics, a full storehouse: this meaning is not Aristotle's, but it is already that of the Sophists who had felt the necessity of having a table of things commonly spoken of and on which one must not be "cornered." This reification of the Topics has been regularly extended, beyond Aristotle, through the Latin authors; it has triumphed in neo-rhetoric and was absolutely general in the Middle Ages. Curtius has given a list of these obligatory themes, accompanied by their fixed treatment. Here are some of these reified places (in the Middle Ages): 1. *topos* of affected modesty: every orator

---

[22] These topical grids are "stupid," they have no relation to "life," "truth," and have rightly been banished from modern instruction, etc.: no doubt: yet the "subjects" (of themes, of dissertations) must still follow this fine movement. Even as I write, I understand that one of the "subjects" of the last baccalaureate exam was something like "Must we still respect the elderly?" For a stupid subject, an indispensable topics.

must declare that he is crushed by his subject, that he is incompetent, that it is certainly no coquetry to say as much, etc. (*excusatio propter infirmitatem*);[23] 2. *topos* of the *puer senilis*: this is the magical theme of the youth endowed with perfect wisdom or of the old man endowed with the grace and beauty of youth; 3. *topos* of the *locus amoenus*: the ideal landscape, Elysium or Paradise (trees, groves, spring, and meadows) has furnished a good number of literary "descriptions" (cf. *ekphrasis*, A.5.2), but its origin is judicial: any demonstrative relation of a case made necessary the *argumentum a loco*: one had to establish proofs on the nature of the place where the action occurred; topography then invaded literature (from Virgil to Barrès); once reified, the *topos* has a fixed content, independent of context: olive trees and lions are set in northern regions: *landscape* is detached from *place*, for its function is to constitute a universal sign, that of Nature: landscape is the cultural sign of Nature; 4. the *adynata* (*impossibilia*): this *topos* describes as suddenly compatible contrary phenomena, objects, and beings, a paradoxical conversion functioning as the disturbing sign of a world "upside down": *the wolf flees before the sheep* (Virgil); this *topos* flourishes in the Middle Ages, when it permitted a criticism of the times: it is the theme of the grumbler, of the old man who says "now I've seen everything" or "this is really too much."[24] All these *topoi*, and even before the Middle Ages, are detachable pieces (a proof of their powerful reification) that can be mobilized, transported: they are the elements of a syntagmatic combine; their placement was subject

---

[23] The *excusatio propter infirmitatem* still prevails quite commonly in our writings. Consider this humorous *excusatio* by Michel Cournot (*Le Nouvel Observateur*, March 4, 1965): "I am not going to laugh this week, the Gospel is my subject, and why not say so right off, I am not up to it, etc."

[24] Two examples of *adynata*:

Delille: "Soon to the black crow the swallow shall be joined; soon to his love the faithless dove, far from the conjugal nest, shall fearless bear to the savage kite his heart and all his love."

Théophile de Viau: "This stream flows backward to its source, an ox ascends the steeple, blood flows from this rock, a viper couples with a bear. Atop an ancient tower, a serpent tears apart a vulture; fire burns within the ice, the sun has turned black, I see the moon about to fall, that tree has left its place."

to a single reservation: they could not be put in *peroratio* (peroration), which is entirely contingent, for it must summarize the *oratio*. However, ever since and even today, how many stereotyped conclusions!

### B.1.22.  Some Topics

Let us return to our Topics-grid, for that is what will allow us to follow the "descent" of our rhetorical tree, of which it is the great distributive place. Antiquity and classicism have produced several Topics defined either by the affinitive grouping of places, or by that of subjects. In the first case, we can cite the general Topics of Port-Royal, inspired by the German logician Clauberg (1654); the Topics of Lamy, already cited, affords some notion of it: there are places of grammar (etymology, *conjugata*), places of logic (genus, property, accident, species, difference, definition, division), the places of metaphysics (final cause, efficient cause, effect, whole, parts, opposing terms): this is evidently an Aristotelian Topics. In the second case, which is that of Topics by subjects, we can cite the following Topics: 1. the *oratorical Topics* proper, which includes three topics: a topics of reasoning, a topics of *mores* (*ethé*: practical intelligence, virtue, affection, devotion) and a topics of passions (*pathé*: anger, love, fear, shame, and their contraries); 2. a *topics of the laughable*, part of a possible rhetoric of the comic; Cicero and Quintilian listed several places of the laughable: bodily defects, mental defects, incidents, exteriors, etc.; 3. a *theological topics*: this includes the various sources from which the theologians can draw their arguments: Scripture, Fathers, Councils, etc.; 4. a *topics of sensibility* or *topics of imagination*; we find this sketched in Vico: "The founders of civilization [allusion to the anteriority of Poetry] turned to a *topics of sensibility*, in which they united the properties, the qualities, or the relations of individuals or of races and employed them concretely to form their poetic genre"; Vico speaks elsewhere of the "*universals of the imagination*"; in this topics of sensibility we may see an ancestor of our thematic criticism, which proceeds by categories and not by authors: Bachelard's in short: the ascensional, the cavernous, the torrential, the mirroring, the slumbering, etc. are so many "places" to which the poets' images may be referred.

### B.1.23. Commonplaces

The Topics, strictly speaking (the oratorical, Aristotelian topics), the one which depends on *pisteis entechnoi*, as opposed to the topics of characters and the topics of passions, includes two parts, two subtopics: 1. a general topics, that of commonplaces; 2. an applied topics, that of special places. For Aristotle, *commonplaces* (*topoi koinoi, loci communissimi*) have a meaning quite different from the one we attribute to the expression (under the influence of the third meaning of the word *Topics, cf. supra*, B.1.21). Commonplaces are out-and-out stereotypes, but on the contrary formal places: being general (the general is appropriate to the probable), they are common to all subjects. For Aristotle, these commonplaces are of three sorts: 1. the *possible/impossible*; confronted by time (past, future), these terms afford a topic question: can the thing have been done or not, could it be done or not? This place can be applied to relations of contrariety: if it was possible for a thing to begin, it is possible for it to end, etc.; 2. *existent/non-existent* (or *real/unreal*); like the preceding, this place can be confronted by time: if a thing unlikely to occur has nonetheless occurred, what is more likely has certainly occurred (happened); there are building materials here: it is likely that a house will be built (future); 3. *more/less*: this is the place of the great and the small; its mainspring is "with all the more reason" (*a fortiori*): there is a strong chance that X has attacked his neighbors, since he has attacked his own father. —Although commonplaces, by definition, are unspecialized, each is better suited to one of the three oratorical genres: the *possible/impossible* matches the deliberative (is it possible to do this?), the *real/unreal* matches the judicial (did the crime take place?), the *more/less* matches the epideictic (praise or blame).

### B.1.24. Special places

Special places (*eidè, idia*) are places (*topoi*) appropriate to specific subjects; these are generally accepted particular truths, special propositions; they are the experimental truths attached to politics, law, finances, to war, naval actions, etc. However, since these places (*topoi*) are inextricably linked to the practice of disciplines, of genres, of particular subjects, they cannot be enumerated. The theoretical problem must be posed nevertheless. The extension of our "tree" will thus depend on confronting *inventio*, such as we have known it to this point, with the special nature of the content. This confrontation is the *quaestio*.

### B.1.25. Thesis and hypothesis: causa

The *quaestio* is the form of the special nature of discourse. In all the operations ideally posed by the rhetorical "machine," a new variable is introduced (which is, actually, when it is a matter of *creating* the discourse, the variable of the point of departure): the content, the point at debate, in short, the referential. This referential, by contingent definition, can nonetheless be classified into two major forms, which constitute the two chief types of *quaestio*: 1. The *position* or *thesis* (*thèsis, propositum*): this is a general question—"abstract," we would say today—but specified, referred (otherwise it would not call for any special places), though without (and this is its mark) any parameter of place or of time (for example: *must one marry?*); 2. The *hypothesis* (*hypothèsis*): this is a particular question that specifies facts, circumstances, persons, in short a time and a place (for instance: *should X marry?*)—it is evident that in rhetoric the words *thesis* and *hypothesis* have an entirely different meaning from that we are accustomed to. Now, the hypothesis, that temporalized and localized point at debate, has another, prestigious name: *causa*. *Causa* is a *negotium*, an affair, a deal, a combination of various contingencies; a problematic point in which contingency is engaged, especially temporal contingency. Since there are three tenses (past, present, future), we shall have three types of *causa*, and each type will correspond to one of the three oratorical genres that we already know: here, then, they are—structurally established, located on our rhetorical tree. We can assign them their attributes:

| | Genre | Audience | End | Subject | Time | Reasoning (a) | Common-places |
|---|---|---|---|---|---|---|---|
| 1 | DELIBER-ATIVE | members of an assembly | to per-suade/dissuade | useful/harmful | future | exempla | possible/impossible |
| 2 | JUDICIAL | judges | to accuse/defend | just/unjust | past | enthy-meme | real/unreal |
| 3 | EPIDEICTIC | spectators, public | to praise/blame | beautiful/ugly | present | amplifying comparison (b) | more/less |

(a) The dominant method of reasoning
(b) A variety of induction, an *exemplum* oriented toward the exaltation of the person praised (by implicit comparisons)

### B.1.26.   Status causae

Of these three genres, it is the judicial which received the most thorough commentary in Antiquity; the rhetorical tree extends it beyond its neighbors. The special places of the judicial are called *status causae*. A *status causae* is the heart of the *quaestio*, the point to be judged; this is the moment where the first shock between adversaries, parties, occurs; anticipating this conflict, the orator must seek out the *bearing* of the *quaestio* (whence the words: *stasis*, *status*). The *status causae* greatly excited the taxonomic passion of Antiquity. The simplest classification lists three *status causae* (we are dealing with the *forms* the contingent can take): 1. *conjecture*: did this occur or not (*an sit*)? is the first place because it is the immediate result of a first conflict of assertions: *fecisti/non feci: an fecerit?* (did you do it? no, it wasn't me, is it he?); 2. definition (*quid sit?*): what is the legal qualification of the fact, under what (juridical) name is it to be classified? is it a crime? a sacrilege? 3. quality (*quale sit?*): is the deed permitted, useful, excusable? This is the order of attenuating circumstances. To these three places is sometimes added a fourth, of a procedural order: this is the state (*status*) of disclaiming competence (realm of Cassation). —Once the *status causae* are posited, *probatio* is exhausted; we proceed from the theoretical elaboration of discourse (rhetoric is a *technè*, a speculative practice) to discourse itself; we come to the point where the "machine" of the orator, of the *ego*, must be articulated around the machine of the adversary, who on his side will have covered the same ground, performed the same tasks. This articulation, this meshing, is obviously agonistic: it is the *disceptatio*, friction point between the two parties.

### B.1.27. Subjective or ethical proofs

The entire *probatio* (the body of logical proofs whose end is *to persuade*) having been passed through, we must return to the initial dichotomy that opened the field of *Inventio* and go back up to the subjective or ethical proofs, those that depend on *moving the hearers*. This is the department of psychological Rhetoric. Two names prevail here: Plato (types of discourse must be found that are adapted to types of souls) and Pascal (the inner movement of the other's thought must be discovered). As for Aristotle, he acknowledges a psychological rhetoric, but since he continues to make it depend on a *technè*, it is a "projected" psychology: psychology as everyone imagines it: not "what is in the mind" of the public, but what the public believes others "have in mind": this is an *endoxon*, a "probable" psychology, as opposed to "true" psychology, as the enthymeme is opposed to the "true" (demonstrative) syllogism. Before Aristotle, technographers recommended taking into account such psychological states as pity; but Aristotle was innovative in carefully classifying the passions not according to what they are, but according to what they are believed to be: he does not describe them scientifically, but seeks out the arguments which can be used with respect to the public's ideas about passion. The passions are specifically premises, places: Aristotle's rhetorical "psychology" is a description of the *eikos*, of passional probability. The psychological proofs are divided into two major groups: *ethè* (characters, tones, qualities) and *pathè* (passions, sentiments, affects).

### B.1.28.  Ethè, characters, tones

Ethè are the attributes of the orator (and not those of the public, pathè): these are the character traits which the orator must *show* the public (his sincerity is of little account) in order to make a good impression: these are his "airs," his qualities, his expressions. Hence there is no question here of an expressive psychology; it is a psychology of the imaginary (in the psychoanalytic sense: of the imaginary as an image-repertoire): I must signify what I want to be *for the other*. This is why—in the perspective of this theatrical psychology—it is better to speak of *tones* than of characters: tone in the musical and ethical sense which the word had in Greek music. *Ethos* is, strictly speaking, a connotation: the orator gives a piece of information and *at the same time* says: I am this, I am not that. For Aristotle, there are three "airs" which as a group constitute the orator's personal authority: 1. *phronèsis*: the quality of one who deliberates carefully, who weighs the *pro* and the *con*: this is an objective wisdom, a paraded good sense; 2. *arété*: the showing of a frankness which does not fear the consequences and expresses itself by means of direct remarks, stamped with a theatrical straightfor- wardness; 3. *eunoia*: a matter of not shocking, of not being pro- vocative, of being sympathetic (and perhaps even lovable), of entering into a pleasing complicity with the public. In short, while he speaks and unfolds the protocol of logical proofs, the orator must also keep saying: follow me (*phronèsis*), esteem me (*arété*) and love me (*eunoia*).

### B.1.29.  Pathè, sentiments

Pathè are affects of the listener (and no longer of the speaker), at least what he imagines them to be. Aristotle does not deal with them except from the perspective of a *technè*, that is to say, as protases of the argumentative links: a distance he marks by the *esto* (*granted that*) which precedes the description of each passion and which, as we have seen, is the operator of the "probable." Each "passion" is identified in its habitus (the general dispositions which favor it), according to its object (for whom it is felt), and according to the circumstances which provoke "crystallization" (*anger/calm, hatred/friendship, fear/trust, envy/emulation, ingratitude/helpfulness*, etc.). The point must be insisted on, for this marks Aristotle's profound modernity and makes him the ideal patron of a society of "mass culture": all these passions are deliberately taken *in their banality*: anger is what everyone thinks about anger, passion is never anything but what people say it is: pure intertextuality, "citation" (this is how Paolo and Francesca understood it, who loved each other only because they had read about Lancelot's love). Rhetorical psychology is therefore quite the opposite of a reductive psychology which would try to see what is *behind* what people say and which would attempt to reduce anger, for instance, to *something else*, something hidden. For Aristotle, public opinion is the first and last datum; he has no hermeneutic notion (of decipherment); for him, the passions are ready-made pieces of language which the orator must simply be familiar with; whence the notion of a *grid of passions*, not as a collection of essences but as a collection of opinions. For the reductive psychology (prevailing today) Aristotle substitutes (in advance) a classificatory psychology which distinguishes "languages." It may seem quite banal (and no doubt wrong) to say that young men are more easily angered than old men; but this platitude (and this mistake) becomes interesting if we realize that such a proposition is merely an element of that *general language of the other* which Aristotle reconstitutes, according perhaps to the arcanum of Aristotelian philosophy: "what everyone believes to be true is actually true" (*Eth. Nic.*, X.2.1173a1).

### B.1.30. Semina probationum

Thus closes the field or the network of *Inventio*, the heuristic preparation of the materials of discourse. Now we must approach *Oratio* itself: the order of its parts (*Dispositio*) and its realization in words (*Elocutio*). What are the "programmatic" relations of *Inventio* and *Oratio*? Quintilian puts it in a word (an image): he recommends using even in *narratio* (*i.e.*, before the argumentative part proper) certain "seeds of proofs" (*semina quaedam probationum spargere*).

Thus between *Inventio* and *Oratio* there is a relation of *dispersal*: one must suggest, then be silent, reintroduce, start up later on. In other words, the materials of *Inventio* are already pieces of language, posited in a state of *reversibility*, which now must be inserted into an inevitable and irreversible order, which is that of the discourse. Whence the second major operation of *technè*: *Dispositio*, or treatment of the constraints of succession.

## B.2.   Dispositio

We have seen that the situation of *Dispositio* (*Taxis*) in *technè* constituted an important stake. Without returning to this problem, we shall define *dispositio* as the arrangement (either in the active, operational sense, or in the passive, reified sense) of the major parts of the discourse. The best translation is perhaps: *composition*, recalling that in Latin *compositio* is something else: it refers solely to the arrangement of words within the sentence; *conlocatio* designates the distribution of materials within each part. According to an augmentative syntagmatics, then, we have: the level of the sentence (*compositio*), the level of the part (*conlocatio*), the level of discourse (*dispositio*). The main parts of the discourse were posited very early by Corax (cf. *supra* A.1.2.) and their distribution has not varied much subsequently: Quintilian articulates five parts (he doubles the third part into *confirmatio* and *refutatio*), Aristotle four: it is the latter division that will be adopted here.

### B.2.1.   Egressio

Before enumerating these fixed parts, we must indicate the optional existence of a movable part: *egressio* or *digressio*: this is a ceremonial piece, outside the subject or attached to it by a very loose link, and whose function is to show the orator at his best; it is most often a eulogy of places or persons (for example, the praise of Sicily in Cicero's *Verres*). This movable unit, outside classification, and one might say, supernumerary—origin of neo-rhetoric's *ekphrasis*—is an operator of spectacle, a sort of stamp, a signature of the "sovereign language" (Gorgias's *kurôsis*, Jakobson's *poetic*).

Yet just as a painting is always signed in the same place, so *digressio* has ended up by being placed more or less regularly between *narratio* and *confirmatio*.

### B.2.2. Paradigmatic structure of the four parts

*Dispositio* starts from a dichotomy which was already, in other terms, that of *Inventio*: *impellere animos* (to move)/*rem docere* (to inform, to convince). The first term (appeal to the sentiments) covers the *exordium* and the *epilogue*, *i.e.*, the two extremities of the discourse. The second term (appeal to facts, to reason) covers *narratio* (relation of facts or deeds) and *confirmatio* (establishment of proofs or means of persuasion), *i.e.*, the two median parts of the discourse. The syntagmatic order therefore does not follow the paradigmatic order, and we are faced with a chiasmus-construction: two slices of "passional" material frame a demonstrative *bloc*:

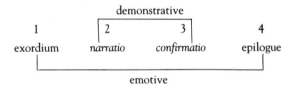

We shall treat the four parts according to the paradigmatic order: exordium/epilogue, narration/confirmation.

### B.2.3. The beginning and the end

The formalization of beginnings and ends, of openings and closings, is a problem which exceeds rhetoric (rites, protocols, liturgies). The opposition of the exordium and the epilogue, in clearly constituted forms, has doubtless something archaizing about it; hence, in developing and secularizing itself, the rhetorical code has come to tolerate discourses without exordium (in the deliberative genre), according to the rule of *in medias res*, and even to recommend abrupt ends (Isocrates, for example). In its canonical form, the opposition *beginning/end* involves a differentiation: in the exordium, the orator must commence with prudence, reserve, proportion; in the epilogue he need no longer contain himself, he commits himself deeply, brings forth all the resources of the machinery of pathos.

### B.2.4. The proem

In archaic poetry, that of the bards, the *prooïmon* (proem) is what comes before the song (*oimê*): it is the prelude of the lyre players who, before the contest, limber their fingers and take advantage of the occasion to win over the jury in advance (traces of this persist in Wagner's *Die Meistersinger*). The *oimê* is an old epic ballad: the reciter began to tell the story at a more or less arbitrary moment: he could have "taken it up" earlier or later (the story is "infinite"); the first words *cut* the virtual thread of a narrative without origin. This arbitrariness of the beginning was marked by the words *ex ou* (starting from which): I am beginning starting from here; the bard of the *Odyssey* asks the Muse to sing the return of Ulysses *"starting wherever she pleases."* The function of the proem is, then, to exorcise the arbitrariness of any beginning. Why begin here rather than there? For what reason does speech cut into what Ponge (author of *Proèmes*) calls the *raw analogical magma*? This cut of the knife must be made less harsh, this anarchy requires a protocol of decision: this is the *prooïmon*. Its evident role is to *tame*, as if beginning to speak, encountering language were to risk waking the unknown, the scandalous, the monstrous. In each of us, there is a terrifying formality about "breaking" silence (or the *other* language), except for those babblers who fling themselves headlong into speech and "take" it by force, anywhere and everywhere: this is what is called "spontaneity." Such, perhaps, is the basis from which the rhetorical exordium, the regulated inauguration of discourse, proceeds.

### B.2.5. The exordium

The exordium canonically includes two moments: 1. the *captatio benevolentiae*, or enterprise of seduction with regard to the public, which must immediately be conciliated by an assay of complicity. The *captatio* has been one of the most stable elements of the rhetorical system (it flourished well into the Middle Ages, and is still found today); it follows a highly elaborate model, codified according to the classification of *causes*: the means of seduction varies according to the relation of the cause to the *doxa*, to current, normal opinion; *a.* if the cause is identified with the *doxa*, if it is a "normal" cause, in good repute, there is no use subjecting the judge to any seduction, to any pressure; this is the genre known as *endoxon*, *honestum*; *b.* if the cause is more or less neutral in relation to the *doxa*, a positive action is required in order to conquer the judge's inertia, to waken his curiosity, to make him attentive (*attentum*): this is the genre known as *adoxon*, *humile*; *c.* if the cause is ambiguous, if for instance two *doxai* are in conflict, the judge's favor must be won, the judge must be rendered *benevolum*, be made to side with the speaker; this is the genre known as *amphidoxon*, *dubium*; if the cause is confused, obscure, the judge must be made to follow you as his guide, as an enlightener, he must be rendered *docilem*, receptive, malleable; this is the genre known as *dysparakoloutheton*, *obscurum*; finally, if the cause is extraordinary, provokes astonishment by its location very far from the *doxa* (for instance: to plead against a father, an old man, a child, a blind man, to proceed counter to the "human touch"), a vague action (a connotation) upon the judge no longer suffices, a true remedy is required, but this remedy must nonetheless be indirect, for the judge must not be openly affronted or shocked: this is *insinuatio*, an autonomous fragment (and no longer a simple tone) which is placed after the beginning: for example, to pretend to be overwhelmed by the adversary. Such are the modes of the *captatio benevolentiae*. 2. The *partitio*, second moment of the exordium, announces the divisions that will be adopted, the plan that will be followed (the *partitiones* can be multiplied, one can be placed at the beginning of each part); the advantage, Quintilian says, is that we never find long something whose end is announced in advance.

### B.2.6. The epilogue

How are we to know if a discourse is finished? This is quite as arbitrary as the beginning. Hence there must be a sign for the end, a sign of closure (as in certain manuscripts: *"ci falt la geste que Turoldus declinet"*). This sign has been rationalized under the alibi of pleasure (which would prove how conscious the Ancients were of the "tedium" of their speeches!). Aristotle has mentioned it, not apropos of the epilogue, but apropos of the period: the period is an "agreeable" sentence because it is the contrary of the one which does not come to an end; on the contrary is it disagreeable not to be able to anticipate what is coming, to have no ending in sight. The epilogue (*peroratio, conclusio, cumulus,* crowning touch) includes two levels: 1. the level of "things" (*posita in rebus*): a question of continuing and summarizing (*enumeratio, rerum repetitio*); 2. the level of "sentiments" (*posita in affectibus*): this pathetic, even tearful conclusion was little used by the Greeks, where an usher would impose silence upon the orator who tugged the heartstrings too hard and too long; but in Rome the epilogue was the occasion for a great piece of theater, for the advocate's gestures: to reveal the accused surrounded by his relatives and children, to exhibit a bloody dagger, fragments of bone taken from the wound: Quintilian lists all these devices.

### B.2.7. Narratio

*Narratio* (*diegesis*) is indeed the account of the facts involved in the cause (since *causa* is the *quaestio* imbued with contingency), but this account is conceived solely from the point of view of the proof, it is "the persuasive exposition of a thing done or claimed to have been done." The narration is therefore not a *recital* (in the disinterested sense of the word) but an argumentative protasis. It has, consequently, two obligatory characteristics: 1. its nakedness: no digressions, no prosopopeia, no direct argumentation; there is no *technè* proper to *narratio*; it must be merely *clear, probable, brief*; 2. its functionality: it is a preparation for argumentation; the best preparation is the one whose meaning is concealed, whose proofs are disseminated as imperceptible seeds (*semina probationum*). *Narratio* involves two types of elements: facts and descriptions.

### *B.2.8.* Ordo naturalis/ordo artificialis

In ancient rhetoric, the exposition of facts is subject to a single structural rule: that the connections be probable. But later, in the Middle Ages, when Rhetoric was completely detached from the judicial, *narratio* became an autonomous genre and the arrangement of its parts (*ordo*) became a theoretical problem: this is the opposition of *ordo naturalis* and *ordo artificialis*. "Every order," says a contemporary of Alcuin, "is either natural or artificial. The order is natural if the facts are told in the very order in which they occurred; the order is artificial if one sets out, not from the beginning of what has happened, but from the middle." This is the problem of the flashback. *Ordo artificialis* requires a segmentation of the sequence of facts, since it is a question of obtaining movable, reversible units; it implies or produces a special intelligibility, one deliberately shown, since it destroys the (mythic) "nature" of linear time. The opposition of the two "orders" may bear not on the facts but on the very parts of the discourse: then *ordo naturalis* is what respects the traditional norm (exordium, *narratio, confirmatio,* epilogue), and *ordo artificialis* is what disrupts this order according to circumstances; paradoxically (and this paradox is no doubt a frequent one) *naturalis* then means *cultural*, and *artificialis* means spontaneous, contingent, natural.

### *B.2.9.   The descriptions*

Alongside the strictly chronological—or diachronic, or diegetic—axis, *narratio* admits of an aspectual, durative axis formed by a hovering sequence of stases: *descriptions*. These have been powerfully encoded. There have been chiefly: *topographies*, or descriptions of places; *chronographies*, or descriptions of time, of periods, of ages; *prosopographies*, or portraits. We know the fortune of these "pieces" in our literature, outside the judicial. —Lastly we must indicate, to finish with *narratio*, that the discourse can sometimes include a second narration; the first having been very short, it is resumed subsequently in detail ("Here in detail is how the thing I have just spoken of transpired"): this is the *epidiegesis*, the *repetita narratio*.

### B.2.10.  Confirmatio

*Narratio*, or the account of the facts, is followed by *confirmatio*, or the account of the arguments: it is here that the "proofs" elaborated in the course of *inventio* are uttered. *Confirmatio (apodeixis)* can include three elements: 1. *propositio (prothèsis)*: a concentrated definition of the cause, of the point in debate; it can be simple or multiple, depending on the headings ("Socrates was accused of corrupting the young and of introducing new superstitions"); *argumentatio*, which is the account of convincing reasons; no particular structuration is recommended, except this: one must begin by the strong reasons, continue by the weak proofs, and end by some very strong proofs; 3. occasionally, at the end of the *confirmatio*, the continuous discourse (*oratio continua*) is interrupted by a very lively dialogue with the adversary lawyer or a witness: another voice breaks into the monologue: this is *altercatio*. This oratorical episode was unknown to the Greeks; it is attached to the genre *Rogatio* or accusatory interrogation (*"Quousque tandem, Catilina . . ."*).

### B.2.11.  Other segmentations of discourse

The powerful encoding of the *Dispositio* (of which a deep trace remains in our pedagogy of the "plan") attests to the fact that humanism, in its conception of language, was deeply concerned with the problem of syntagmatic units. *Dispositio* is one segmentation among others. Here are several of these segmentations, starting from the largest units: 1. the discourse as a whole can form a unit, if we set it in opposition to other discourses; this is the case of classification by genres or by styles; it is also the case of *figures of subjects*, a fourth type of figure after tropes, figures of words, and figures of thought: the *figure of subject* embraces the whole of the *oratio*; Dionysius of Halicarnassus distinguished three: *a.* the *direct* (saying what one means); *b.* the *oblique* (indirect discourse: Bossuet threatening the kings, *under the color of religion*); *c.* the contrary (antiphrasis, irony); 2. the parts of the *Dipositio* (which we know); 3. the piece, the fragment, *ekphrasis* or *descriptio* (which we also know); 4. in the Middle Ages, *articulus* is a unit of development: in a collective work, an anthology of *Disputationes* or a *Summa*, a summary is given of the disputed question (introduced by *utrum*); 5. *period* is a sentence structured according to an organic model (with beginning and end); it has at least two members (elevation and lowering, *tasis* and *apotasis*) and at most four. Below this (and in truth, starting from the period or periodic sentence), begins the sentence, object of *compositio*, a technical operation deriving from *Elocutio*.

## B.3.   Elocutio

The arguments found and broadly distributed in the parts of the discourse remain to be "put into words": this is the function of this third part of the *technè rhétorikè* known as *lexis* or *elocutio*, to which we are accustomed to pejoratively reducing rhetoric because of the interest the Moderns have taken in the figures of rhetoric, a part (but only a part) of *Elocutio*.

### B.3.1.   *Development of* Elocutio

Since the origin of Rhetoric, *Elocutio* has in fact considerably evolved. Missing from Corax's classification, it appears when Gorgias wants to apply esthetic criteria (drawn from poetry) to prose; Aristotle treats it less abundantly than the rest of rhetoric; it develops chiefly with the Latins (Cicero, Quintilian), flowers spiritually with Dionysius of Halicarnassus and the anonymous author of the *Peri Hypsos*, and ends by absorbing all Rhetoric, identified solely as "figures." However, in its canonical state, *Elocutio* defines a field which bears on *all* language: it includes both our grammar (until the heart of the Middle Ages) and what is called *diction*, the theater of the voice. The best translation of *elocutio* is perhaps not *elocution* (too limited) but *enunciation* or even *locution* (locutory activity).

### B.3.2.  The network

The internal classifications of *Elocutio* are many, doubtless for
two reasons: first, because this *technè* had to pass through different
idioms (Greek, Latin, Romance languages), each of which could
inflect the nature of the "figures"; second, because the growing
promotion of this part of rhetoric compelled terminological rein-
ventions (a patent fact in the bewildering naming of figures). We
shall simplify this network here. The mother-opposition is that of
the paradigm and the syntagm: 1. *to choose* the words (*electio, eglogè*);
2. *to assemble* them (*synthesis, compositio*).

### B.3.3.  "Colors"

*Electio* implies that in language we can substitute one term for
another: *electio* is possible because synonymy is part of the system
of language (Quintilian): the speaker can substitute one signifier
for another, he can even, in this substitution, produce a secondary
meaning (connotation). All the kinds of substitutions, whatever
their scope and fashion, are *Tropes* ("conversions"), but the meaning of the word is ordinarily reduced in order to be able to set it
in opposition to "Figures." The truly general terms, which cover
equally all the classes of substitutions, are "*ornaments*" and "*colors.*"
These two words clearly show, by their very connotations, how the
Ancients conceived language: 1. there is a naked base, a proper
level, a normal state of communication, starting from which we
can elaborate a more complicated expression, *ornamented*, endowed
with a greater or lesser *distance* in relation to the original ground.
This postulate is decisive, for it seems that even today it determines
all the attempts at reinvigoration of rhetoric: to recover rhetoric is
inevitably to believe in the existence of a *gap* between two states
of language; conversely, rhetoric is always condemned in the name
of a rejection of the hierarchy of languages, between which only a
"fluctuating" and not a fixed hierarchy based on nature is admitted;
2. the secondary layer (rhetoric) has an animating function: the
"proper" state of language is inert, the secondary state is "living":
colors, lights, flowers (*colores, lumina, flores*); the ornaments are on

the side of passion, of the body; they render speech desirable; there is a *venustas* of language (Cicero); 3. the *colors* are sometimes used "to spare modesty the embarrassment of too naked an exposition" (Quintilian); in other words, as a possible euphemism, *color* indexes a taboo, that of language's "nudity": like the blush which reddens a face, *color* exposes desire by hiding its object: it is the very dialectic of the garment (*schéma* means costume, *figura* appearance).

### B.3.4.  Taxonomic frenzy

What we call generically figures of rhetoric, but which with historical rigor and to avoid the ambiguity between *Tropes* and *Figures* it would be better to call "ornaments," have been for centuries and again today are the object of a veritable frenzy of classification, indifferent to the mockery which nonetheless sprang up very early. It appears that these figures of rhetoric can be invented merely by naming and classifying them: hundreds of terms, either very banal in form (*epithet, reticence*) or very barbaric (*anantapodoton, epanadiplosis, tapinosis,* etc.), dozens of groupings. Why this rage for segmentation, for denomination, this sort of delirious activity of language upon language? No doubt (at least this is one structural explanation) because rhetoric tries *to code speech* [*parole*] and no longer language [*langue*], *i.e.*, the very space where, in principle, the code ceases. This problem was seen by Saussure: what to do with the stable amalgams of words, of fixed syntagms, which participate both in language and in speech, in structure and in combination? It is to the degree that Rhetoric has prefigured a linguistics of speech (other than statistical), which is a contradiction in terms, that it has exhausted itself trying to hold within a necessarily more and more discriminating network the "manners of speaking," *i.e.*, trying to master the unmasterable: a true mirage.

### B.3.5.  Classification of ornaments

All these ornaments (hundreds of them) have been distributed down through history according to certain binary oppositions:

*tropes/figures, grammatical tropes/rhetorical tropes, figures of grammar
/figures of rhetoric, figures of words/figures of thought, tropes/figures of
diction.* From one author to the next, the classifications are contradictory: the *tropes* are here set in opposition to the *figures*, and
there are said to belong to them; for Lamy hyperbole is a trope, for
Cicero a figure of thought, etc. A word concerning the three most
frequent oppositions: 1. *Tropes/Figures*: this is the oldest of the
distinctions, that of Antiquity; in the Trope, the conversion of
meaning bears on one unit, on a word (for example, catachresis:
the *arm* of a windmill, the *leg* of a table); in the Figure, the conversion requires several words, a whole little syntagm (for instance,
the periphrasis: *the decent obscurity of a learned language*). This opposition would correspond by and large to that of the system and
the snytagm. 2. *Grammar/Rhetoric*: the tropes of grammar are conversions of meaning which have passed into current usage, to the
point where we no longer "sense" the ornament: *step on the gas*
(metonymy for *accelerator*), *primrose path* (trivialized metaphor),
whereas the tropes of rhetoric are still felt to be an unusual usage:
*Nature's laundry* for the Flood (Tertullian), *the ice floe of the keyboard*,
etc. This opposition would correspond by and large to that of denotation and connotation. 3. *Words/Thought*: the opposition of
figures of words and of figures of thought is the most banal: figures
of words exist where the figure would disappear if we changed the
words (*i.e.*, the anacoluthon, which depends entirely on the order
of the words: *Cleopatra's nose, had it been shorter, the face of the world
. . .* ); the figures of thought remain whatever words are chosen
(*i.e.*, the antithesis: *I am the wound and the knife*, etc.); this third
opposition is a mental one, it brings into play signifieds and signifiers, the former able to exist without the latter. —It is still
possible to conceive of new classifications of figures, and indeed
one can suggest that no one concerned with rhetoric fails to be
tempted to classify the figures in his turn and in his way. Yet we
still lack (but perhaps such a thing is impossible to produce) a purely
operational classification of the principal figures: dictionaries of
rhetoric, indeed, permit us to discover what a *chleuasmus* is,

or an *epanalepsis*, or a *paralepsis*, to proceed from the often quite hermetic name to the example; but no book allows us to make the converse trajectory, to proceed from the sentence (found in a text) to the name of the figure; if I read: *so much marble trembling over so much shadow*, what book will tell me this is a *hypallage*, if I do not already know this? We lack an inductive instrument, useful if we want to analyze the classical texts according to their actual metalanguage.

### B.3.6.  Review of some figures

There can of course be no question of giving a list of the "ornaments" acknowledged by the ancient rhetoric under the general name of "figures": dictionaries of rhetoric exist. Yet I believe it is useful to review the definition of ten or so figures, taken at random, so as to give a concrete perspective to these remarks about *electio*. 1. *Alliteration* is a close repetition of consonants in a brief syntagm (*the zeal of Lazarus*); when it is the timbres that are repeated, we have *apophony* (*il pleure dans mon coeur comme il pleut sur la ville*). It has been suggested that alliteration is frequently less intentional than the critics and stylisticians tend to believe; B. F. Skinner has shown that in Shakespeare's sonnets the alliterations do not exceed what one might expect from the normal frequency of letters and groups of letters. 2. *Anacoluthon* is a break in (sometimes defective) construction (*Rather proclaim it, Westmoreland, through my host, / that he which hath no stomach to this fight, /let him depart . . .* ). 3. *Catachresis* occurs where the language lacks the "proper" term and it is necessary to use a "figure" (*legs* of a table). 4. *Ellipsis* consists in suppressing syntactic elements to the point where intelligibility may be affected (*Je t'aimais inconstant, qu'eussé-je fait fidèle?*); ellipsis has often been said to represent a "natural" state of the language: the "normal" mode of speech, in pronunciation, in syntax, in dreams, in children's language. 5. *Hyperbole* consists in exaggerating: either by augmenting (*auxesis: to ride faster than the wind*), or by diminishing (*tapinosis: slower than a tortoise*). 6. *Irony* or *antiphrasis* consists in saying one thing that is meant to be understood as something else (connotation); as F. de Neufchateau says: *"She chooses her words: they all seem caressing, but the tone she uses gives them quite another meaning."* 7. *Periphrasis* is at its origin a detour of language made to avoid a taboo notation. If periphrasis is deprecatory, it is called *perissologia.* 8. *Reticence* or *aposiopesis* marks an interruption in discourse due to a sudden change in feeling (as in the Virgilian *Quos ego*). 9. *Suspension* delays the utterance, by addition of interpolated clauses, before resolving it: on the level of the sentence this is *suspense.*

### B.3.7.  Proper *and* Figured

As we have seen, every structure of "figures" is based on the notion that there exist two languages, one proper and one figured, and that consequently Rhetoric, in its elocutionary part, is a table of *deviations* of language. Since Antiquity, the meta-rhetorical expressions which attest to this belief are countless: in *elocutio* (field of figures), words are *"transported," "strayed," "deviated"* from their normal, familiar habitat. Aristotle sees in it a taste for alienation: one must "distance oneself from ordinary locutions . . . : we feel in this respect the same impressions as in the presence of strangers or foreigners: style is to be given a foreign air, for what comes from far away excites admiration." Hence there is a relation of *strangeness* between the "commonplace words" each of us uses (but who is this "we"?), and the "unaccustomed words," words alien to everyday use: "barbarisms" (words of foreign peoples), neologisms, metaphors, etc. For Aristotle there must be a mixture of the two terminologies, for if only ordinary words are used, the result is a *low* discourse, and if only unaccustomed words are used, the result is an *enigmatic* discourse. From *national/foreign* and *normal/strange,* the opposition has gradually shifted to *proper/figured.* What is the proper meaning? "It is the first signification of the word" (Dumarsais): "When the word signifies that for which it was originally established." Yet the proper meaning cannot be the earliest meaning (archaism is alienating), but the meaning *immediately anterior to the creation of the figured:* the proper, the true is, once again, the *foregoing* (the Father). In classical Rhetoric, the *foregoing* has been *naturalized*. Whence the paradox: how can the proper meaning be the "natural" meaning and the figured meaning be the "original" meaning?

### B.3.8. Function and origin of the figures

We may here distinguish two groups of explanations. 1. *Explanations by function*: *a.* the secondary language derives from the necessity to euphemize, to evade the taboos; *b.* the secondary language is a technique of *illusion* (in the sense of painting: perspective, shadows, *trompe-l'oeil*); it redistributes things, makes them seem other than they are, or as they are but in an impressive manner; *c.* there is a pleasure inherent in the association of ideas (we should say: a *ludism*). 2. *Explanations by origin*: these explanations start from the postulate that the figures exist "in nature," *i.e.*, in the "people" (Racine: "One need merely listen to a dispute between women of the lowest condition: what abundance in the figures! They lavish metonymy, catachresis, hyperbole, etc."); and F. de Neufchateau: "In town, at the court, in the fields, at market, the eloquence of the heart breathes forth in tropes." How then are we to reconcile the "natural" origin of the figures and their secondary, posterior rank in the structure of language? The classic answer is that art *chooses* the figures (with regard to a just evaluation of their distance, which must be *measured*), it does not create them; in short the figured is an artificial combination of natural elements.

### B.3.9. Vico and poetry

Starting from this last hypothesis (the figures have a "natural" origin), we may further distinguish two kinds of explanations. The first is mythic, romantic, in the very broad sense of the term: the "proper" language is poor, it does not suffice for all needs, but it is supplemented by the explosion of another language, "those divine blossomings of the spirit which the Greeks called *Tropes*" (Hugo); or again (Vico, cited by Michelet), Poetry being the original language, the four great archetypal figures were invented *in order*, not by writers but by humanity in its poetic age: *Metaphor*, then *Metonymy*, then *Synecdoche*, then *Irony*; originally, they were employed *naturally*. Then how could they have become "figures of rhetoric"? Vico gives a very structural answer: when abstraction was born, *i.e.*, when the "figure" was apprehended in a paradigmatic opposition with another language.

### B.3.10.  *The language of the passions*

The second explanation is psychological: it is that of Lamy and the classical writers: the Figures are the language of passion. Passion distorts the perspective of things and compels special words: "If men conceived all the things which present themselves to their minds, simply, as they are in themselves, they would all speak of them in the same manner: geometers almost always employ the same language" (Lamy). This is an interesting view, for if the figures are the "morphemes" of passion, by the figures we can know the classical taxonomy of the passions, and notably that of the passion of love, from Racine to Proust. For example: *exclamation* corresponds to the abrupt seizure of speech, to an emotive aphasia; *doubt, dubitation* (name of a figure) to the uncertainties of behavior (What to do? this? that?), to the difficult reading of the "signs" emitted by the other; *ellipsis*, to the censoring of everything which hampers passion; *paralepsis* (saying that one is not going to say what one finally will say), to the renewal of the "scene," to the demon of wounding; *repetition*, to the obsessional rehearsing of "one's due"; *hypotyposis*, to the scene which one imagines vividly to oneself, to the inner fantasy, to the mental scenario (desire, jealousy), etc. Whereby we understand better how the figured can be a language at once *natural* and *secondary*: it is natural because the passions are in nature; it is secondary because morality requires that these same passions, though "natural," be distanced, placed in the region of Sin; it is because, for a classical writer, "nature" is evil, that the figures of rhetoric are at once basic and suspect.

### B.3.11.  Compositio

Now we must return to the first opposition, the one which serves as the point of departure for the network of *Elocutio*: to *electio*, the substitutive field of the ornaments, is opposed *compositio*, the associative field of the words within the sentence. We shall not take sides here as to the linguistic definition of the "sentence": it is merely, for us, that unit of discourse intermediary between *pars orationis* (major part of *oratio*) and *figura* (small group of words). The ancient Rhetoric codified two types of "constructions": 1. a "geometric" construction: that of the *period* (Aristotle) "a sentence having in itself a beginning, an end, and an extent which can be readily encompassed"; the structure of the period depends on an internal system of *commas* (strokes) and of *colons* (members); their number is variable and disputed; in general, three or four colons are required, subject to opposition (1/3 or 1–2/3–4); the reference of this system is vitalized (the oscillation of the breath) or sportive (the period reproduces the ellipsis of the stadium: a course, a turn, a return); 2. a "dynamic" construction (Dionysius of Halicarnassus): the sentence is then conceived as a sublimated, vitalized period transcended by "movement"; no longer a question of a course and a return, but of a rise and a descent; this kind of "swing" is more important than the choice of words: it depends on a kind of innate sense on the part of the writer. This "movement" has three modes: *a.* wild, jolting (Pindar, Thucydides); *b.* *gentle*, encased, smooth-flowing (Sappho, Isocrates, Cicero); *c.* *mixed*, a storehouse of these hovering cases.

*Thus concludes the rhetorical network—since we have decided to leave aside the parts of the* technè rhétorikè *that are strictly theatrical, hysterical, linked to the voice:* actio *and* memoria. *Any historical conclusion whatever (aside from the fact that there is a certain irony in ourselves encoding the second metalanguage we have just used by a* peroratio *derived from the first) would exceed the purely didactic intention of this simple manual. Yet, upon leaving the ancient Rhetoric, I should like to say what remains for me personally of this memorable journey (a*

descent through time, a descent through the network, as down a double
river). "What remains for me" means: the questions which reach me
from this ancient empire in my present enterprise and which I can no
longer avoid, having come this close to Rhetoric.

First of all, the conviction that many features of our literature, of our
instruction, of our institutions of language (and is there a single institution
without language?) would be illuminated or understood differently if we
knew thoroughly (i.e., if we did not censor) the rhetorical code which
has given its language to our culture; neither a technique, nor an esthetic,
nor an ethic of Rhetoric are now possible, but a history? Yes, a history
of Rhetoric (as research, as book, as teaching) is today necessary, broad-
ened by a new way of thinking (linguistics, semiology, historical science,
psychoanalysis, Marxism).

Next, this notion that there is a kind of stubborn agreement between
Aristotle (from whom rhetoric proceeded) and our mass culture, as if
Aristotelianism, dead since the Renaissance as a philosophy and as logic,
dead as an esthetic since Romanticism, survived in a corrupt, diffused,
inarticulate state in the cultural practice of Western societies—a practice
based, through democracy, on an ideology of the "greatest number," of
the majority-as-norm, of current opinion: everything suggests that a kind
of Aristotelian vulgate still defines a type of trans-historical Occident, a
civilization (our own) which is that of the endoxa: how to avoid this
realization that Aristotle (by his poetics, by his logic, by his rhetoric)
furnishes for the entire language—narrative, discursive, and argumentative—of "mass communications," a complete analytical grid (starting
from the notion of "the probable") and that he represents that optimal
homogeneity of a metalanguage and of a language-as-object which can
define an applied science? In a democratic system, Aristotelianism would
then be the best of cultural sociologies.

Lastly, this observation, disturbing as it is in its foreshortened form,
that all our literature, formed by Rhetoric and sublimated by humanism,
has emerged from a politico-judicial practice (unless we persist in the
error which limits Rhetoric to the "Figures"): in those areas where the
most brutal conflicts—of money, of property, of class—are taken over,
contained, domesticated, and sustained by state power, where state in-

stitutions regulate feigned speech and codifies all recourse to the signifier: there is where our literature is born. This is why reducing Rhetoric to the rank of a merely historical object; seeking, in the name of text, of writing, a new practice of language; and never separating ourselves from revolutionary science—these are one and the same task.

Communications, 1970

## APPENDIX TO THE MANUAL

### Structural classification of the figures of rhetoric

Rhetoric can be defined as the connotative level of language; the signifieds of the rhetorical Sign have long since been constituted by the different "styles" recognized by the code and today by the very concept of literature; its signifiers, formed of units of different sizes (chiefly larger than the moneme), correspond in large part to the figures of rhetoric.

The figures can be classified in two main groups; the first, or group of *metabolas*, includes all the connotators which involve a semantic conversion; either metaphor: *traveler by night = old age*; the semantic chain is established in the following manner: Signifier[1] ( */traveler by night/* = Signified[1] (*"traveler by night"*) = Signified[2] (*"old age"*) = Signifier[2] ( */old age/* ); in this chain, the conversion retains Signifier[1] = Signified[2]; the canonical form of the chain corresponds to most of the known figures (metaphor, metonymy, antiphrasis, litotes, hyperbole), which are differentiated only by the nature of the relation between Signified[1] and Signified[2]; this relation can be defined by reference to different methods (logical analysis; semic analysis, contextual analysis); the semantic chain may include two aberrant cases: 1. Signifier[2] = $\emptyset$; this is the case of catachresis, in which the "proper" word is lacking in the language itself; 2. Signified[1] = Signified[2]; this is the case with a pun.

The second group, or group of *parataxes*, includes all the codified accidents which can affect a "normal" syntagmatic sequence (A.B.C.D. . . .): break (anacoluthon), disappointment (aposiopesis), delay (suspension), defection (ellipsis, asyndeton), amplification (repetition), symmetry (antithesis, chiasmus).

*Le Français moderne*, 1966

# Introduction to the Structural Analysis of Narratives

Numberless are the world's narratives. First of all in a prodigious variety of genres, themselves distributed among different substances, as if any material were appropriate for man to entrust his stories to it: narrative can be supported by articulated speech, oral or written, by image, fixed or moving, by gesture, and by the organized mixture of all these substances; it is present in myth, legend, fable, tale, tragedy, comedy, epic, history, pantomime, painting (think of Carpaccio's *Saint Ursula*) stained-glass window, cinema, comic book, news item, conversation. Further, in these almost infinite forms, narrative occurs in all periods, all places, all societies; narrative begins with the very history of humanity; there is not, there has never been, any people anywhere without narrative; all classes, all human groups have their narratives, and very often these are enjoyed by men of different, even opposing culture:[1] narrative never prefers good to bad literature: international, transhistorical, transcultural, narrative is *there*, like life.

Is such universality a reason for us to infer narrative's unim-

---

[1] This is not the case, it will be recalled, with poetry nor with the essay, dependent on the cultural level of their consumers.

portance? Is narrative so general that we have nothing to say about it, except modestly to describe a few of its extreme varieties, as literary history sometimes does? But how are we to master these very varieties, how are we to establish our right to distinguish them, to recognize them? How are we to set novel against novella, tale against myth, drama against tragedy (as has been done a thousand times) without reference to a common model? This model is implied by all speech concerning the most individual, the most historical of narrative forms. Hence it is legitimate that, far from renouncing all ambition to speak of narrative on the excuse that it is, after all, a universal phenomenon, there should have been periodic concern with narrative form (Aristotle); and it is normal that a nascent structuralism should make this form one of its first preoccupations: is it not a permanent preoccupation of structuralism to master the infinity of words by describing the language by which they are produced and out of which they can be engendered? Confronting the infinity of narratives, the multiplicity of the points of view from which we can speak of them (historical, psychological, sociological, ethnological, esthetic, etc.), the analyst is virtually in the same situation as Saussure, confronting the heteroclite nature of language and attempting to perceive in the apparent anarchy of its messages a principle of classification and a focus of description. To remain within the present period, the Russian Formalists, Propp, and Lévi-Strauss have taught us to recognize the following dilemma: either narrative is a simple chronicling of events, in which case we can discuss it only by relying on the teller's (the author's) art, talent, genius—all mythic forms of chance[2]—or else it shares with other narratives a structure accessible to analysis, whatever patience is necessary in order to articulate that structure; for there is an abyss between the most complex aleatory world and the simplest com-

---

[2] The storyteller's "art" exists, of course: it is the power to engender narratives (messages) from the structure (code); this art corresponds to Chomsky's notion of *performance*, and this notion is quite remote from an author's "genius," romantically conceived as a scarcely explicable individual secret.

binatory one, and no one can combine (produce) a narrative without referring to an implicit system of units and rules.

Where then are we to look for the structure of narrative? In the narratives themselves no doubt. *All* narratives? Many commentators, who accept the notion of a narrative structure, cannot bring themselves to separate literary analysis from the model of the experimental sciences: they intrepidly insist that a purely inductive method be applied to narration and that the first step be to study all the narratives of a genre, of a period, of a society, and then to undertake the sketch of a general model. This commonsense view is utopian. Linguistics itself, which has only some three thousand languages to survey, cannot manage this; wisely, it has remained deductive, and it was moreover from the day of that decision that linguistics actually constituted itself and has advanced with giant strides, managing even to anticipate phenomena which had not yet been discovered.[3] What then are we to say of narrative analysis, confronting millions of narratives? It is necessarily doomed to a deductive program; it is obliged to conceive, first of all, a hypothetical model of description (which the American linguists call a "theory"), and then to descend gradually from this model to the species which, simultaneously, participate in it and depart from it: it is only on the level of these conformities and these departures that narrative analysis will recognize, armed with a unique instrument of description, the plurality of narratives, their historical, geographic, cultural diversity.[4]

In order to describe and classify the infinite number of narratives,

[3] See the history of Hittite *a*, postulated by Saussure and actually discovered fifty years later, in Emile Benveniste, *Problèmes de linguistique générale*, Paris: Gallimard, 1966, p. 35; *Problems of General Linguistics*, Coral Gables: University of Florida, 1971, p. 32.

[4] We may note the present conditions of linguistic description: ". . . linguistic 'structure' is always relative not just to the data or corpus but also to the grammatical theory describing the data." (E. Bach, *An Introduction to Transformational Grammars*, New York, 1964, p. 29); "it has been recognized that language must be described as a formal structure, but that the description first of all necessitates specification of adequate procedures and criteria and that, finally, the reality of the object is inseparable from the method given for its description" (Benveniste, *op. cit.*, p. 119, trans. p. 101).

we must therefore have a "theory" (in the pragmatic sense just given), and our first task will be to find it and sketch it out. The elaboration of this theory can be greatly facilitated if we begin with a model which provides it with its first terms and its first principles. In the present state of research, it seems reasonable[5] to take linguistics itself as a founding model for the structural analysis of narrative.


## I  THE LANGUAGE OF NARRATIVE

### 1.  Beyond the sentence

As we know, linguistics stops at the sentence, which is the last unit it considers itself entitled to deal with; if the sentence, being an order and not a series, cannot be reduced to the sum of words composing it and thereby constitutes an original unit, a larger discourse, on the contrary, is nothing but the sequence of sentences which compose it: from the linguistic point of view, there is nothing in discourse which is not to be found in the sentence: "The sentence," Martinet says, "is the smallest segment which is perfectly and integrally representative of discourse."[6] Hence linguistics cannot take an object superior to the sentence, because, beyond the sentence, there is never anything but more sentences: having described the flower, the botanist cannot be concerned with describing the bouquet.

And yet, it is obvious that discourse itself (as a group of sentences) is organized and that by this organization it appears as the message of another language, superior to the language of the linguists;[7]

---

[5] But not imperative (see Claude Bremond, "La logique des possibles narratifs," *Communications,* #8 (1966), more logical than linguistic).

[6] André Martinet, "Réflexions sur la phrase," in *Language and Society* (Studies presented to Jansen), Copenhagen, 1961, p. 113.

[7] It follows, as Jakobson has observed, that there are transitions from the sentence to what lies beyond it: coordination, for example, can function beyond the sentence.

discourse has its units, its rules, its "grammar": beyond the sentence and although composed solely of sentences, discourse must naturally be the object of a second linguistics. This linguistics of discourse has for a very long time possessed a celebrated name: Rhetoric; but since Rhetoric, through a complex historical development, had become linked to belles lettres and since belles lettres had been separated from the study of language, it has seemed necessary, in recent years, to take up the question anew: the new linguistics of discourse has not yet developed, but it has at least been postulated, and by the linguists themselves.[8] This fact is significant: though constituting an autonomous object, discourse is to be studied from a linguistic basis; if we must grant a working hypothesis to an analysis whose task is enormous and whose materials are infinite, the most reasonable thing is to postulate a homologous relation between sentence and discourse, insofar as the same formal organization apparently regulates all semiotic systems, whatever their substances and dimensions: discourse would be one huge "sentence" (whose units would not necessarily be sentences), just as the sentence, allowing for certain specifications, is a little "discourse." This hypothesis fits in with certain propositions of contemporary anthropology: Jakobson and Lévi-Strauss have observed that humanity could be defined by the power to create secondary, "multiplying" systems (tools serving to fabricate other tools, the double articulation of language, the incest taboo permitting the proliferation of families), and the Soviet linguist Ivanov speculates that artificial languages can be acquired only after natural language: since what is important for humanity is being able to use several systems of meaning, natural language helps in elaborating artificial languages. Hence it is legitimate to postulate between sentence and discourse a "secondary" relation—which we shall call homological, in order to respect the purely formal character of the correspondences.

[8] See especially: Benveniste, *op. cit.*, chapter x; Zelig Harris, "Discourse Analysis" in *Language*, #28 (1952), pp. 18–23 & 474–494; Nicolas Ruwet, *Language, Musique, Poésie*, Paris: Éd. du Seuil, 1972, pp. 151–175.

The general language of narrative is obviously but one of the idioms available to the linguistics of discourse,[9] and is consequently subject to the homological hypothesis: structurally, narrative participates in the sentence without ever being reducible to a total of sentences: narrative is a great sentence, just as every constative sentence is, in a way, the sketch of a little narrative. Though afforded there with original (often highly complex) signifiers, we in effect recognize in narrative, enlarged and transformed in proportion, the main categories of the verb: tenses, aspects, modes, persons; further, the "subjects" themselves set in opposition to the verbal predicates do not fail to submit to the sentence model: the actantial typology Greimas proposes (cf. *infra*, III,1) acknowledges in the host of characters of narrative the elementary functions of grammatical analysis. The homology we are suggesting here has not only a heuristic value: it implies an identity between language and literature (inasmuch as literature is a kind of privileged vehicle of narrative): it is no longer possible to conceive of literature as an art unconcerned with any relation to language, once it has used language as an instrument to express ideas, passion, or beauty: language does not cease to accompany discourse, holding up to it the mirror of its own structure: does not literature, especially today, make a language out of the very conditions of language?[10]

## 2. The levels of meaning

From the start, linguistics provides the structural analysis of narrative with a decisive concept, because, immediately accounting

[9] It would be, specifically, one of the tasks of the linguistics of discourse to establish a typology of discourses. For the time being, we can recognize three major types of discourse: metonymic (narrative), metaphoric (lyric poetry, sapiential discourse), enthymematic (intellectual discourse).

[10] Here is the place to recall Mallarmé's intuition, formed just when he was planning a work of linguistics: "Language appeared to him the instrument of fiction: he will follow the method of language (determine this method). Language reflecting itself. Finally fiction seems to him the very process of the human mind—it is fiction which brings every method into play, and man is reduced to will" (*Oeuvres complètes*, Bibiliothèque de la Pléiade, Paris, 1961, p. 851). It will be recalled that for Mallarmé: "Fiction or Poetry" (cf. *ibid.*, p. 335).

for what is essential in any system of meaning, *i.e.*, its organization, it permits both the demonstration of how a narrative is not a simple total of propositions and the classification of an enormous mass of elements which participate in the composition of a narrative. This concept is that of the *level of description*.[11]

A sentence, as we know, can be described, linguistically, on several levels (phonetic, phonological, grammatical, contextual); these levels are in a hierarchical relation, for if each has its own units and its own correlations, necessitating for each an independent description, no level can in and of itself produce meaning: every unit which belongs to a certain level assumes meaning only if it can be integrated into a higher level: a phoneme, though perfectly describable, in itself means nothing; it participates in meaning only when integrated into a word; and the word itself must be integrated into the sentence.[12] The theory of levels (as articulated by Benveniste) provides two types of relations: distributional (if the relations are situated on the same level), integrative (if they are apprehended from one level to another). It follows that the distributional levels do not suffice to account for meaning. In order to achieve a structural analysis, we must therefore first distinguish several instances of description and place these instances in a hierarchical (integrative) perspective.

The levels are operations.[13] Hence it is normal that as it proceeds linguistics tends to multiply them. The analysis of discourse can as yet work on only rudimentary levels. In its fashion, rhetoric had assigned to discourse at least two planes of description: *dispositio*

[11] "Linguistic descriptions are not, so to speak, monovalent. A description is not simply 'right' or 'wrong' in itself . . . it is better thought of as more useful or less" (M. A. K. Halliday, "General Linguistics and its Application to Language Teaching," *Patterns of Language*, London, 1966, p. 8).

[12] The levels of integration were postulated by the Prague School (*vide* J. Vachek, *A Prague School Reader in Linguistics*, Bloomington, 1964, p. 468) and subsequently adopted by many linguists. It is Benveniste, it seems to me, who has produced their most enlightening analysis (*op. cit.*, chapter 10).

[13] "In somewhat vague terms, a level may be considered as a system of symbols, rules, and so on, to be used for representing utterances" (Bach, *op. cit.*, p. 57).

and *elocutio*.[14] In our own day, in his analysis of the structure of myth, Lévi-Strauss has already specified that the constitutive units of mythic discourse (mythemes) acquire meaning only because they are grouped in bundles and because these bundles themselves are combined;[15] and Tzvetan Todorov, adopting the distinction of the Russian formalists, has proposed to work on two main levels, themselves subdivided: *story* (the argument), including a logic of actions and a "syntax" of characters, and *discourse*, including tenses, aspects, and modes of narrative.[16] Whatever the numbers of levels proposed and whatever definition given of them, there can be no doubt that narrative is a hierarchy of instances. To understand a narrative is not only to follow the process of the story, it is also to recognize in it certain "stages," to project the horizontal concatenations of the narrative "thread" on an implicitly vertical axis; to read (to hear) a narrative is not only to pass from one word to the next, but also to pass from one level to the next. Let me offer a kind of fable here: in his *Purloined Letter*, Poe acutely analyzed the failure of the Paris police chief, who was unable to find the letter: his investigations were perfect, Poe says, "so far as his labors extended": the police chief omitted no location, he entirely "saturated" the level of "search"; but in order to find the letter— protected by its conspicuousness—it was essential to pass to another level, to substitute the concealer's pertinence for that of the policeman. In the same way, complete as the "search" performed on a horizontal group of narrative relations may be, in order to be effective it must also be oriented "vertically": meaning is not "at the end" of narrative, it traverses it; quite as conspicuous as the *purloined letter*, it similarly escapes any unilateral exploration.

Much groping will still be necessary before we can determine the levels of narrative. Those which we are going to propose here constitute a temporary outline, whose advantage is still almost ex-

---

[14] The third part of rhetoric, *inventio*, did not concern language: it dealt with *res*, not with *verba*.

[15] Claude Lévi-Strauss, *Structural Anthropology*, New York & London, 1963, p. 213.

[16] Tzvetan Todorov, "Les catégories du récit littéraire," *Communications*, #8 (1966).

clusively didactic: they permit locating and grouping the problems, without disagreeing, it would appear, with the various analyses made so far. We propose to distinguish in the narrative work three levels of description: the level of *"functions"* (in the meaning this word is given by Propp and Bremond), the level of *"actions"* (in the meaning this word is given by Greimas when he speaks of characters as actants), and the level of *"narration"* (which is, by and large, the level of "discourse" in Todorov). It must be recalled that these three levels are linked together according to a mode of progressive integration: a function has meaning only insofar as it occurs in the general action of an actant; and this action itself receives its ultimate meaning from the fact that it is narrated, entrusted to a discourse which has its own code.

## II  FUNCTIONS

### 1.  The determination of units

Every system being the combination of units whose classes are known, we must first segment the narrative and determine the segments of the narrative discourse which can be distributed into a small number of classes; in a word, we must define the smallest narrative units.

According to the integrative perspective defined here, the analysis cannot be limited to a purely distributional definition of the units: meaning must from the first be the criterion of the unit: it is the functional character of certain segments of the story which makes them units: whence the name "functions," immediately given to these first units. Since the Russian Formalists,[17] any segment of

[17] See especially B. Tomashevski, "Thématique" (1925), in *Théorie de la littérature*, Paris: Éd. du Seuil, 1965. —Somewhat later, Propp defined function as "the action of a character, defined from the point of view of its signification in the course of the Plot" (*Morphology of the Folktale*, Austin & London, 1968, p. 21). See also Todorov's definition: "The meaning (or the function) of an element of the work is its possibility of entering into correlation with other elements of this work and with the work as a whole" (*op. cit.*) and the clarifications provided by Greimas, who has just defined the unit by its paradigmatic correlation, but also by its place within the syntagmatic unit of which it constitutes a part.

the story is constituted as a unit which is presented as the term of a correlation. The soul of any function is, so to speak, its seed, what allows it to sow the narrative with an element which will ripen later, on the same level, or elsewhere, on another level: if, in *Un Coeur simple*, Flaubert tells us at a certain point, apparently without insisting on it, that the daughters of the sub-prefect of Pont-l'Évêque owned a parrot, it is because this parrot will later have a great importance in Félicité's life: the statement of this detail (whatever its linguistic form) therefore constitutes a function, or narrative unit.

Is everything, in a narrative, functional? Does everything, down to the least detail, have a meaning? Can the narrative be entirely segmented into functional units? As we shall shortly see, there are doubtless several types of functions, for there are several types of correlations. Nonetheless a narrative always consists of nothing but functions: everything in it, to varying degrees, signifies. This is not a question of art (of the narrator's share), it is a question of structure: in the order of discourse, what is noted is, by definition, notable: even when a detail seems irreducibly insignificant, refractory to any function, it will nonetheless ultimately have the very meaning of absurdity or uselessness: everything has a meaning or nothing has. We might say in other words that art does not acknowledge "noise" (in the meaning that word has in information theory):[18] it is a pure system, there is never a "wasted" unit,[19] however long, loose, and tenuous the thread linking it to the levels of the story.[20]

---

[18] It is this that makes art different from "life," which acknowledges only "blurred" communications. "Blurring" (what one cannot see beyond) can exist in art, but then as a coded element (Watteau, for instance); again, this "blurring" is unknown to the written code: writing is fatally distinct.

[19] At least in literature, where the freedom of notation (consequent upon the abstract character of articulated language) involves a stronger responsibility than in the "analogical" arts, such as the cinema.

[20] The functionality of the narrative unit is more or less immediate (hence apparent), according to the level where it functions: when the units are placed on the same level (in the case of suspense, for instance), functionality is very sensitive; much less so when the function is saturated on the narrational level: a modern text, weakly signifying on the anecdotal plane, recovers a great strength of meaning only on the plane of writing.

Function is obviously, from the linguistic point of view, a unit of content: it is what a statement "means" which constitutes it as a functional unit,[21] not the way in which it is said. This constitutive signified can have different signifiers, often very complicated ones: if I am told (in *Goldfinger*) that *"James Bond saw a man of about fifty,"* etc., the information simultaneously harbors two functions, of unequal pressure: on the one hand, the age of the character is integrated into a certain portrayal (whose "usefulness" for the rest of the story is not nil, but diffused, delayed), and on the other, the immediate signified of the statement is that Bond does not know his future interlocutor: the unit therefore implies a very strong correlation (initiation of a threat and obligation to identify the character). In order to determine the first narrative units, it is therefore necessary never to lose sight of the functional character of the segments being examined, and to admit in advance that they will not inevitably coincide with the forms traditionally identified with the different parts of narrative discourse (actions, scenes, paragraphs, dialogues, interior monologues, etc.), and still less with the "psychological" classes (kinds of behavior, feelings, intentions, motivations, rationalizations of characters).

In the same way, since the language of narrative is not that of articulated speech—though often supported by it—the narrative units will be substantially independent of the linguistic units: they may of course coincide, but occasionally, not systematically; the functions will be represented sometimes by units superior to the sentence (groups of sentences of various dimension, up to the work in its entirety), sometimes by units inferior to it (the syntagm, the word, and even, within the word, only certain literary elements);[22] when we are told that—while he is on duty in his office at Secret

---

[21] "Syntactical units (beyond the sentence) are actually units of content" (A. J. Greimas, *Sémantique structurale*, Paris: Larousse, 1966, VI, 5). —Hence the exploration of the functional level is part of general semantics.

[22] "We must not treat the word as if it were an indivisible element of literary art, the brick with which the building is constructed. It can be decomposed into much finer 'verbal elements'" (J. Tynyanov, quoted by Todorov in *Langages*, #1, 1966, p. 18).

Service headquarters—"*Bond picked up one of the four receivers,*" the moneme *four* constitutes by itself a functional unit, for it refers to a concept necessary to the whole of the story (that of an elaborate bureaucratic technique); as a matter of fact, the narrative unit here is not the linguistic unit (the word), but only its connoted value (linguistically, the word/*four*/never means "*four*"); this explains how certain functional units can be inferior to the sentence, without ceasing to belong to the discourse: they then overflow not the sentence, to which they remain materially inferior, but the level of denotation, which belongs, like the sentence, to linguistics properly speaking.

## 2. Classes of units

These functional units must be distributed within a small number of formal classes. If we want to determine these classes without resorting to the substance of the content (a psychological substance, for example), we must again consider the different levels of meaning: certain units have for correlates units on the same level; on the contrary, in order to saturate the others, we must pass to another level. Hence, at the start, two major classes of functions, some distributional, others integrative. The former correspond to Propp's functions, adopted notably by Bremond, but which we are considering here in an infinitely more detailed fashion than these authors; it is to them that we shall apply the name "*functions*" (though the other units, too, are functional); the model for them has been classical since Tomashevsky's analysis: the purchase of a revolver has for its correlate the moment when it will be used (and if it is not used, the notation is reversed as a sign of indecision, etc.); to pick up the telephone has for its correlate the moment when it will be hung up again; the intrusion of the parrot into Félicité's house has for its correlate the episode of the parrot's being stuffed, worshipped, etc. The second major class of units, of an integrative nature, includes all the "*indices*" (in the very general sense of the word),[23] when the unit refers not to a complementary and consequential action, but to a more or less diffused concept, though one necessary to the meaning of the story: characterial indices concerning the characters, information relative to their identity, notations of "atmosphere," etc.; the relation of the unit and its correlate is then no longer distributional (frequently several indices refer to the same signified and their order of appearance in the discourse is not necessarily pertinent), but integrative; in order to understand the "use" of an indicial notation, we must pass to a higher level (actions of the characters or narration), for it is only here that the index is explained; the administrative power which is behind Bond, indexed by the number of telephones, has no bearing on the sequence of actions in which Bond is engaged by answering the call; it assumes its meaning only on the level of a general typology of actants (Bond is on the side of order); the indices, by the more or less vertical nature of their relations, are truly semantic units, for contrary to the true "functions," they refer to a signified, not to an "operation"; the sanction of the indices is "higher up," sometimes even virtual, outside the explicit syntagm (the "character" of a character can never be named, though ceaselessly indexed), it is a paradigmatic sanction; on the contrary, the sanction of the "functions" is always "farther on," it is a syntagmatic sanction.[24] *Functions* and *indices* thus cover another classical distinction: the functions imply metonymic *relata*, the indices imply metaphoric *relata*; the former correspond to a functionality of doing, the latter to a functionality of being.[25]

These two major classes of units, Functions and Indices, should already permit a certain classification of narratives. Certain nar-

---

[23] These designations, like those that follow, may all be provisional.

[24] Which does not keep the syntagmatic display of functions from *finally* being able to cover paradigmatic relations between separate functions, as has been acknowledged since Lévi-Strauss and Greimas.

[25] We cannot reduce the functions to actions (verbs) and the indices to qualities (adjectives), for there are actions which are indicial, being "signs" of a character, of an atmosphere, etc.

ratives are powerfully functional (such as folktales), and on the other hand others are powerfully indicial (such as "psychological" novels); between these two poles, a whole series of intermediary forms, dependent on history, society, genre. But this is not all: within each of these two major classes, it is immediately possible to determine two subclasses of narrative units. With regard to the class of Functions, its units do not all have the same "importance"; some constitute veritable hinges of the narrative (or of a narrative fragment); others merely "fill" the narrative space separating the hinge-functions: let us call the former *cardinal functions* (or *nuclei*) and the latter, given their completive nature, *catalyses*. For a function to be cardinal, it suffices that the action to which it refers opens (or sustains, or closes) an alternative consequential for the rest of the story, in short, that it inaugurate or conclude an uncertainty; if, in a narrative fragment, *the telephone rings*, it is equally possible that it will or will not be answered, which will not fail to lead the story in two different directions. On the other hand, between two cardinal functions, it is always possible to arrange subsidiary notations, which agglomerate around one nucleus or another without modifying their alternative nature: the space which separates "*the telephone rang*" and "*Bond answered*" can be saturated by a host of tiny incidents or tiny descriptions: "*Bond went over to the desk, picked up a receiver, put down his cigarette,*" etc. Such catalyses remain functional, insofar as they enter into correlation with a nucleus, but their functionality is attenuated, unilateral, parasitic: we are concerned here with a purely chronological functionality (what is being described is what separates two moments of the story), while, in the link which unites two cardinal functions, is invested a double functionality, both chronological and logical: the catalyses are merely consecutive units, the cardinal functions are both consecutive and consequential. There is every reason to believe, as a matter of fact, that the mainspring of narrative activity is the very confusion of consecution and consequentiality, what comes *after* being read in the narrative as *caused by*; the narrative would in this case be a systematic application of the logical error condemned by Scholasticism in the formula *post hoc, ergo propter hoc*, which might well be the motto of Fate, of which the narrative is in fact merely the "language"; and this "squeezing together" of logic and temporality is achieved by the armature of the cardinal functions. These functions may seem at first glance quite insignif- icant; what constitutes them is not spectacle (the importance, vol- ume, rarity, or power of the action articulated), it is, so to speak, risk: the cardinal functions are the moments of risk of the narrative; between these points of alternative, between these "dispatchers," the catalyses set up zones of security, rests, luxuries; these "luxuries" are not, however, useless: from the story's point of view, let us repeat, the functionality of the catalysis may be weak but not nil: were it purely redundant (in relation to its nucleus), it would par- ticipate no less in the message's economy; but this is not the case: a notation, apparently expletive, always has a discursive function: it accelerates, delays, resumes the discourse, it summarizes, antic- ipates, sometimes even misleads or baffles:[26] what is noted always appearing as notable, catalysis constantly wakens the semantic ten- sion of the discourse, constantly says: there has been, there is going to be meaning; the constant function of catalysis is therefore, ul- timately, a phatic one (to adopt Jakobson's word): it sustains the contact between the narrator and the receiver of the narrative. Let us say that we cannot suppress a nucleus without altering the story, but that we also cannot suppress a catalysis without altering the discourse. As for the second major class of narrative units (the Indices), an integrative class, the units which occur here have in common the fact that they can be saturated (completed) only on the level of the characters or of the narration; they therefore belong to a *parametric* relation[27] whose second, implicit term is continuous, extensive to an episode, a character or an entire work; yet we can

[26] Valéry used to speak of "dilatory signs." The detective story makes great use of these "baffling" signs.
[27] Nicolas Ruwet calls a parametric element one which is constant throughout an entire piece of music (for example, the tempo of an allegro by Bach, or the monodic character of a solo).

distinguish here certain *indices*, strictly speaking, referring to a character, to a feeling, to an atmosphere (for instance, one of suspicion), to a philosophy, from *items of information*, which serve to identify, to situate in time and in space. To say that Bond is on duty in an office whose open window reveals the moon between huge, rolling clouds is to index a stormy summer night, and this deduction itself forms an atmospheric index which refers to the heavy, oppressive climate of an action which is not yet known. The indices therefore always have implicit signifieds; the items of information, on the contrary, do not, at least on the level of the story: they are pure data, immediately signifying. The indices imply an activity of deciperment: the reader must learn to know a character, an atmosphere; the items of information supply a ready-made knowledge; their functionality, like that of the catalyses, is therefore weak, but it too is not nil: whatever its "matte" nature in relation to the story, the item of information (for instance, the exact age of a character) serves to authenticate the reality of the referent, to implant the fiction in reality: it is a realist operator, and thus possesses an incontestable functionality, not on the level of the story but on the level of the discourse.[28]

Nuclei and catalyses, indices and items of information (once again, the names are of little importance)—such are, it would seem, the first classes among which the units of the functional level can be distributed. We must complete this classification by two remarks. First of all, a unit can belong at the same time to two different classes: to drink a whisky (in an airport lounge) is an action which may serve as a catalysis to the (cardinal) notation of *waiting*, but it is also and at the same time the index of a certain atmosphere (modernity, relaxation, memories, etc.): in other words, certain units can be mixed. Thus a whole play of possibilities arises in the

---

[28] Gérard Genette distinguishes two kinds of descriptions: ornamental and significant (in *Figures II*: Paris: Éd. du Seuil, 1969). The significant description must obviously be attached to the level of the story and the ornamental description to the level of the discourse, which explains why for so long it formed a perfectly coded rhetorical "piece": *descriptio* or *ekphrasis*, a highly prized exercise of neo-rhetoric.

narrative economy; in the novel *Goldfinger*, Bond, having to search his adversary's bedroom, receives a skeleton key from his partner: the notation is a pure (cardinal) function; in the film, this detail is altered: Bond manages to relieve an unprotesting chambermaid of her keys; the notation is not only functional now, but also indicial, it refers to Bond's character (his offhandedness and his success with women). Secondly, we must remark (what will moreover be taken up again later on) that the other classes we have just mentioned can be subject to another distribution, one more in accord, moreover, with the linguistic model. The catalyses, the indices and the items of information have a common character: they are all *expansions*, in relation to the nuclei: the nuclei (as we shall soon see) form finite groups of a small number of terms, they are governed by a logic, they are at once necessary and sufficient; given this armature, the other units fill it out according to a mode of proliferation which is in principle infinite; as we know, this is what happens in the case of the sentence, consisting of simple propositions, complicated to infinity by duplications, by paddings, insertions, etc.: like the sentence, the narrative is infinitely catalyzable. Mallarmé attached such importance to this type of structure that he used it to construct his poem *Un Coup de dès*, which we may well consider, with its "nodes" and its "loops," its "node-words" and its "lace-words," as the emblem of all narrative—of all language.

## 3.  Functional syntax

How—according to what "grammar"—do these different units link up with each other throughout the narrative syntagm? What are the rules of the functional combinatory system? The items of information and the indices can freely combine among themselves: for example in the character sketch, which unconstrainedly juxtaposes data of civil status and character traits. A relation of simple implication unites the catalyses and the nuclei: a catalysis necessarily implies the existence of a cardinal function to which it is attached, but not vice versa. As for the cardinal functions, they are united by a relation of solidarity: a function of this kind requires another of the same kind, and vice versa. It is this last relation which we must attend to briefly: first of all because it defines the very armature of the narrative (the expansions can be suppressed, but not the nuclei), then because it chiefly concerns those who are seeking to structure narrative.

We have already observed that, by its very structure, narrative instituted a confusion between consecution and consequentiality, time and logic. It is this ambiguity which forms the central problem of narrative syntax. Is there behind narrative time an atemporal logic? This point divided investigators quite recently. Propp, whose analysis as we know opened the way to contemporary studies, insists on the irreducibility of the chronological order: time in his eyes is reality, and for this reason it seems necessary to root the tale in time. Yet Aristotle himself, setting tragedy (defined by the unity of action) in opposition to history (defined by the plurality of actions and the unity of time), already attributed primacy to logic over chronology (*Poetics*, 1459a). As do all contemporary researchers (Lévi-Strauss, Greimas, Bremond, Todorov), all of whom might subscribe (though diverging on other points) to Lévi-Strauss's proposition: "The order of chronological succession is reabsorbed into an atemporal matrix structure."[29] Contemporary analysis tends, as a matter of fact, to "dechronologize" narrative content and to "relogicize" it, to subject it to what Mallarmé called, apropos of the French language, "the primitive thunderbolts of logic."[30] Or more exactly—at least, so we hope—the task is to produce a structural description of the chronological illusion; it is up to narrative logic to account for narrative time. We might say in another fashion that temporality is only a structural class of narrative (of discourse), just as, in language, time exists only in a systematic form; from the point of view of narrative, what we call time does not exist, or at least exists only functionally, as an element of a semiotic system: time does not belong to discourse properly speaking, but to the

[29] Quoted by Claude Bremond, "Le message narratif," in *Logique du récit*, Paris: Éd. du Seuil, 1973.
[30] *Quant au Livre*, in *Oeuvres complètes*, op. cit., p. 386.

referent; narrative and language know only a semiologic time; "real" time is a referential, "realist" illusion, as Propp's commentary shows, and it is as such that structural description must treat it.[31]

What then is this logic which governs the chief functions of narrative? This is what current investigation is attempting to establish, and what has hitherto been most widely debated. Hence we shall refer to the contributions of Greimas, Bremond, and Todorov in *Communications* (#8, 1966), all of which deal with the logic of the functions. Three main directions of investigation are notable, set forth by Todorov. The first (Bremond) is more strictly logical: it seeks to reconstruct the syntax of human behavior utilized in narrative, to retrace the trajectory of the "choices" which, at each point of the story, a character is inevitably compelled to make,[32] and thus to reveal what we might call an energetic logic,[33] since it apprehends the characters at the moment when they choose to act. The second model is linguistic (Lévi-Strauss, Greimas): the essential concern of this investigation is to identify in the functions certain paradigmatic oppositions, these oppositions, according to the Jakobsonian principle of "poetics," being "extended" throughout the narrative (yet we shall see the new developments by which Greimas corrects or completes the paradigmatism of the functions). The third way, sketched by Todorov, is somewhat different, for it establishes the analysis on the level of the "actions" (*i.e.*, of the characters), by attempting to establish the rules by which the narrative combines, varies, and transforms a certain number of basic predicates.

[31] In his fashion, as always perspicacious though undeveloped, Valéry has well expressed the status of narrative time: "Belief in time as agent and guiding thread is based *on the mechanism of memory and on that of combined discourse*" (*Tel Quel*, in *Oeuvres*, Vol. II, Bibliothèque de la Pléiade, Paris, 1957, p. 348; our italics): the illusion is actually produced by the discourse itself.

[32] This conception recalls an Aristotelian view: *proairesis*, rational choice of the actions to be made, establishes *praxis*, a practical science which produces no distinct work of the agent, contrary to *poeisis*. In these terms, we shall say that the analyst tries to reconstitute the *praxis* inherent in narrative.

[33] This logic, based on an alternative (*to do this or that*), has the merit of accounting for the process of dramatization of which narrative is ordinarily the seat.

There is no question of choosing among these working hypotheses; they are not competitive but concurrent, and moreover they are still being elaborated. The only addition we shall attempt to make here regards the dimensions of the analysis. Even if we set aside the indices, the items of information, and the catalyses, there still remains in a narrative (particularly in speaking of the novel rather than the tale) a very great number of cardinal functions; many cannot be mastered by the analyses we have just cited, which have so far been concerned with major articulations of narrative. Yet we must anticipate a sufficiently dense description to account for *all* the narrative units, for its smallest segments; the cardinal functions, we recall, cannot be determined by their "importance," but only by the (doubly implicative) nature of their relations: a "telephone call," however trivial it may appear on the one hand, involves in itself several cardinal functions (ringing, picking up the receiver, speaking, hanging up), and moreover, taking these all together, we must be able to attach them as closely as possible to the major articulations of the anecdote. The functional covering of narrative compels an organization of relays, whose basic unit can only be a small group of functions, which we shall here call (following Bremond) a *sequence*.

A sequence is a logical succession of nuclei, linked together by a relation of solidarity:[34] the sequence opens when one of its terms has no solidary antecedent and it closes when another of its terms has no consequent. To take a deliberately trivial example, to order a drink, to receive it, to drink it, to pay for it—these various functions constitute an evidently closed sequence, for it is not possible to put something before the ordering of the drink or to put something after the payment without leaving the homogeneous group "Having a drink." The sequence is in fact always nameable. Determining the major functions of the folktale, Propp, then Bremond, have already been led to name them (*Fraud, Betrayal, Struggle, Contract, Seduction*, etc.); the nominative operation is just as

[34] In the Hjelmslevian sense of double implication: two terms presuppose each other.

inevitable for trivial sequences, which one might call "micro-sequences," those which frequently form the finest texture of the narrative fabric. Are these nominations solely the province of the analyst? In other words, are they purely metalinguistic? No doubt they are, since they deal with the narrative code, but we can suppose that they belong to a metalanguage internal to the reader (to the auditor) himself, who apprehends any logical succession of actions as a nominal whole: to read is to name; to hear is not only to perceive a language, it is also to construct it. The titles of sequences are rather analogous to those cover-words of translation machines, which more or less adequately cover a wide variety of meanings and nuances. The language of narrative, which is in ourselves, initially involves these essential rubrics: the closed logic which structures a sequence is indissolubly linked to its name: any function which inaugurates a *seduction*, say, prescribes upon its appearance, in the name which it produces, the whole process of seduction that we have learned from all the narratives which have formed in us the language of narrative.

Whatever its lack of importance, being composed of a small number of nuclei (*i.e.*, actually, of "dispatchers"), the sequence always involves moments of risk, and this is what justifies our analysis of it: it might seem absurd to constitute as a sequence the logical succession of tiny actions which compose the offer of a cigarette (*to offer, to accept, to light, to smoke*); but the fact is that precisely at each of these points an alternative, hence a freedom of meaning, is possible: Du Pont, James Bond's partner, offers him a light from his lighter, but Bond refuses; the meaning of this bifurcation is that Bond instinctively fears a booby-trapped device.[35] Hence the sequence is, so to speak, a *threatened logical unit*: that is its justification *a minimo*. It is also founded *a maximo*: closed over its functions,

---

[35] It is quite possible to identify, even at this infinitesimal level, an opposition of the paradigmatic type, if not between two terms, at least between two poles of the sequence: the sequence *Offer of a cigarette* displays, while suspending it, the paradigm *Danger/Safety* (shown by Shcheglov in his analysis of the Sherlock Holmes cycle), *Suspicion/Protection, Aggressiveness/Friendliness*.

subsumed under a name, the sequence itself constitutes a new unit, ready to function as the simple term of another, larger sequence. Here is a micro-sequence: *hold out a hand, shake the hand, release the hand*; this *Greeting* becomes a simple function: on the one side, it takes the part of an index (Du Pont's slackness, Bond's distaste), and on the other, it forms *in toto* the term of a larger sequence called *Meeting*, whose other terms (*approach, halt, interpellation, greeting, sitting down*) can themselves be micro-sequences. A whole network of subrogations thus structures the narrative, from the tiniest matrices to the largest functions. We are here concerned, of course, with a hierarchy which remains internal to the functional level: it is only when it has been possible to enlarge the narrative, step by step, from Du Pont's cigarette to Bond's battle against Goldfinger, that the functional analysis is concluded: the pyramid of functions then touches the following level (that of Actions). There is both a syntax internal to the sequences and a (subrogating) syntax of the sequences among themselves. The first episode of *Goldfinger* thus assumes a "stemmatic" aspect:

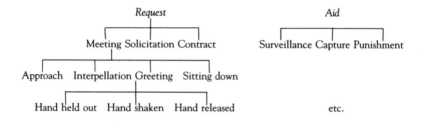

This representation is obviously analytical. The reader perceives a linear succession of terms. But what must be noted is that the terms of several sequences can very well be imbricated one within the other: a sequence is not finished when, already, inset, the initial term of a new sequence can appear: the sequences move in counterpoint[36]; functionally the narrative structure is "fugued": this

---

[36] This counterpoint was anticipated by the Russian Formalists, who outlined its typology; it suggests the main "intricate" structures of the sentence (cf. *infra*, V,1).

is how narrative simultaneously "holds" and "aspires." The imbrication of the sequences can only be allowed to cease, within a single work, by a phenomenon of radical rupture if the several closed blocks (or "stemmas") which then compose it are somehow recuperated at the higher level of Actions (of characters): *Goldfinger* is composed of three functionally independent episodes, for their functional stemmas twice cease to communicate: there is no sequential relation between the episode of the swimming pool and that of Fort Knox; but there remains an actantial relation, for the characters (and consequently the structure of their relations) are the same. Here we recognize the epic ("group of several fables"): the epic is a narrative broken on the functional level but unitary on the actantial level (as can be verified in the *Odyssey* or in Brecht's "epic theater"). Hence we must crown the level of functions (which furnishes the main part of the narrative syntagm) by a higher level, from which, step by step, the units of the first level draw their meaning, and which is the level of Actions.

## III  ACTIONS

### 1.  Toward a structural status of characters

In Aristotelian poetics, the notion of character is secondary, entirely subsidiary to the notion of action: there can be stories without "characters," Aristotle says; there cannot be characters without a story. This view was adopted by the classical theoreticians (Vossius). Later, the character, who hitherto was merely a name, the agent of an action,[37] assumed a psychological consistency, became an individual, a "person," in short a fully constituted being, even when he performed no action, and of course, even before acting,[38] the character ceased to be subordinate to the action,

---

[37] Let us not forget that classical tragedy still knows only "actors," not "characters."

[38] The "character-person" prevails in the bourgeois novel: in *War and Peace*, Nicholas Rostov is from the start a good boy, loyal, courageous, ardent; Prince Andrew is a disillusioned man of noble birth, etc.: what happens to them illustrates them, it does not constitute them.

embodying from the start a psychological essence; such essences could be subject to an inventory, whose purest form was the bourgeois theatre's list of "roles" (the coquette, the noble father, etc.). From its first appearance, structural analysis has shown the greatest reluctance to treat the character as an essence, even to classify it; as Todorov observes, Tomashevsky went so far as to deny the character any narrative importance whatever, a point of view which he subsequently modified. Without going so far as to withdraw characters from his analysis, Propp reduced them to a simple typology, based not on psychology but on the unity of the actions the narrative imparted to them (Giver of a magical object, Helper, Villain, etc.).

Since Propp, the character continues to raise the same problem for the structural analysis of narrative: on one hand, the characters (whatever they are called: *dramatis personae* or *actants*) form a necessary plan of description, outside which the trivial "actions" reported cease to be intelligible, so that we might say that there does not exist a single narrative the world over without "characters,"[39] or at least without "agents"; but on the other hand, these very numerous "agents" can be neither described nor classified in terms of "persons," whether because we consider the "person" as a purely historical form limited to certain genres (though the best known ones), so that we must set aside the enormous case of all the narratives (folktales, contemporary texts) which involve agents but not persons; or because we regard the "person" as nothing but a critical rationalization imposed by our period on pure narrative agents. Structural analysis, scrupulous not to define character in terms of psychological essences, has sought till now, through various hypotheses, to define character not as a "being" but as a "partici-

---

[39] If one part of contemporary literature has attacked the "character," it has done so not in order to destroy it (an impossibility) but to depersonalize it, a very different affair. A novel apparently without characters, such as Philippe Sollers's *Drame*, entirely subjugates the person to language, but nonetheless retains a fundamental play of actants, confronting the very action of speech. Such literature still knows a "subject," but this "subject" is henceforth that of language.

pant." For Claude Bremond, each character can be the agent of sequences of actions which are proper to it (*Fraud, Seduction*); when the same sequence implicates two characters (as is usually the case), the sequence involves two perspectives or, one might say, two names (what is *Fraud* for one is *Gullibility* for the other); in short, each character, even a secondary one, is the hero of his own sequence. Todorov, analyzing a "psychological" novel (*Les Liaisons dangereuses*), starts not from character-persons but from three main relations in which they can engage and which he calls basic predicates (love, communication, help); these relations are subjected by the analysis to two kinds of rules: of *derivation* when it is a matter of accounting for other relations and of *action* when it is a matter of describing the transformation of these relations in the course of the story: there are many characters in *Les Liaisons dangereuses*, but "what is said of them" (their predicates) can be classified.[40] Finally, Greimas has proposed describing and classifying the characters of narrative not according to what they are but according to what they do (whence their name, *actants*), insofar as they participate in three main semantic axes, which we identify moreover in the sentence (subject, object, indirect object, adjunct) and which are communication, desire (or quest) and ordeal[41]; since this participation is organized in pairs, the infinite world of characters is also subject to a paradigmatic structure (*Subject/Object, Giver/Receiver, Helper/Opponent*), projected throughout the narrative; and since the actant defines a class, it can be filled with different actors, mobilized according to the rules of multiplication, substitution, or deficiency.

These three conceptions have many points in common. The main one, we repeat, is to define the character by its participation in a sphere of actions, such spheres being few in number, typical, classifiable; this is why we have here called the second level of description, though that of the characters, the level of Actions: this

---

[40] *Littérature et Signification*, Paris: Larousse, 1967.
[41] *Sémantique structurale, op. cit.*, p. 129ff.

word must therefore not be understood here in the sense of the trivial actions which form the fabric of the first level, but in the sense of the major articulations of *praxis* (to desire, to communicate, to struggle).

## 2. The problem of the subject

The problems raised by a classification of the characters in narrative are not yet properly solved. Of course there is agreement that the countless characters of narrative can be subject to rules of substitution and that, even within a work, one and the same figure can absorb different characters[42]; on the other hand, the actantial model proposed by Greimas (and adopted in a different perspective by Todorov) seems to stand the test of a great number of narratives: like every structural model, it has value less for its canonical form (a matrix of six actants) than for the regulated transformations (deficiencies, confusions, duplications, substitutions) to which it lends itself, thereby holding out hope for an actantial typology of narrative[43]; however, when the matrix has a high classifying power (as is the case with Greimas's actants), it accounts poorly for the multiplicity of participations when these are analyzed in terms of perspectives; and when these perspectives are respected (in Bremond's description), the system of characters remains too segmented; the reduction proposed by Todorov avoids both dangers, but has so far been applied to only one narrative. All this can be readily and harmoniously resolved, it would seem. The real difficulty raised by the classification of characters is the place (hence the existence) of the *subject* in any actantial matrix, whatever its formula. *Who* is the subject (the hero) of a narrative? Is there—or is

[42] Psychoanalysis has widely accredited these operations of condensation—already Mallarmé had said of *Hamlet*: "Supernumeraries, there must be! for in the ideal painting of the stage everything moves according to a symbolic reciprocity of types among themselves or relative to a single figure" (*Crayonné au Théâtre*, in *Oeuvres complètes, op. cit.*, p. 301).

[43] For example: narratives in which object and subject are identified in the same character are narratives of the quest for oneself, for one's own identity (*The Golden Ass*); narratives in which the subject pursues successive objects (*Madame Bovary*), etc.

there not—a privileged class of actors? Our novel has accustomed us to accentuating in one way or another, sometimes intricately (negatively), one character among the others. But this prerogative is far from being typical of all narrative literature. Thus, many narratives bring to grips, in their contention for a goal, two adversaries whose "actions" are thereby equalized; the subject is then really double, without our being any further enabled to reduce it by substitution; this may even be a common archaic form, as if the narrative, in the fashion of certain languages, had also known a *duel* of characters. This duel is all the more interesting in that it relates the narrative to the structure of certain (very modern) games in which two equal adversaries seek to gain possession of an object placed in circulation by a referee; this schema recalls the actantial matrix proposed by Greimas, which is hardly surprising if we realize that the game, being a language, also derives from the same symbolic structure that we recognize in language and in narrative: the game too is a sentence.[44] If then we keep a privileged class of actors (the subject of the quest, of the desire, of the action), it is at least necessary to inflect it by subjecting this actant to the very categories of *the person*, not psychological but grammatical: once again, we shall have to turn to linguistics in order to describe and classify the personal (I/you) or impersonal (he), singular, dual, or plural instance of the action. It will be—perhaps—the grammatical categories of the person (accessible in our pronouns) which will provide the key to the actional level. But since these categories can be defined only in relation to the instance of discourse, and not to that of reality[45], the characters, as units of the actional level, find their meaning (their intelligibility) only if we integrate them into the third level of description, which we shall here call the level of Narration (as opposed to Functions and to Actions).

---

[44] Umberto Eco's analysis of the James Bond cycle in *Communications*, #8 refers more to games than to language.

[45] See the analyses of person given by Benveniste, in *Problèmes de linguistique générale*, *op. cit.*

## IV  NARRATION

### 1.  Narrative communication

Just as there is, within narrative, a major function of exchange (distributed between a giver and a receiver), so, homologically, narrative, as object, is the stake of a communication: there is a giver of the narrative, there is a receiver of the narrative. As we know, in linguistic communication, *I* and *you* are absolutely presupposed by each other; in the same way, there cannot be a narrative without a narrator and without an auditor (or reader). This may be commonplace, but it is as yet undeveloped. Of course the role of the sender has been abundantly paraphrased (we study the "author" of a novel, without wondering, moreover, if he is in fact the "narrator"), but when we turn to the reader, literary theory is much more modest. As a matter of fact, the problem is not to introspect the motives of the narrator nor the effects which the narration produces upon the reader; it is to describe the code through which narrator and reader are signified through the narrative itself. The signs of the narrator seem at first glance more visible and more numerous than the signs of the reader (a narrative more frequently says *I* than *you*); in reality, the latter are simply more intricate than the former; thus, each time the narrator, ceasing to "represent," reports phenomena which he knows perfectly well but which the reader does not, there occurs, by a signifying deficiency, a sign of reading, for it would be meaningless for the narrator to offer a piece of information to himself. "Leo was the owner of this joint,"[46] we are told in a first-person novel: this is a sign of the reader, close to what Jakobson calls the conative function of communication. Lacking an inventory, we shall nonetheless leave aside for the moment the signs of reception (though they are also important), to say a word about the signs of narration.[47]

---

[46] *Double Bang à Bangkok.* The sentence functions as a wink to the reader, as if he were being given a sign of recognition. On the contrary, the statement "So Leo had just left" is a sign of the narrator, for this belongs to a reasoning performed by a "person."

[47] Todorov moreover deals with the image of the narrator and the image of the reader in "Les catégories du récit littéraire", *op. cit.*

Who is the giver of the narrative? Three conceptions seem to have been formulated so far. The first considers that the narrative is produced by a person (in the fully psychological meaning of the word); this person has a name, he is the author, in whom are ceaselessly exchanged the "personality" and the art of a fully identified individual, who periodically takes up his pen to write a story: the narrative (notably the novel) is then merely the expression of an *I* which is external to it. The second conception makes the narrator into a sort of total, apparently impersonal consciousness who produces the story from a superior point of view, that of God:[48] the narrator is at once internal to his characters (since he knows everything that is happening in them) and external (since he is never identified with one more than with the other). The third, most recent conception (Henry James, Sartre) states that the narrator must limit his narrative to what the characters can observe or know: everything occurs as if each character were in turn the sender of the narrative. These three conceptions are equally difficult, insofar as all three seem to regard the narrator and the characters as real, "living" persons (we recognize the unfailing power of this literary myth), as if the narrative originally determined itself at its referential level (it is a matter of equally "realist" conceptions). Now, at least from our point of view, narrator and characters are essentially "paper beings"; the (material) author of a narrative cannot in any way be identified with its narrator;[49] the signs of the narrator are immanent to the narrative, and consequently quite accessible to a semiologic analysis; but to decide that the author himself (whether he parades himself, hides, or withdraws) possesses "signs" with which he strews his work, we must suppose between the "person" and his language a descriptive relation which makes

[48] "When will someone write from the point of view of a *supreme joke*, that is, the way the good Lord sees things from on high?" (Flaubert, *Préface à la vie d'écrivain*, Paris: Éd. du Seuil, 1965, p. 91).

[49] A distinction all the more necessary, on the level which concerns us, in that, historically, a considerable mass of narratives have no author (oral narratives, folktales, epics entrusted to bards, to reciters, etc.).

the author a full subject and the narrative the instrumental expression of that plenitude: this is unacceptable to structual analysis:
*who speaks* (in the narrative) is not *who writes* (in life) and *who
writes* is not *who is.*[50]

As a matter of fact, narration strictly speaking (or the code of
the narrator) knows, like language, only two sign systems: personal
and apersonal; these two systems do not necessarily offer the linguistic marks attached to the person and to the non-person; there
may be, for example, narratives or at least episodes written in the
third person whose true instance is nonetheless in the first person.
How to determine in this case? It suffices to rewrite the narrative
(or the passage), substituting "he" for "I": so long as this operation
involves no other alteration in the discourse besides the change in
grammatical pronouns, it is clear that we remain within a system
of the person: the entire beginning of *Goldfinger*, though written
in the third person, is in fact spoken by James Bond; for the instance
to change, the rewriting must become impossible; thus the sentence:
"he noticed a man of about fifty, still young-looking, etc.," is
entirely within the person system, despite the "*he*" ("I, James Bond,
noticed, etc.") but the narrative statement "the clink of ice against
the glass seemed to give Bond a sudden inspiration" cannot be
within the personal system, by reason of the verb "to seem," which
becomes the sign of the apersonal system (and not by reason of
"he"). It is clear that the apersonal system is the traditional mode
of narrative, language having elaborated a whole temporal system
proper to narrative (articulated on the aorist),[51] meant to eliminate
the present of the speaker: "In narrative," Benveniste says, "no one
speaks." Yet the personal instance (in more or less disguised forms)
has gradually invaded narrative, narration being referred to the *hic
et nunc* of locution (this is the definition of the personal system);
hence we see today many narratives, and of the most ordinary kind,
mixing at an extremely rapid rate, frequently within the confines

[50] Jacques Lacan: "Is the subject I speak of when I speak the same as he who speaks?"
[51] Emile Benveniste, *op. cit.*

of a single sentence, the personal and the apersonal; for example, this sentence from *Goldfinger*:

> His eyes were fixed on those of Du Pont,
> who didn't know where to look,                    *personal*
>
> for that stare combined candor,
> irony and self-deprecation                        *apersonal*

The mixture of systems is obviously experienced as an accommodation, one that can become a kind of deception: a detective story by Agatha Christie (*The Sittaford Mystery*) sustains the mystery only by deceiving us as to the person of the narration: a character is described from within, whereas he is already the killer:[52] everything happens as if, within the same person, there were a witness's consciousness, immanent to the discourse, and a killer's consciousness, immanent to the referent: the abusive alternation of the two systems is what enables the mystery. Hence we understand that at the opposite pole, of "serious" literature, the rigor of the chosen system should be made into a necessary condition of the work—though still without being able to honor it all the way.

Such rigor—sought by certain contemporary writers—is not necessarily an esthetic imperative; what is called the psychological novel is usually marked by a mixture of the two systems, successively mobilizing the signs of the non-person and those of the person; "psychology" cannot, in fact—paradoxically—accommodate a pure system of the person, for by confining the entire narrative to the mere instance of the discourse, or one might say to the act of locution, it is the very content of the person which is threatened: the psychological person (referential order) has no relation with the linguistic person, never defined by arrangements, intentions, or features, but only by (coded) place within the discourse. It is this formal person whom we are attempting currently to speak of;

---

[52] Personal mode: "It even seemed to Burnaby that nothing looked changed," etc. The device is even cruder in *The Murder of Roger Ackroyd*, since here the killer actually says *I*.

it is a matter of an important subversion (moreover the public has the impression that no one is writing "novels" any longer) for it attempts to shift the narrative from the purely constative order (which it occupied till now) to the performative order, according to which the meaning of an utterance is the very action which utters it:[53] today, to write is not "to tell," it is to say that one is telling, and to shift the entire referent ("what one says") to this act of locution; this is why a part of contemporary literature is no longer descriptive, but transitive, attempting to accomplish in speech a present so pure that the entire discourse is identified with the act which delivers it, the whole *logos* being confined—or extended— to a *lexis*.[54]

## 2. Narrative situation

The narrational level is thus occupied by the signs of narrativity, the group of operators which reintegrate functions and actions within narrative communication, articulated around its giver and its receiver. Some of these signs have already been studied: in oral literatures, we know certain codes of recitation (metrical formulas, conventional protocols of presentation), and we know that the "author" is not the one who invents the best stories, but the one who best masters the code whose use he shares with the listeners: in such literatures, the narrational level is so distinct, its rules so constraining, that it is difficult to conceive of a "tale" without coded signs of narrative (*"Once upon a time,"* etc.). In our written literatures, the "forms of discourse" (which are actually signs of narrativity) were very early identified: classification of the author's modes of intervention, outlined by Plato, adopted by Diomedes,[55]

---

[53] On the performative, cf. Todorov, "Les catégories du récit littéraire," *op. cit.* —The classic example of a performative is the statement: *I declare war*, which neither "constates" nor "describes" anything, but exhausts its meaning in its own utterance (in contrast to the statement: *The king has declared war*, which is constative and descriptive).

[54] For the *logos/lexis* opposition, see Genette, "Frontières du récit," *op. cit.*

[55] *Genus activum vel imitativum* (no intervention on the part of the narrator in the discourse: theater, for example); *genus ennarativum* (only the poet speaks: *sententiae*, didactic poems); *genus commune* (mixture of the two genres: epic poems).

coding of the beginnings and ends of narratives, definition of the various styles of representation (*oratio directa, oratio indirecta*, with its *inquit, oratio tecta*),[56] study of "points of view," etc. All these elements belong to the narrational level. To them must obviously be added writing as a whole, for its role is not to "transmit" the narrative, but to parade it.

It is actually in a parading of narrative that the units of the lower levels are integrated: the ultimate form of narrative, as narrative, transcends its contents and its strictly narrative forms (functions and actions). This explains why the narrational code should be the final level which our analysis can reach, unless it departs from the narrative-as-object, *i.e.*, unless it transgresses the rule of immanence which establishes it. Narration can actually receive its meaning only from the world which makes use of it: beyond the narrational level begins the world, *i.e.*, other systems (social, economic, ideological), whose terms are no longer only the narratives, but elements of another substance (historical phenomena, determinations, behaviors, etc.). Just as linguistics halts at the sentence, the analysis of narrative halts at discourse: thereafter we must shift to another semiotics. Linguistics knows this kind of frontier, which it has already postulated—if not explored—under the name of *situation*. Halliday defines "situation" (in relation to a sentence) as "the associated non-linguistic factors";[57] Prieto as "the group of phenomena known by the receiver at the moment of the semic act and independently of this act."[58] In the same way we can say that every narrative is dependent on a "narrative situation," a group of protocols according to which the narrative is "consumed." In "archaic" societies, the narrative situation is strongly coded;[59] nowadays, only avant-garde literature still dreams of protocols of reading, spectacular in the case of Mallarmé, who wanted the book to be recited

[56] H. Sörenson, in *Language and Society* (Studies presented to Jansen), *op. cit.*), p. 150.
[57] M. A. K. Halliday, *op. cit.*, p. 4.
[58] L. J. Prieto, *Principes de noologie*, Paris & The Hague, 1964, p. 36.
[59] The tale, as Lucien Sebag observed, can be told at any time and in any place, but not the mythic narrative.

in public according to a precise combinatory process, typographic in the case of Butor, who tries to accompany the book with its own signs. But, in ordinary cases, our society evades as carefully as possible the coding of the narrative situation: countless are the narrative devices which attempt to naturalize the subsequent narrative by feigning to assign it a natural occasion for its origin, and, so to speak, to "disinaugurate" it: novels in letters, manuscripts supposedly recovered, the author who has encountered the narrator, films which start their story before the titles. The reluctance to parade its codes marks bourgeois society and the mass culture which has issued from it: each demands signs which do not seem to be signs. Yet this is, so to speak, only a structural epiphenomenon: however familiar, however casual the act of opening a novel or a newspaper or turning on a television program today, nothing can keep this modest action from setting up in us, at one blow and in its entirety, the narrative code we are going to need. The narrational level thereby has an ambiguous role: contiguous with the narrative situation (and sometimes even including it), it opens out onto the world where narrative is undone (consumed); but at the same time, crowning the previous levels, it closes narrative, definitively constitutes it as the speech of a language which foresees and bears its own metalanguage.

## V   THE SYSTEM OF NARRATIVE

Language proper can be defined by the concurrence of two fundamental processes: articulation, or segmentation, which produces units (this is what Benveniste calls *form*), and integration, which collects these units in units of a higher rank (this is *meaning*). This double process is recognizable in the language of narrative, which also knows an articulation and an integration, a form and a meaning.

## 1.  Distortion and expansion

The form of narrative is essentially marked by two powers: that of distending its signs throughout the story, and that of inserting within these distortions unforeseeable expansions. These two powers appear to be liberties; but the characteristic of narrative is precisely to include these "deviations" in its language.[60]

The distortion of signs exists in language, where Bally has studied it, apropos of French and German;[61] dystaxia occurs when the signs (of a message) are no longer simply juxtaposed, when (logical) linearity is disturbed (the predicate preceding the subject, for example). A notable form of dystaxia occurs when the parts of the same sign are separated by other signs throughout the chain of the message (for instance, the negation *ne jamais* and the verb *a pardonné* in the sentence: *elle ne nous a jamais pardonné*): the sign being split up, its signified is distributed under several signifiers, distant from one another, each of which taken separately cannot be understood. As we have already seen apropos of the functional level, this is exactly what happens in narrative: the units of a sequence, though forming a whole on the level of this sequence itself, can be separated from one another by the insertion of units which come from other sequences: as has been said, the structure of the functional level is fugued.[62] According to Bally's terminology, which opposes the synthetic languages, in which dystaxia predominates (such as German), and the analytic languages, which show a greater respect for logical linearity and monosemy (such as French), narrative is a strongly synthetic language, essentially based on a syntax of embedding and enveloping: each point of the narrative spreads in several directions at once: when James Bond orders a whisky while waiting for his plane, this whisky, as index, has a polysemic value, it is a kind of

---

[60] Valéry: "Formally, the novel is close to the dream; both can be defined by the consideration of this curious property: *that all their deviations belong to them.*"

[61] Charles Bally, *Linguistique générale et Linguistique française*, 4th ed., Berne, 1965.

[62] Cf. Lévi-Strauss (*Structural Anthropology, op. cit.*, p. 211): "Relations pertaining to the same bundle may appear diachronically at remote intervals." —Greimas has insisted on the separation of functions (*Sémantique structurale, op. cit.*).

symbolic node which gathers several signifieds (modernity, wealth, leisure); but as a functional unit, the ordering of a whisky must traverse, step by step, many relays (consumption, waiting, departure, etc.) in order to find its final meaning: the unit is "taken over" by the entire narrative, but also the narrative "holds together" only by the distortion and the spread of its units.

Generalized distortion gives narrative language its characteristic mark: a phenomenon of pure logic, since it is based on an—often remote—relation, and mobilizing a kind of confidence in intellective memory, it constantly substitutes meaning for the pure and simple copy of the events related; according to "life," it is unlikely that, in an encounter, the fact of sitting down would not immediately follow the invitation to do so; in narrative, these units, contiguous from a mimetic point of view, can be separated by a long succession of insertions belonging to entirely different functional spheres: thus is established a sort of *logical time*, which has little relation with real time, the apparent pulverization of the units being always firmly maintained under the logic which unites the nuclei of the sequence. "Suspense" is obviously only a privileged, or if one prefers, exasperated form of distortion: on the one hand, by keeping a sequence open (by empathic processes of delay and reinauguration), it reinforces the contact with the reader (the hearer), possesses a manifestly phatic function; and on the other hand, it offers him the threat of an incomplete sequence, of an open paradigm (if, as we believe, every sequence has two poles), *i.e.*, of a logical disturbance, and it is this disturbance which is consumed with anxiety and pleasure (especially since it is always, ultimately, repaired); "suspense" is therefore a game with structure intended, so to speak, to threaten and to glorify it: it constitutes a veritable "thrill" of the intelligible: by representing order (and no longer series) in its fragility, it fulfills the very idea of language: what seems most pathetic is also the most intellectual: suspense grips the mind, not the guts.[63]

[63] J. P. Faye, apropos of Klossowski's *Baphomet*: "Rarely has fiction (or narrative) so clearly revealed what it always, necessarily, is: an experimentation of "thought" upon "life" (*Tel Quel*, #22, p. 88).

What can be separated can also be filled. Distended, the functional nuclei present intercalary spaces which can be loaded almost to infinity; these interstices can be filled with a very great number of catalyses; yet, here, a new typology can intervene, for the catalytic freedom can be regulated according to the content of the functions (certain functions are more widely exposed than others to catalysis: *Waiting*, for example),[64] and according to the substance of the narrative (writing has possibilities of diaeresis—and therefore of catalysis—much superior to those of film: we can "cut" a narrated gesture more easily than the same gesture visualized).[65] The catalytic power of narrative has for a corollary its elliptical power. On the one hand, a function (*he had a good meal*) can economize all the virtual catalyses it harbors (the detail of the meal),[66] on the other, it is possible to reduce a sequence to its nuclei, and a hierarchy of sequences to its higher terms, without altering the meaning of the story: a narrative can be identified, even if we reduce its total syntagm to its actants and to its main functions, so that they result from the gradual assumption of the functional units.[67] In other words, the narrative is susceptible to *summary* (what used to be called the *argument*). At first glance, this is the case with all discourse; but each discourse has its own type of summary; the lyric poem, for example, being only the vast metaphor of a single signified,[68] is summarized by giving this signified, and the operation

---

[64] Logically, *Waiting* has only two nuclei: 1. waiting posited; 2. waiting satisfied or disappointed; but the first nucleus can be broadly catalyzed, sometimes indefinitely (*Waiting for Godot*): another—extreme—game with structure.

[65] Valéry: "Proust divides up—and gives us the sensation of being able to do so indefinitely—what other writers are accustomed to pass over."

[66] Here again, there are specifications according to substance: literature has an incomparable elliptical power—which the cinema does not.

[67] This reduction does not necessarily correspond to the segmentation of the book into chapters; on the contrary it seems that increasingly the role of the chapters is to set up breaks, *i.e.*, suspense (technique of the serial).

[68] Nicolas Ruwet in *Langage, Musique, Poésie, op. cit.*, p. 199: "The poem can be understood as the result of a series of transformations applied to the proposition 'I love you.' " Ruwet is alluding here to Freud's analysis of paranoiac delirium apropos of President Schreber ("Psychoanalytic Notes on an Autobiographical Account of a Case of Paranoia," Standard Edition, vol. 12).

is so drastic that it cancels out the poem's identity (summarized, lyric poems are reduced to the signifieds *Love* and *Death*): whence the conviction that a poem cannot be summarized. On the contrary, the summary of narrative (if it is conducted according to structural criteria) maintains the individuality of the message. In other words, the narrative is *translatable*, without fundamental damage: what is not translatable is determined only on the last, narrational level: the signifiers of narrativity, for example, can with difficulty pass from novel to film, for film knows personal treatment only exceptionally,[69] and the last layer of the narrational level, to wit writing, cannot pass from one language to the other (or does so very poorly). The translatability of narrative results from the structure of its language; by a converse path, it would therefore be possible to recognize this structure by distinguishing and by classifying the (variously) translatable and untranslatable elements of a narrative: the (present) existence of different and concurrent semiotics (literature, cinema, comics, radio, television) would greatly facilitate this kind of analysis.

## 2. Mimesis and meaning

In the language of narrative, the second important process is integration: what has been disjoined at a certain level (a sequence, for example) is often united again at a higher level (a sequence hierarchically important, total signified of scattered indices, action of a class of characters); the complexity of a narrative can be compared to that of a data flow chart, capable of integrating both backward and forward impulses; or, more exactly, it is integration, in its various forms, which permits compensating for the apparently unmasterable complexity of the units on one level; it is integration which permits orienting the comprehension of discontinuous, contiguous, and heterogeneous elements (as they are given by the

---

[69] Once again, there is no relation between the grammatical "person" of the narrator and the "personality" (or subjectivity) which a film director engages in his way of presenting a story: the *camera-I* (continually identified with the eye of a character) is an exceptional phenomenon in the history of cinema.

syntagm, which knows only one dimension: succession); if we follow Greimas and call the unit of signification *isotopy* (that unit which impregnates a sign and its context), we shall say that integration is a factor of isotopy: each (integrative) level gives its isotopy to the units of the level below, keeping the meaning from dangling, as it would not fail to do, if we did not perceive the staggering of the levels. However, the narrative integration is not presented in a serenely regular fashion, like a fine building which would lead by symmetrical baffles of an infinity of simple elements to several complex masses; very often, one unit can have two correlates, one on one level (function of a sequence), the other on another (index referring to an actant); the narrative thus presents itself as a succession of mediate and immediate elements, powerfully imbricated; dystaxia orients a "horizontal" reading, but integration superimposes a "vertical" reading: there is a kind of structural "limping," a kind of incessant play of potentials, whose different "falls" give the narrative its dynamic or its energy: each unit is perceived in its surfacing and in its depth, and that is how the narrative "proceeds": by the rivalry of these two paths, the structure is ramified, proliferates, is revealed—and recovers itself: what is new does not cease to be regular. There is, of course, a freedom of narrative (as there is a freedom of every speaker with regard to his language), but this freedom is literally *confined*: between the strong code of language and the strong code of narrative, is established, so to speak, a hollow or a trough: the sentence. If we try to comprehend the whole of a written narrative, we see that it starts from the most powerfully coded (the phonematic, or even merismatic level), gradually loosens until it reaches the sentence, extreme point of combinatory freedom, then begins once more to tighten, starting from the small groups of sentences (micro-sequences), still very free, up to the major actions, which form a strong and limited code: the creativity of narrative (at least in its mythic appearance of "life") would thus be located *between two codes*, the linguistic and the translinguistic. This is why we can say, paradoxically, that *art* (in the romantic sense of the word) is a matter of statements of detail, while *imag-*

*ination* is a mastery of the code: "It will be found in fact," wrote
Poe, "that the ingenious are always fanciful, and the *truly* imaginative never otherwise than analytic . . ."[70]

Hence we must discount the "realism" of narrative. Receiving a
phone call in the office where he is on duty, Bond "reflects," the
author tells us: "Communications with Hong-Kong are as bad as
they always were and just as difficult to obtain." Neither Bond's
"reflection" nor the poor quality of telephone connections are the
real information here; such contingency may give the illusion of
"life," but the true piece of information, the one which will ger-
minate later, is the localization of the phone call, to wit, Hong
Kong. Thus in all narrative, imitation remains contingent;[71] the
function of narrative is not to "represent," it is to constitute a
spectacle which still remains very mysterious to us, but which cannot be of a mimetic order; the "reality" of a sequence is not in the
"natural" succession of the actions which compose it, but in the
logic which is revealed and risked and satisfied there; we might say
in another fashion that the origin of a sequence is not the observation of reality, but the necessity to vary and transcend the first
*form* available to man, *i.e.*, repetition: a sequence is essentially a
whole at the heart of which nothing is repeated; logic here has a
liberating value—and the whole narrative with it; it may be that
men ceaselessly reinject into narrative what they have known, what
they have lived; at least they do so in a form which has triumphed
over repetition and instituted the model of a becoming. Narrative
does not show, does not imitate; the passion which can excite us
upon reading a novel is not that of a "vision" (indeed, we "see"
nothing), it is that of meaning, *i.e.*, of a higher order of relation,
which also possesses its emotions, its hopes, its threats, its victories:
"what happens" in narrative is, from the referential (real) point of

---

[70] *The Murders in the Rue Morgue.*

[71] Gérard Genette (cf. "Frontières du récit," *op. cit.*) correctly reduces *mimesis* to the
fragments of dialogue reported; yet even such dialogue always harbors an intelligible and
non-mimetic function.

view, literally, *nothing*,[72] what "takes place" is language alone, the adventure of language, whose coming never ceases to be celebrated. Though we know little more about the origin of narrative than about that of language, we can reasonably suggest that narrative is a contemporary of monologue, a creation, apparently, posterior to that of dialogue; in any case, without wanting to strain the phylogenetic hypothesis, it may be significant that it is at the same moment (around the age of three) that the child "invents" the sentence, narrative, and the Oedipus complex.

*Communications*, 1966

---

[72] Mallarmé: ". . . A dramatic work shows the succession of the externals of action without any moment's keeping its reality and without there happening, ultimately, anything at all" (*Crayonné au théâtre, Oeuvres Complètes, op. cit.*, p. 296).

# The Sequences of Actions

According to the first structural analysis of narrative, a tale is a systematic concatenation of actions, distributed among a small number of characters and whose function is identical from one story to the next. By analyzing some hundreds of Slavic tales, Vladimir Propp has succeeded in establishing the invariability of elements (characters and actions) and of relations (concatenation of actions) which definitively constitutes the *form* of the folktale. This form, however, remains in Propp's work a *schema*, a syntagmatic design, resulting by abstraction from the progress of the action in various tales. Lévi-Strauss and Greimas, completing and correcting Propp, have attempted to structure this progress, by coupling the actions of the narrative series, separated in the tale's course by other actions and a certain temporal distance, but linked among themselves by a paradigmatic relation of oppositions (for example: *a difficulty occurring to the hero/overcoming of this difficulty*). Bremond, finally, has studied the logical relation of the narrative actions, insofar as this relation refers to a certain logic of human behavior, revealing, for example, a certain constant structure of *stratagem* or of *deceit*, very frequent episodes in the tale.[1] We shall now attempt to make a contribution to this problem, which is certainly fundamental for the structural analysis of narrative, by analyzing certain sequences of actions, taken not from the folktale, but from a literary narrative: the examples to be considered here are borrowed from a *nouvelle* by Balzac, *Sarrasine*—published in his *Scenes of Parisian Life*—though without our being concerned to any degree with either Balzac's art or even "realistic" art: we shall deal solely with narrative *forms*, not with historical features or authorial performance.

Two observations, to begin with; first, the analysis of folktales has revealed the major actions, the primordial articulations of the story (contracts, ordeals, or adventures undertaken by the hero); but in literary narrative, once these principal actions are identified, supposing this can be readily done, there remains a host of minor actions, apparently trivial and more or less mechanical (*knocking at a door, engaging in a conversation, making an appointment,* etc.): are we to consider these subsidiary actions as a sort of insignificant background and withhold them from analysis on the pretext that *it goes without saying* that the discourse utters them in order to link two principal actions? No, for this would be to prejudice the final structure of the narrative, this would mean inflecting that structure in a unitary, hierarchical direction; we believe on the contrary that *all* the actions of a narrative, however minute they may seem, should be analyzed, integrated into an order which it is our obligation to describe: in the text (contrary to oral narrative) no feature of speech is insignificant.

Our second observation: even more than in the folktale, the sequences of actions of the literary narrative are caught in an abundant flux of other "details," other features which are not *actions* at all; they are either psychological indices, denoting the nature of a

[1] See especially: A. J. Greimas, "Éléments pour une théorie de l'interprétation du récit mythique," *Communications*, #8 (1966), pp. 28–59; and *Du sens*, Paris: Éd. du Seuil, 1970; Claude Bremond, "Le message narratif," *Communications*, #4 (1964), pp. 4–32; and "La Logique des possibles narratifs," *Communications*, #8 (1966), pp. 60–76.

character or a place, or else conversational interchanges through which the participants seek to reach one another, to convince or deceive one another, or else notations which the discourse advances in order to posit, delay, or solve enigmas, or else general reflections proceeding from particular knowledge or a wisdom, or else, finally, inventions of language (such as metaphor) which the analysis must ordinarily integrate into the symbolic field of the work. None of these features is "spontaneous" or "insignificant": each receives its authority and its familiarity from a systematic group of "ways of thinking," *i.e.*, from collective rules and repetitions, or else from some principal cultural code: Psychology, Science, Wisdom, Rhetoric, Hermeneutics, etc. In this profusion of other signs, the behavior of the characters (insofar as they are linked in coherent sequences) derives from a special code, from a logic of actions which, certainly, profoundly structures the text, gives it its "readable" quality, its appearance of narrative rationality, what the Ancients used to call its *verisimilitude* or probability, but is far from occupying the entire signifying surface of the literary narrative: for entire pages, it is quite likely that *nothing happens* (*i.e.*, no action is described), and, elsewhere, a consequential action can be separated from its antecedent by a great mass of signs produced by other codes that the actional one. And then we must not forget that actions can be articulated only as *indices* of a character (*he was in the habit of* . . .): they are then linked among themselves by a process of accumulation, not by a logical order, or at least the logic to which they refer is of a psychological and not a pragmatic order.

With all these reservations (which represent an enormous part of the literary narrative), there remain nonetheless within the classical text (before the advent of modernity) a certain number of actional data linked among themselves by a *logico-temporal* order (*this* which follows *that* is also its consequence), organized thereby in individuated series or sequences (for example: 1. *to come to a door*; 2. *to knock at this door*; 3. *to see someone appear at it*), whose internal development (even if imbricated in that of other parallel sequences) affords the story its progress and makes the narrative a processive organism, moving toward its "goal" or its "conclusion."

What are we to call this general code of narrative actions, some of which appear important, endowed with a great novelistic density (*to murder, to carry off a victim, to make a declaration of love,* etc.) while others seem quite trivial (*to open a door, to sit down,* etc.), so as to distinguish it from the other codes of culture which are invested in the text (this distinction obviously has no more than an analytic value, for the text presents all the codes mingled and as though *braided*)? Referring to a term from the Aristotelian vocabulary (Aristotle is, after all, the father of the structural analysis of works), I have proposed[2] to call this code of narrative actions the *proairetic code.* Establishing the science of action or *praxis,* Aristotle, in effect, precedes it by a connected discipline, *proairesis,* or the human faculty of deliberating in advance the result of an action, of *choosing* (this is the etymological meaning) between the two terms of an alternative the one which will be realized. Now, in each node of the sequence of actions, the narrative too (better to speak of the narrative and not of the author, for we are referring here to a narrative *language* and not to a storyteller's performance) "chooses" between several possibilities and this choice at every moment commits the very future of the story: from all evidence, the story will change according to whether the door on which one has knocked opens or does not open, etc. (this alternative structure has been specially studied by Claude Bremond); it follows that, placed at each action before an alternative (to give it this or that consequence) the narrative invariably chooses the term profitable to it, *i.e., which assures its survival as narrative;* the narrative never marks a term (by articulating it as fulfilling itself) which would extinguish the story, would make it turn short: there is a sort of instinct of preservation in narrative which, of two possible outcomes implied by an articulated action, always chooses the outcome which makes the story "go on"; this obvious circumstance, banal but in

[2] In a work devoted to the structural analysis of *Sarrasine* (*S/Z*, Paris: Éd. du Seuil, 1970; New York, Hill & Wang, 1975).

truth hardly studied at all, is worth recalling because narrative *art* (which is performance, application of a code) consists precisely in giving these structural determinations (which have uniquely in view the "salvation" of the narrative, and not that of this or that character in it) the guarantee (the alibi) of motives usually psychological, moral, passional, etc.: where the narrative is in fact choosing its own survival, it is the character who seems to choose his own destiny: the instinct of preservation of the one is masked by the freedom of the other: the narrative *economy* (quite as constraining as the monetary kind) sublimates itself into human free will. Such are the implications of this term *proairetism* which I am proposing to apply to any narrative action engaged in a coherent and homogeneous sequence.

We must further know how we can constitute these sequences, how we decide that an action belongs to one sequence and not to another. As a matter of fact, this constitution of the sequence is closely linked to its nomination; and, conversely, its analysis is linked to the unfolding of the name which has been found for it: it is because I can spontaneously subsume various actions such as *leaving, traveling, arriving, remaining* under the general name *Journey*, that the sequence asumes consistency and is individualized (sets itself in opposition to other sequences, other names); conversely, it is because a certain practical experience convinces me that under the term *Appointment* is arranged ordinarily a series of actions such as *proposing, accepting, honoring* that, this term having been in one way or another suggested to me by the text, I am entitled to observe, specifically, its sequential schema; to release the sequences (from the signifying mass of the text, whose heteroclite character we have mentioned) is to classify actions under a generic name (*Appointment, Journey, Excursion, Murder*, etc.); to analyze these sequences is to unfold this generic name into its component parts. That the simple *nomination* is a sufficient criterion of constitution of the phenomenon being observed may seem quite frivolous, left to the quite subjective discretion of the analyst, and, in short, quite "unscientific"; is it not to say, to each sequence: you exist because I am naming you; and I am naming you this way because I choose to do so? To which we must answer that the science of narrative (if it exists) cannot obey the criteria of the exact or experimental sciences; narrative is an activity of language (of signification or of symbolization) and it is in terms of language that it must be analyzed: *to name* is then for the analyst an operation as well established, as homogeneous with its object, as measuring for the geometrician, as weighing for the chemist, as examining through a microscope for the biologist. Further, the name which we find for the sequence (and which constitutes it) is a systematic witness, it proceeds itself from the vast activity of classification of which language consists; if I call a certain sequence *Abduction*, it is because the language itself has classified, has mastered the diversity of certain actions under a unique concept which it transmits to me and whose coherence it thereby authenticates; the *Abduction* which I constitute starting from snatches of actions scattered in the text then coincides with all the abductions I have read; the name is the exact, irrefutable trace, as solid as a scientific fact, of a certain *already-written, already-read, already-done*; to find the name is therefore not at all a whimsical operation, left to my mere caprice; to find the name is to find that *already* which constitutes the code, it is to assure the communication of the text and of all the other narratives which make up the narrative language, for the linguistic or semiological work must always consist in finding the *passage* which joins the anterior of language and the present of the text. Finally, by naming the sequence, the analyst merely reproduces, in a more applied and more reasoned fashion, the very work of the reader, and his "science" is rooted in a phenomenology of reading: to read a narrative is in effect (by the rushing rhythm of reading) to organize it in fragments of structures, it is to tend toward names which "summarize" more or less the profuse sequence of notations, it is to proceed within oneself, at the very moment when one "devours" the story, to nominal adjustments, it is constantly to tame the novelty of what one is reading by known names, proceeding from the vast anterior code of reading: it is because in myself, very rapidly, certain indices produce the name *Murder* that my reception of the tale is effectively a *reading*, and not the simple perception of phrases whose linguistic meaning I would understand, but not the narrative meaning: to read is to name (which is why one might go so far as to say, at least in relation to certain modern texts, to read is to write).

Without claiming to cover all of actional logic, and without even claiming that this logic is such a thing, let us try to reduce several proairetic sequences to a small number of simple relations; thus we might have a first notion of a certain rational conduct of the classical narrative.

1. *Consecutive.* In the narrative (and this is perhaps its mark), there is no pure succession: the temporal is immediately penetrated by the logical, the *consecutive* is at the same time the *consequential*:[3] what comes *after* seems produced by what was *before*. Yet, in the decomposition of certain movements, we approach the purely temporal: thus in the perception of an object, a painting for example (*to glance around/to perceive the object*). The faintly logical character of these (rather rare) sequences is apparent in that each term merely repeats the preceding one, as in a series (which is not a structure): *to leave a first place* (a room for instance)/*to leave a second place* (the structure which contains this room); yet logic is close at hand, in the form of a relation of implication: in order to "perceive," one *must* first "see"; in order to "enter a room" one *must* first "enter the building"; *a fortiori*, if the movement implies a return (*Excursion, Lover's Walk*): then the structure seems quite slight (by dint of being elementary): it is that of the *round trip*; but it suffices to imagine that a term is not noted in order to measure the logical scandal of which the narrative would then suddenly become the bearer: the *journey without return* (by a simple absence of one term of the sequence) is one of the most significant that can be recounted.

[3] See the foregoing essay.

2.  *Consequential.* This is the classical relation between two actions, one of which is the determination of the other (but here again, symmetrically and inversely to the preceding relation, most often, the causal link is imbued with temporality); the consequential articulation is obviously one of the richest, since it supports in some sense the narrative's "freedom": let a consequence be positive or negative, and the whole fate of the story is thereby changed.

3.  *Volitional.* An action (for example: *to get dressed*) is preceded by a notation of intention or of will (*to want to get dressed, to decide to get dressed*); here again the relation can deviate, the will can be severed from its accomplishment (*to want to get dressed and not to do so*), if an incident proceeding from a second sequence disturbs the logical process of the first one (the important thing for us is that this incident is always noted).

4.  *Reactive.* An action (for example: *to touch*) is followed by its reaction (*to scream*); this is a variety of the consequential schema, but the model here is more specifically biological.

5.  *Durative.* After having noted the beginning or the duration of an action (or of a state), the discourse notes its interruption or its cessation: *to bust out laughing/to break off*; *to be hidden/to come out of hiding*; *to meditate/to be roused from one's reverie*, etc. Once again, it is the very banality of these sequences which is significant; for, if it happened to the narrative not to note the end of a state or of an action, there would occur a veritable narrative scandal: the notation of interruption seems to be a veritable constraint of narrative language, or again, transposed to the level of the discourse, one of those *obligatory rubrics* Jakobson speaks of with regard to language.

6.  *Equipollent.* A small number of sequences (reduced to their nucleus) merely fulfill oppositions inscribed in the lexicon; thus *to question/to answer* (or: *to pose a problem/to work out the solution*); the

two terms are of course linked by a simple logic of implication (one answers because one has questioned), but the structure is that of a formal *complement*, such as one recognizes in the lexical pairs of contraries.

There are certainly other logical relations in the sequences of actions, and, further, the six relations identified can no doubt be further reduced and formalized; the important thing, for the analysis, is less the *nature* of the logical link than the necessity of its notation; the narrative *must* note the two terms of the relation, or else become "unreadable." Now, if the logical link seems less pertinent than its expression, this is because the logic to which the narrative refers is nothing other than a logic of the *already-read*: the stereotype (proceeding from a culture many centuries old) is the veritable ground of the narrative world, built altogether on the traces which experience (much more bookish than practical) has left in the reader's memory and which constitutes it. Hence we can say that the perfect sequence, the one which affords the reader the strongest logical certainty, is the most "cultural" sequence, in which are immediately recognized a whole *summa* of readings and conversations; such as (in Balzac's *nouvelle*) the sequence *Career: to go up to Paris/to work for a great master/to leave the master/to win a prize/ to receive the stamp of approval of a great critic/to leave for Italy*: how many times has this sequence not been imprinted upon our memory? Narrative logic, it must be admitted, is nothing other than the development of the Aristotelian *probable* (common opinion and not scientific truth); hence it is normal that, when an attempt is made to legalize this logic (in the form of esthetic constraints and values), it should still be an Aristotelian notion which the first classical theoreticians of narrative have advanced: that of *verisimilitude*.

It remains to be said in what ways the sequence of actions is present in the text.

1.   The preceding analysis has focused on several logical nuclei or nodes, and might suggest that the sequences, while deriving by

definition from a syntagmatic order, have a binary (paradigmatic) structure, but this would be an analytic illusion. If we accept as a criterion of the sequence its aptitude to be named (*i.e.*, to be covered by a generic term proceeding from the lexicon-as-culture), we must acknowledge sequences whose number of terms is very variable. When the sequence denotes a trivial operation, its terms are generally very few; the contrary is the case when it refers to a great novelistic model (*Lover's Walk, Murder, Abduction*, etc.). Further, in these principal sequences, different structures can be superimposed: for example, the discourse can mix the denotation of "real" events (in their logico-temporal sequence) and the ordinary terms of rhetorical *dispositio* (announcement, parts, summary), which extends the sequence without dispersing it; the discourse can also posit two or three principal (and different) terms and repeat each of them several times (varying their signifier): a character, thanks to a certain situation, can *hope/be disappointed/compensate*, but hope, disappointment, and compensation are repeated several times (by the rhythm of the subject's reflections and with the help of flashbacks); finally, we must not forget that the repetition of terms (cause of a proliferation of the sequence) can have a semantic value (be endowed with a content of its own, *as* repetition); this is the case of the sequences *Danger* and *Threat*, in which the multiplication of the same term (*to incur a danger, to undergo a threat*) has the value of dramatic oppression.

2.    In general the structural analysis of narrative does not classify the actions (called *functions* by Propp) before having specified them by the character who is their agent or patient; in this regard, the analysis should note that the sequences are worked out almost always with two or three partners; in a sequence such as *act/react*, there are obviously two distinct agents; but this is an ulterior degree of the analysis; from the point of view of a simple structuration (which has concerned us here), it is legitimate (and no doubt profitable) to consider the actional term as a verb released from any personal engagement and apprehended on the contrary in its state as a pure

semanteme (further, the semantism of certain verbs already implies in itself the duality of agents; as *unite*).

3.   A sequence, once it is of a certain length, can include subsidiary sequences, which are inserted within its general development, as "subprograms" (which would be called "bits" in cybernetics). The sequence *To Narrate* can at a certain moment include the term *Appointment/*(*to make an appointment in order to tell the story*); this term can in its turn cover a sequence (*to ask for an appointment/to accept it/to refuse it/to honor it*, etc.). The actional network is in effect constituted, in principle, by an amplifying or reductive substitution, according to the case: sometimes the discourse *decomposes* a term and thereby produces a new sequence of actions; sometimes it *summarizes* several operations under a single word: this freedom of oscillation is proper to articulate speech (it is much more guarded in cinematic language, for instance).

4.   When a sequence seems to present a certain illogicality, it suffices in most cases to extend the analysis and to proceed to certain elementary substitutions in order to restore its rationality thereafter. In the sequence *To Narrate*, the term *to accept the appointment proposed* is equivalent to *to agree that you be told the story in question*; if a "hole" appears between the order of recounting a story and the effect of this story (on the one who has heard it), this is because the act of narrating, without being explicitly denoted, is represented by the very text of the story: the missing term is then the whole story, signified as such by the quotation marks which open its utterance.

5.   These substitutions (these "restitutions," one ought to say) are inevitable because it is constant that, in classical narrative, the sequence tends to cover the event related as completely as possible: there is a kind of narrative obsession to surround the fact by the

greatest number of determinations possible: *To Narrate*, for instance, will be preceded both by the *conditions* and by the *causes* of the action; the fact (or the actional node in which it is expressed) is constantly extended by its precedents (the typical case of this process is the flashback). From the actional point of view, the principle of narrative art (one might say: its ethic) is the *complement*: it is a matter of producing a discourse which best satisfies a requirement of *completeness* and spares the reader the "horror of the void."

These observations relative to a certain level of the narration (which includes many others) have as their goal to introduce (in the form of a sort of preliminary inventory of obvious materials) a specific problem: what is it that makes a narrative "readable"? What are the structural conditions of a text's "readability"? Everything which has been identified here may seem "self-evident"; but if these conditions of narrative seem "natural," it is then because there exists potentially, in reverse, an "anti-nature" of narrative (of which no doubt certain modern texts constitute the new experience): by staking out an elementary rationality with sequences of actions, we approach the *limits* of narrative, beyond which begins a new art, which is that of narrative transgression. Now, the sequence of actions is in a sense the privileged depository of that readability: it is by the pseudo-logic of its sequences of actions that a narrative seems to us "normal" (readable); this logic, as we have said, is empirical, we cannot relate it to a "structure" of the human mind; what matters in it, is that it assures to the sequence of events narrated an *irreversible* (logico-temporal) *order: it is irreversibility which constitutes the readability of the classical narrative.* Hence we understand that the narrative subverts itself (modernizes itself) by intensifying in its general structure the work of reversibility. Now, the reversible level *par excellence* is that of symbols (the dream, for instance, is removed from the logico-temporal order). As a romantic work, Balzac's text to which we have made some reference is historically situated at the crossroads of the actional and the symbolic:

it well represents the *passage* from simple readability, marked by a constraining irreversibility of actions (of the classical type) to a complex (threatened) readability subject to forces of dispersion and reversibility of symbolic elements, destroyers of time and of rationality.

1969; in *Patterns of Literary Style*,
Pennsylvania State University Press, 1971

# TWO

# DOMAINS

# Saussure, the Sign, Democracy

Popular speech and Rousseau himself use "traisait" for "trayait": this because "traire" is conjugated on the model of "plaire," which in the imperfect takes "plaisait." This is a four-term proportion which Saussure calls an *analogy* (*analogia* actually means *proportion*, but nowadays we should probably say *homology*).

Analogy, Saussure believes, is the mainspring, the very being of language: "The role of analogy is vast"; "The principle of analogy is ultimately identical with that of the mechanism of language." Saussure treats this primacy with an impassioned accent: he sings the strength, the virtue, the wisdom of analogy; he raises it to the rank of a creative, demiurgic principle, and thus remodels the linguistic hierarchy of his time: the swarming of analogical phenomena, he thinks, is much more important than changes in sound (this was the warhorse of the earlier linguistics); over centuries of evolution, elements of the language are preservd (simply: distributed differently); Saussure magnifies the language: resistance, stability, identity (he has always tended to absorb diachrony into synchrony), and the reason for this permanence is analogy: "Analogy is eminently conservative"; "The innovations of analogy are more apparent than real. Language is a gown covered with patchwork made of its own fabric": four-fifths of French is Indo-European. Analogy puts an eternity into language.

This enthusiastic promotion of analogy shows, on its underside, a profound hostility to geneticism. With Saussure, there is an epistemological change: analogism takes the place of evolutionism, imitation substitutes for derivation. Do not say, as everyone does, that "magasinier" comes from "magasin"; say rather that "magasin/magasinier" has been formed on the model of "prison/prisonnier." Do not say that the object of etymological science is to "trace back" from a present form to an original form; be satisfied to place the word in a configuration of neighboring terms, in a network of relations, which Time—this is its faint power—merely distorts topologically.

It is easy to glimpse the ideology of such a conception (as a matter of fact, quite often, nothing is more *directly* ideological than linguistics). On the one hand, the promotion of analogy joins a whole sociology of Imitation, codified, at the time, by Tarde (whom Saussure had doubtless read, more than Durkheim), and readily conforming to the beginnings of a mass society; in the cultural order, and singularly in that of the garment, the lower middle classes begin to appropriate bourgeois values by imitating them; Fashion, a frenzied imitation of a novation ceaselessly overtaken, is the triumph of this social imitation (it compels the bourgeoisie to affirm itself outside Fashion, in the simple but difficult category "distinction"); Saussure, like many of his contemporaries, from Herbert Spencer to Mallarmé, was struck by the importance of Fashion, which he calls, in the realm of language, *inter-course*. Further, by eternalizing language, Saussure manages to dismiss Origin (whence his indifference with regard to etymology): language is not caught up in a process of filiation, inheritance is devalued; scientific procedure ceases to be explicative (filial, seeking cause, anteriority), it becomes descriptive: the space of the word is no longer that of an ancestry or a descent, it is that of a collaterality: the elements of language—its individuals—are no longer sons, but fellow citizens: language, in its very becoming, is no longer a lordship but a democracy: the rights and duties of words (which actually form their meaning) are limited by coexistence, the cohabitation of equal individuals.[1]

Omnipotent, the principle of analogy nonetheless has, in Saussure, a cause: it proceeds from the status of the sign; in language, the sign is "arbitrary," no natural link binds signifier and signified, and this arbitrary relation must be compensated for by a power of stabilization, which is analogy; since the sign does not stand "naturally" (its signifying verticality is fallacious), it must depend, in order to last, on its surroundings; the relations of neighborhood (of fellow-citizenship) will take up the relay in relations of signification, the contract will be substituted for a failing (because uncertain) nature. Let us review this trajectory, which has assumed, in Saussure, the tone of a little scientific drama—so much did this linguist suffer, apparently, from the lacunae of signification, before he managed to bring forth his theories of value into the light of day.

Saussure sees signs in the form of divided, isolated, and closed-off individuals; they are veritable monads; each encloses in its circle—in its being—a signifier and a signified: this is signification. Two difficulties then appear: on the one hand, if it were articulated only around its monads, language would be nothing but a dead collection of signs, a nomenclature—which from all evidence it is not; on the other hand, if we reduce meaning to the vertical and apparently enclosed relation of signifier and signified, since this relation is not natural, we cannot understand the stability of language: "A language [if it is only a collection of monads] is radically impotent to defend itself against factors which shift, from moment to moment, the relation of signifier and signified. This is one of the consequences of the arbitrary nature of the sign"; hence, if we

---

[1] Chomsky, as we know, has opposed the Saussurian principle of analogy—in the name of another principle, that of creativity. This is to determine another option; for Chomsky, what matters is to distinguish man from animal and from the machine; this distinction must be respected *in the sciences as in government*; whence that same movement which establishes at once Chomskian linguistics and Chomsky's opposition to the authoritarian, technocratic, and warmongering state.

relied upon signification, Time and Death would constantly threaten language; this risk is the fruit of a kind of original Sin—for which Saussure seems inconsolable—the arbitrary nature of the sign. How beautiful that time, that order, that world, that language would be in which a signifier, without the aid of any human contract, of any sociality, would account through all eternity for its signified, in which a salary would be the "fair" price of labor, in which paper money would forever be worth its weight in gold! For we are dealing here with a general meditation on exchange: for Saussure, Labor and Gold are the signifieds of Sound, of Salary, and of the Banknote: *the Gold of the Signified!* That is the cry of all Hermeneutics, those semiologies which halt at signification: for them, the signified *certifies* the signifier, just as, in good finance, gold certifies currency; a strictly Gaullist conception: *let us keep the gold standard* and *be clear*, such were the general's two watchwords.

Saussure's little drama is that, contrary to the proud conservers, he trusts neither the Sign nor Gold: he sees quite clearly that the connection of paper to gold, of the signifier to the signified, is mobile, precarious; nothing certifies it; it is subject to the vicissitudes of time, of History. In his notion of signification, Saussure is actually at the point of the present monetary crisis: gold and its factitious substitute, the dollar, are collapsing: one dreams of a system in which currencies would stand among themselves, without reference to a natural standard: Saussure is, in short, "European."

Finally, Saussure—in this, happier than Europe's present-day politicians—found this system of support. Starting from the observation that the sentence functions otherwise than by a simple juxtaposition, down the spoken chain, of signs closed over themselves, and that something more is required for language to "take," he discovers *value*: now he can escape the impasse of signification: the relation to the signified (to gold) being uncertain, fragile, the whole system (of language, of currency) is stabilized by the behavior of the signifiers among themselves (of the currencies among themselves).

What is value? It is hardly necessary to observe that Saussure's *Lectures* are explicit on this point. Let us simply give one example, which will not be that of the linguistic manuals (*sheep/mutton*): on the lavatories of the University of Geneva we find a singular (though official) inscription: the two doors, whose obligatory duality ordinarily consecrates the difference of the sexes, are here marked *Messieurs* and *Professeurs*. On the level of pure signification, the inscription has no meaning: are not "professors" "gentlemen"? It is on the level of value that the opposition, as bizarre as it is ethical, is explained: two paradigms enter into collision, of which we read no more than the ruins: *messieurs*/dames//*professeurs*/étudiants: in the play of language, it is indeed value (and not signification) which possesses the apparent, symbolic, and social charge: here that of segregation, pedagogic and sexual.

In the Saussurian enterprise, value is the redeeming concept which permits saving language's permanence and surmounting what we must call *fiduciary anxiety*. Saussure has a conception of language which is very close to Valéry's—or vice versa: it is of little consequence: they knew nothing of each other. For Valéry, too, commerce, language, currency, and law are defined by one and the same system, that of reciprocity: they cannot function without a social contract, for only the contract can correct the lack of a standard. In language, this lack obsessed Saussure (more anxiety-prone than Valéry): does not the sign's arbitrary nature constantly risk introducing Time, Death, Anarchy into language? Whence the vital necessity for language, and behind it for society (a necessity linked to their survival), to posit a system of rules: economic rules, democratic rules, structural rules (of analogy and of value), which relate all these systems to a game (the game of chess, central metaphor of Saussurian linguistics): language is brought close to the economic system the moment the latter abandons the gold standard, and to the political system the moment society shifts from the *natural* (eternal) relation of the prince and his subjects to the social contract of the citizens among themselves. The model of Saussurian linguistics is democracy: we draw no argument from Saussure's biographical situation—a prominent citizen of Geneva, belonging to one of the oldest democracies in Europe, and in this nation to the city of Rousseau; let us merely note the incontestable homology which, on the epistemological level, links the social contract and the linguistic contract.

There exists another Saussure, as we know: the one of the *Anagrams*. This Saussure already *hears* modernity in the phonic and semantic swarming of archaic verses: then, no more contract, no more clarity, no more analogy, no more value: the order of the signified is replaced by the gold of the signifier, a metal no longer monetary but poetic. We know how much such hearing troubled, even maddened Saussure, who seems to have seen his entire life pass between the anxiety of the lost signified and the terrifying return of the pure signifier.

*Le Discours social,* 1973

# The Kitchen of Meaning

---

A garment, an automobile, a dish of cooked food, a gesture, a film, a piece of music, an advertising image, a piece of furniture, a newspaper headline—these indeed appear to be heterogeneous objects.

What might they have in common? This at least: all are signs. When I walk through the streets—or through life—and encounter these objects, I apply to all of them, if need be without realizing it, one and the same activity, which is that of a certain *reading*: modern man, urban man, spends his time reading. He reads, first of all and above all, images, gestures, behaviors: this car tells me the social status of its owner, this garment tells me quite precisely the degree of its wearer's conformism or eccentricity, this *apéritif* (whiskey, Pernod, or white wine and cassis) reveals my host's lifestyle. Even with regard to a written text, we are constantly given a second message to read between the lines of the first: if I read in the headlines: PAUL VI AFRAID, this also means: *if you read what follows, you will know why.*

All these "readings" are too important in our life, they imply too many social, moral, ideological values, not to attempt to account for them by systematic reflection: it is this reflection which, at least for the moment, we call *semiology*. Science of social messages? of cultural messages? of secondary information? Apprehension of everything which is "theatre" in the world, from ecclesiastical pomp to the hairstyle of the Beatles, from lounging pajamas to the debates of international politics? For the moment, the diversity or the vagueness of the definitions is of little importance.

What matters is to be able to subject an enormous mass of apparently anarchic facts to a principle of classification, and it is signification which affords this principle: beside various determinations (economic, historical, psychological), we must henceforth foresee a new quality of phenomena: meaning.

The world is full of signs, but these signs do not all have the fine simplicity of the letters of the alphabet, of highway signs, or of military uniforms: they are infinitely more complex. Most of the time, we take them for "natural" information; a Czech machine gun has been found in the hands of Congolese rebels: this is an incontestable piece of information; yet, to the very degree that we do not at the same moment recall the number of American weapons used by governments around the world the information becomes a secondary sign, it *parades* a political choice.

To decipher the world's signs always means to struggle with a certain innocence of objects. We all understand our language so "naturally" that it never occurs to us that it is an extremely complicated system, one anything but "natural" in its signs and rules: in the same way, it requires an incessant shock of observation in order to deal not with the content of messages but with their making: in short the semiologist, like the linguist, must enter the "kitchen of meaning."

This is a tremendous undertaking. Why? Because a meaning can never be analyzed in an isolated fashion. If I establish that blue jeans are the sign of a certain adolescent dandyism, or the *pot-au-feu* photographed by a luxury magazine that of a rather theatrical rusticity, and if I even multiply these equivalences in order to constitute lists of signs resembling the columns of a dictionary, I shall have discovered nothing at all. *The signs are constituted by differences.*

At the start of the semiological project, it was thought that the main task was, in Saussure's phrase, to study the life of signs at the heart of social life, and consequently to reconstitute the semantic systems of objects (garments, food, images, rituals, protocols, music, etc.). This has yet to be done. But as semiology advances into this already vast project, it encounters new tasks; for example, to study that mysterious operation by which any message may be impregnated with a secondary meaning, a meaning that is diffuse, generally ideological, and which is known as the *"connoted meaning"*: if I read the following headline in a newspaper: *"An atmosphere of fervor prevails in Bombay, excluding neither luxury nor triumph,"* I receive of course a certain amount of literal information as to the atmosphere of the Eucharistic Congress; but I also perceive a certain sentence stereotype, consisting of a subtle balancing of negations, which refers me to a sort of equilibrating vision of the world; such phenomena are constants, we must henceforth study them writ large with all the resources of linguistics.

If the tasks of semiology are constantly enlarging, this is indeed because we are constantly discovering more of signification's importance and extent in the world; signification becomes the mode of thought of the modern world, rather as "fact" previously constituted the unit of reflection of positivist science.

*Le Nouvel Observateur*, 1964

# Sociology and Socio-logic

## Apropos of two recent works by Claude Lévi-Strauss

Studying the psychosocial organization of tent villages set up by vacation clubs on certain points of the Mediterranean coast, a young French sociologist[1] has made this observation: the structure of these artificial villages, the interior distribution of their "sites," half-functional, half-ceremonial, seems indifferent to the landscape in which they develop; nothing prevents installing a complete village, with its tents, its sites for meals, dancing, conversation, sports, and bathing, in a desolate locale, with monstrous geological features: there is manifestly no conflict between the festive function of the vacation village and the austerity, even the disharmony, of the site which receives it. Such an example would doubtless be of interest to Claude Lévi-Strauss: not, superficially, because there is an analogy of object between the tent village and the "primitive" village, but because one and the other are constructed according to certain

[1] Henri Raymond, in an unpublished work. See however by the same author, on this subject: "Recherches sur un village de vacances," *Revue française de sociologie*, July–September, 1960, pp. 323–333.

relations of space, *i.e.*, according to a certain logic, and because this logic involves, in both cases, a whole representation of the world, thereby attesting that there is everywhere, from "primitive" Australia to the "civilized" Mediterranean, a responsibility of forms. For if Henri Raymond's observation is warranted, if the tent village, a modern phenomenon *par excellence* and thereby pertaining to a sociology of leisure, can be defined, outside of any geographical or psychological determinism, as an organization of functions, there is an obligation to proceed to analyses of a new type, and the possible birth of a structural sociology (or at least the encounter of ethnology and sociology within a structural anthropology). On what conditions? This is what must be examined.

The two latest works by Claude Lévi-Strauss, *Totemism Today* (*Le Totémisme aujourd'hui*, 1962) and *The Savage Mind* (*La Pensée sauvage*, 1962), compel such an examination (however summary it must be here); the first because, despite its strictly ethnological object (totemism), it attacks one of the constant attitudes of contemporary science, which consists in assigning a preeminence to the content of social symbols, and not to their forms; the second because, aside from the deepening and widening of structural thought to which it bears witness, it suggests and sketches in several places certain analyses of modern phenomena, of a strictly sociological adherence (*bricolage*, contemporary art, food, proper names, dress). The sociologist, or to speak more broadly, the analyst of contemporary society, thus possesses here principles of research and examples which he can relate to his own reflection.

We have seen that the tent village constituted an excellent object of structural analysis, insofar as its construction (and consequently its use) implied a socio-logic, which the analyst is responsible for reconstituting. Is this example a singular one? What are the objects in modern society which are available to structural analysis? What might be the field of a sociology of functions (in the logical sense of the term)? We have here a postulate of method which answers for itself: it is probable that, for Lévi-Strauss, no human "productions," objects, rites, arts, institutions, roles, usages, ever reach the

point of consumption (or consummation) without being subjected
by society itself to the mediation of the intellect: there is no *praxis*
which the human mind does not seize upon, dissect, and reconstruct
in the form of a system of practices.[2] If the intellect is a sovereign
mediator, if it necessarily imposes a form upon substance and upon
the actions which transform or consume it (but this form obviously
varies with each society), there is no reason to exclude from structural analysis any object whatever, if it is social (but are there any
other kinds?): whatever is presented to him, the analyst must identify in it the trace of the mind, the collective work which has been
performed by thought in order to subject reality to a logical system
of forms; whether we are dealing, then, with a village, a garment,
a meal, a festival, a usage, a role, a tool, an institution, or an
action, even a "creative" one, if it is normalized; whether all these
elements of social raw material belong to a "primitive," historical,
or modern society; they all derive from this socio-logic postulated,
demanded, and in many points established by the work of Lévi-
Strauss. In short, for the essentials of the superstructures, nothing
can validly separate ethnology from sociology and from history (on
condition that history ceases to be merely factual): it is because the
intelligible is everywhere that there cannot be "reserved objects"
in the human sciences; it is because society, any society, is concerned immediately to structure reality that structural analysis is
necessary.

The structural ethnology elaborated by Lévi-Strauss hence implies, by its method and its goals, a universality of field which brings
it into contact with all the objects of sociology. Yet we must remark
(without reviving an old argument) that the sociological object
differs from the ethnological object on two points (we are speaking
here only of differences offering a structural interest). First of all

---

[2] "Without questioning the incontestable primacy of infrastructures, we believe that between *praxis* and practices there always intervenes a mediator, which is the conceptional
schema by whose operation a substance and a form, each lacking an independent existence,
are fulfilled as structures, *i.e.*, as beings at once empirical and intelligible" (*La Pensée sauvage*,
*op. cit.*, p. 173).

this: what is called *massification* seems to fail the structural method insofar as number can apparently be dominated only by statistical methods: where structural analysis seeks qualitative gaps (between units), statistical sociology seeks averages; the former aims at being exhaustive, the latter at being total. We must still specify what it is that number modifies. Mass society is characterized by the mechanical multiplication of each model it elaborates: a newspaper, an automobile, an overcoat are reproduced in thousands, millions of examples; the same tent village is to be met with at ten different points in the Mediterranean coast. But if the original models are limited in number (and this is the case), nothing, in truth, forbids their structuration: to structure (need we be reminded?) does not consist in counting units, but in noting differences; it is of little importance, from the point of view of intelligibility, that the number of 2CV Citroëns greatly exceeds that of Facel-Vegas; what counts, in order to understand not the automobile market but the automobile "image," is that these two models exist through a body (a "system") of institutional differences.[3] In this regard, a structural sociology would be likely to respect much more than any other the delicate, aberrant, deviant features of a mass society, which statistical sociology regards as insignificant: it is not because a phenomenon is rare that it signifies less; for what signifies is not the phenomenon itself but its relation to other, antagonistic or correlative phenomena; statistical sociology more or less implies a sociology of normality; what, on the contrary, we can look for from a structural sociology is that it be truly a sociology of totality, for in its eyes no relation, even if it unites rare elements, can be "exceptional": there are many fewer mad men than sane; but what matters a great deal, *first of all*, is that society institutionalizes a relation of exclusion;[4] good literature is a product consumed by only

[3] We rediscover here the Saussurian distinction between Language (*Langue*), an abstract system of constraints, and Speech (*Parole*), the process of actualization of the Language.

[4] Cf. Michel Foucault, *Madness and Civilization* (*Histoire de la folie*, 1963). —The relation of exclusion can be variously determined by societies and periods, and number has no structural value in it: it is not necessarily the minority which is excluded.

a few, but what counts is that society establishes a structural relation between two literatures: good and bad: what defines "good" literature is not *first of all* an esthetic content, but a certain place in a general system of written productions. Hence it would suffice to collect the (relatively few) models which our societies massively put into circulation in order to obtain the body of forms, then of relations, thanks to which society makes its literatures or its automobiles intelligible to itself, or more specifically, makes the world intelligible to itself through its automobiles and its literatures.

Naturally, the number of buyers of the 2CV or of the Facel-Vega is not a matter of indifference: there is a decisive importance when it comes to studying the economy of the automobile market and the life-style of the consumers. But from a structural point of view, this is not a sign, it is only an index: the number of buyers of the 2CV reminds us of the special use of a word, whose repetition in discourse "betrays" the speaker's situation, mood, and even, if you like, his unconscious; the fact that a given society prefers, at the same price, one model of automobile to another informs us not about the structure but about the particular way in which a social group (the buyers of the model) make use of that structure. This is why, paradoxically, the relations of class society and of mass society can doubtless be analyzed only on the level of a structural sociology which can distinguish between the *meaning* of all the models and their particular consumption.

There is, however, another point on which ethnological societies and sociological societies differ more consequentially, it appears, than on that of number. The so-called primitive societies are societies without writing. It follows that writing and all the institutional forms of discourse which are derived from it serve to define, by this very peculiarity, sociological societies (including, of course, historical societies): sociology is the analysis of "writing" societies. This is in no way to limit its role: it is difficult to imagine anything, in modern society, which does not pass, at a given moment, through the mediation of writing; not only does writing double all the functions devolved elsewhere upon oral communication (myths, narratives, information, games), but further it develops vigorously in the service of other means of communication: in the service of the image (in the illustrated press), in the service of objects them-selves (objects "encounter" writing on the level of the catalogue and of advertising, which are, obviously, powerful factors of structuration[5]). Now, writing has for its function to constitute re-serves of language; these reserves are inevitably linked to a certain solidification of linguistic communication (a reification of language[6]): writing engenders *writings*, or, if you like, "literatures," and it is through these writings or literatures that mass society coins its reality in institutions, practices, objects, and even in events, since the event is henceforth always *written*. In other words, there is always a moment when mass society manages to structure reality through language, since it "writes" not only what other societies "speak" (narratives), but also what they manage to fabricate (tools) or to "perform" (rites, customs). Now language, as we know, is already itself a structure—and among the strongest structures that exist. Mass society therefore structures reality in two concomitant fash-ions: by producing it and by writing it: an automobile is at the same time the element of an "automobile" structure and the object of a discourse (advertising, conversation, literature); it presents itself to intelligibility by two paths: that of forms and that of words. To determine the relation of these two structures is crucial: does writing confirm, inflect, or oppose the agraphic version of intelligibility already provided by the practices themselves? Is the real (or at least material) tent village the same as the tent village of prospectuses and conversations? In other words, has language, in "writing" so-cieties, a function of pure denotation or, on the contrary, of com-plex connotation? In the second case, structural analysis must develop, one might say, a sociology of connotation, whose raw

[5] Advertising has hitherto been conceived in terms of motivation, not in terms of sig-nification.

[6] Cf. J. Gabel, *La Fausse Conscience*, Paris: Éd. de Minuit, 1962, p. 127 and p. 209.

materials would obviously be linguistic, and whose object would be the second structure which society imposes, by writing it, upon a reality which it already structures by fabricating it.

There remains the problem of method. What is involved? A rediscovery of a society's system or systems of classification:[7] each society classifies objects in its own way, and this way constitutes the very intelligibility it grants itself: sociological analysis must be structural, not because the objects are structured "in themselves," but because societies do not cease to structure them;[8] taxonomy would be, in short, the heuristic model of a sociology of superstructures. Now, as a general science, taxonomy does not exist; there are, of course, partial taxonomies (botanical, zoological, mineralogical), but, beyond the fact that such classifications are temporary (and nothing better illustrates the historical and ideological character of the modes of classification; to the point where a history of forms, still to be made, would teach us as much, perhaps, as the history of contents to which we are so dedicated), they have not yet been observed on the level of our mass society: we know nothing of the way in which such a society classifies, distributes, conjoins, opposes the countless objects it produces and whose very production is an immediate act of classification; there still remains to be reconstituted an important number of particular taxonomies, but also to be constructed from that effort, we might say, a taxonomy of taxonomies: for if there is really such a thing as mass society, we must admit that there is always either a contagion of a typical mode of classification by an infinity of objects, or homological correspondences between several modes of classification.

What are the classifications which taxonomic research can reveal? Not necessarily those which "common sense" would suggest (though these classifications by "common sense" have their own signification). Dealing with modern foodstuffs, we classify products

---

[7] "As Durkheim seems on occasion to have understood, it is in a *socio-logic* that the basis of sociology resides" (*La Pensée sauvage*, *op. cit.*, p. 101).

[8] "Arranging in a structure possesses . . . an intrinsic effectiveness, whatever the methods and the principles which inspire it" (*ibid*, p. 19).

according to a rational typology: fruits here, drinks there, etc.:[9] this is a lazy, verbal classification (it concerns a linguistic typology which determines groups wherever the generic term exists; but Lévi-Strauss shows that other groupings can be made: a certain "logic of perception" will lead to grouping wild cherries, cinnamon, vanilla, and sherry here, and there Labrador tea, lavender, bananas, identifying in these associations, moreover, the results of chemical analysis, since the latter detects a common element in each group (here aldehyde and there esters).[10] It would be specifically the task of a "sociological" taxonomy to rediscover the systems of objects which society consumes, through language, beyond it, and sometimes perhaps against it. If, from this point of view, we as yet know nothing of the order of our alimentary representations,[11] color already affords some observations; Lévi-Strauss has concerned himself with this matter from the ethnological point of view;[12] his observations are entirely corroborated by a semantic analysis of the texts of Fashion: despite appearances (Fashion appears to wield a great profusion of colors), contemporary Fashion knows only two main signifying groups of colors (they are, of course, in opposition): the "marked" colors (*high-colored*) and the "neutral" colors; carried in a sense by this opposition, intelligibility can nicely divide one and the same color: there are brilliant blacks and dull blacks, and it is this very opposition which signifies, not the opposition, for example, of black and white.

It appears then that the categories of intelligibility are specific. Whence the enormous advantage in determining them. And, on this point, the great methodological contribution which Lévi-Strauss has made, no doubt the one which will meet with most resistance, since it touches upon the formalist taboo, is, if you like, resolutely

[9] By and large, this is a "commercial" classification whose unit would be the specialized shop. But we know that with polyvalent stores, a new alimentary classification is being born.

[10] *La Pensée sauvage, op. cit.*, p. 20.

[11] Roland Barthes, "Pour une psycho-sociologie de l'alimentation contemporaine," *Annales*, September–October 1961, pp. 977–986.

[12] *La Pensée sauvage, op. cit.*, particularly p. 75.

to have "unhooked" forms from "contents." We must recall here
that not only ethnology but even a large part of sociology—insofar
as it deals with these problems—usually describe the correspondences of the perceptible and the "rest" (ideas, beliefs, affects) in
the form of *symbols* (this is the term consecrated by sociology); now,
the symbol is defined by the solitary union, so to speak, of a signifier
and a signified, whose equivalence is read in depth, each form being
only the more or less analogical materialization of a specific content
(for example, an unconscious archetype). For this rather "deep"
image of the relation between superstructure and infrastructure,
Lévi-Strauss's analysis tends to substitute an *extensive* image of the
relation of forms among themselves; by studying, after Lévi-Strauss,
first the "differential gaps" of the forms of a given society, then the
way in which these gaps are grouped and correspond according to
certain procedures of homology,[13] we can hope to attain no longer
scattered images, at once erratic and analogical, of the social, but
a structured body of formal functions, and thereby to substitute for
a sociology of *symbols* a sociology of *signs*: contrary to the symbol,
the sign is in effect defined not by its analogical and in some sense
*natural* relation to a content, but essentially by its place within a
system of differences (of oppositions on the paradigmatic level and
of associations on the syntagmatic level). It is this system of signs
by which a society marks reality, *its* reality; in other words, the
mediation of the perceptible is not established on the level of the
fragmentary image (symbol), but of a general system of forms (signs).
By leading to a socio-logic, or if you prefer to a semiology (and not
to a symbolics), Lévi-Strauss's ethnology merely attacks frontally a
problem which has always hampered the sociology of superstructures, and which is that of the mediation society arranges between
reality and its images; hitherto, this mediation seems to have been
conceived in too summary a fashion; recourse to dialectics has not
prevented historicizing sociologists from in fact conceiving of the

---

[13] "If we may be permitted the expression, *it is not the resemblances but the differences which resemble each other*" (Lévi-Strauss, *Totemism Today*, p. 111).

collective image as a sort of analogic product of reality, according to the implicit idea that each content directly determines its form. Lévi-Strauss urges us, on the contrary, to describe *in extenso* the mediational forms elaborated by society, and to substitute for the old causal chains on the analogical model, new systems of signification on a homological model. Thus, whereas for a whole period we inquired (without much result) into the *reasons* which impelled a certain clan to take a certain animal as its totem (a symbolic, hence analogical problem), Lévi-Strauss proposes that we confront not the clan and the animal, but the relations between clans and the relations between animals; the clan and the animal vanish, the one as signified, the other as signifier: it is the organization of the former which signifies the organization of the latter, and the relation of signification itself refers to the real society which is elaborating it. We can similarly imagine (simply to suggest that such a method can be applied to contemporary material) that, in a system of representations such as that of present-day images of royalty (whose importance in the press we are familiar with), each "role" does not refer directly to a social or psychological archetype (King, Chief, Father), but that it is only on the level of the royal "world" (extended family or "gens"), as a formal system of roles, that signification begins.[14]

It seems then that on at least two points (specificity of semantic categories and formal analysis of differential gaps), the socio-logic sought by Lévi-Strauss can be extended, *mutatis mutandis*, from ethnological societies to sociological societies. There remains the problem of the formal nature of this logic. Lévi-Strauss, here following the linguistic model, believes that it is essentially a matter of a binary logic:[15] the mind always constructs pairs of antagonistic

[14] The "formalization" of the royal family would then explain how it is that the charismatic role can be indifferently entrusted to a king or to a queen, provided that the formal distribution of the roles be respected: the couple Elizabeth-Philip is perfectly homological to the couple Shah-Farah.

[15] Lévi-Strauss speaks of the "emergence of a logic working by means of binary oppositions, and coinciding with the first manifestations of symbolism" (*Totemism Today, op. cit.*, p. 145).

terms (of the *marked/non-marked* type), but the substance of these contraries is not stable and obviously has no anthropological value: one society can oppose black to white, another shiny black to dull black. Binarism is a seductive logical hypothesis: we know its success in phonology, in cybernetics, and perhaps even in physiology.[16] Yet limits are already appearing, and certain compromises are required; Martinet refuses to grant a universal status to the binarism of phonological oppositions, and Jakobson has completed the schema of the binary opposition (*a/b*), by the adjunction of two derived terms, one neutral (neither *a* nor *b*), the other mixed (both *a* and *b*); Lévi-Strauss himself has often acknowledged the importance of the neutral term or zero degree.[17] We may speculate (though this is merely an idea, not even a hypothesis) whether in fact, as opposed to ethnological societies whose logic is binary (even when they practice a zero degree of the sign), sociological societies do not tend to develop more complex logics (or quite simply, less affirmed ones), either because they multiply recourse to terms derived from the matrix-opposition, or because they have the power to imagine *series* of terms, *i.e.*, intensive paradigms in which language introduces an entirely relative discontinuity. This would obviously be the essential task of a socio-logic applied to modern societies: to establish, in its most formal generality, the type of logic—binary, complex, serial, or other—used by these societies in order to conceive their reality. It would remain to be established, of course, whether complication or abandonment of binaries derives from the fact that our societies tend to elaborate an original logic, or if, on the contrary, this is only a way of masking a real (but guilty) binarism under the appearance of a purely discursive reason: the logical confusion of modernity might then constitute a process of perfectly historical reification. As "primitive" societies establish their own logic in order to pass from nature to culture, in the same way, but con-

---

[16] Cf. V. Belevitch, *Langage des machines et Langage humain*, Paris: Hermann, 1956, pp. 74–75.

[17] Notably apropos of *mana* as a zero symbolic value ("Introduction à l'oeuvre de Marcel Mauss," in M. Mauss, *Sociologie et Anthropologie*, Paris: PUF, 1950, pp. xlix *et seq.*).

versely, modern societies, by "blurring" their logic, merely take shelter behind that mythic return from the cultural to the natural which paradoxically marks most ideologies and moralities of our time. If this is the case, formal analysis would succeed in the humanist function of sociological work, since it is the task of such analysis to determine, behind the rationales of mass society, or if one prefers, in its narratives, the socio-logic of which these rationales are the mask and these narratives the vehicle.

For we must emphasize, by reason of the power of the taboo on formalism in a large segment of our intellectual society, Lévi-Strauss's thought (and consequently what it can contribute to a sociology of intelligibility) is a profoundly responsible thought. To condemn formal analysis on the pretext that it is merely a "refuge" from history and from the social, one must first decree, begging the question, that form is irresponsible. Lévi-Strauss's entire effort seems to be on the contrary to extend the field of human freedom to an order of functions hitherto reputed to be insignificant, futile, or inevitable. To keep to the two works we have just alluded to, the dynamism of this thought—and, since there can be no science without ethics, its profound generosity—are here affirmed on several levels: first of all on the level of history: the latter offers little purchase to ethnology: yet the way in which Lévi-Strauss has described the historical context of the conceptions of totemism is a model of historical sociology;[18] next, on the level of the very ethics of the social: the socio-logic presented by Lévi-Strauss is not a game indifferent to the goals of the men who construct it; it is, on the contrary, described as an effort made by men to master the discontinuity of things and so that "opposition, instead of being an obstacle to integration, might rather serve to produce it";[19] on this point socio-logic will perhaps be in a position, one day, to account for the ethical ambiguities of mass society, alienated from the social (and no longer from nature), and yet making use of this alienation

[18] *Totemism Today*, *op. cit.*, introduction.
[19] *Ibid.*, p. 128.

in order to understand the world; finally, on the level of culture itself: insofar as it applies to acts of the intellect, the sociology Lévi-Strauss envisions is a sociology of the "truly human": it grants men the limitless power to make things signify.

*Informations sur les sciences sociales*, 1962

# The Advertising Message

All advertising is a message: it involves a source of utterance, which is the firm owning the product being launched (and praised), a point of reception, which is the public, and a channel of transmission, which is precisely what is called the support of advertising; and, since the science of messages is today a very current matter, we can try to apply to the advertising message a method of analysis which has come to us (quite recently) from linguistics; to do this, we must adopt a position *immanent* to the object we wish to study, *i.e.*, must deliberately abandon any observation relative to the emission or to the reception of the message, and place ourselves at the level of the message itself: semantically—that is, from the point of view of communication—how is an advertising text constituted (the question is also valid for the image, but it is much more difficult to answer)?

As we know, every message is the encounter of a level of expression (or signifier) and a level of content (or signified). Now, if we examine an advertising sentence (the analysis would be identical for longer texts), we readily see that such a sentence contains in fact *two* messages, whose very imbrication constitutes the specialty of advertising language: it is what we shall observe apropos of two slogans, taken as examples here by reason of their simplicity: *Cook Gold with Astra* and *Gervais Ice Cream—You'll melt with pleasure.*

The first message (the order is arbitrary) is constituted by the sentence taken (if it were possible) in its literalness, setting aside, precisely, its advertising intention; in order to isolate this first message, we need merely imagine some Iroquois, or some Martian, in short someone from another world who has suddenly appeared in our own and who, on the one hand, knows our language perfectly (at least its vocabulary and its syntax, if not its rhetoric), and on the other is utterly ignorant of business, of cooking, of *gourmandise*, and of advertising; magically endowed with this knowledge and with this ignorance, this Iroquois or Martian would receive a message that is perfectly clear (but to our eyes, to us who *know*, utterly alien); in the case of Astra, he will take it as a literal command to prepare food, and as an indisputable assurance that the food thus prepared will have as its result a substance related to the metal known as gold; and in the case of Gervais, he would learn that ingestion of a certain brand of ice cream is infallibly followed by a fusion of the entire being under the effect of pleasure. Naturally, our Martian's intellection takes no account of the metaphors of our language; but this particular deafness does not prevent him from receiving a perfectly constituted message; for this message includes a level of expression (this is the phonic or graphic substance of the words, the syntactic relations of the sentence received) and a level of content (this is the literal meaning of these same words and of these same relations): in short, there is indeed, here on this first level, a sufficient set of signifiers and this set refers to a body, no less sufficient, of signifieds; in relation to the reality which every language is supposed to "translate," this first message is called the message of *denotation.*

The second message has nothing of the analytical character of the first; it is a total message, and it derives this totality from the singular character of its signified: *this signified is unique and it is always the same, in all advertising messages*: it is, in a word, the excellence of the product announced. For it is certain that, whatever I am literally told about Astra or Gervais, I am *finally* being told only one thing: that Astra is the best of shortenings, and Gervais the best of ice creams; this signified is the depth of the message, one might say, it entirely exhausts the intention of communication: the advertising goal is achieved the moment this second signified is perceived. As for the signifier of this second message (whose signified is the excellence of the product), what is it? First of all, stylistic features resulting from rhetoric (figures of style, metaphors, turns of phrase, linkages of words); but, since these features are incorporated in the literal sentence which has already been abstracted from the total message (and sometimes even impregnate it entirely, if we are dealing for example with a rhymed, or rhythmic advertisement), it follows that the signifier of the second message is in fact formed by the *first message in its entirety*, which is why it is said that the second message *connotes* the first (which we have seen was a simple denotation). Hence we are here confronted with a veritable architecture of messages (and not a simple addition or succession): itself constituted by an encounter of signifiers and signifieds, the first message becomes the simple signifier of the second message, according to a kind of disconnected movement, since a single element of the second message (its signifier) is extensive with the totality of the first message.

This phenomenon of "disconnection" or of "connotation" is of a very great importance, and far beyond the advertising phenomenon itself: it seems, in effect, that it is closely linked to mass communication (whose development in our civilization is well known): when we read our newspaper, when we go to the movies, when we watch television and listen to the radio, when we glance at the wrapping of the product we are buying, it is virtually certain that we never receive anything but connoted messages. Without yet deciding whether connotation is an anthropological phenomenon (common, under various forms, to all histories and all societies), we can say that we—men and women of the twentieth century—live in a civilization of connotation, and this leads us to examine the ethical bearing of the phenomenon; advertising constitutes no doubt a special connotation (insofar as it is "frank"), hence we cannot side, according to it, with just any connotation; but, by the very clarity of its constitution, the advertising message at least allows us to formulate the problem and to see how a general reflection can be articulated upon the "technical" analysis of the message, as we have just outlined it here.

What is happening, then, when we receive a double message, denoted-connoted (this is the very situation of millions of individuals who "consume" advertising)? We must not suppose that the second message (of connotation) is "hidden" beneath the first (of denotation); quite the contrary: what we immediately perceive (we who are neither Iroquois nor Martians) is the advertising character of the message, its second signified (Astra, Gervais are marvelous products): the second message is not surreptitious (contrary to other systems of connotation where the connotation is slipped, like contraband merchandise, into the first message, which thus lends it a certain innocence). In advertising, what must be explained, on the contrary, is the role of the message of denotation: why not simply say, without a double message: *buy Astra, buy Gervais?* We might no doubt reply (and this is perhaps the viewpoint of the ad writers) that denotation helps to develop certain arguments, in short to persuade; but it is more likely (and more in accord with the possibilities of semantics) that the first message serves more subtly to *naturalize* the second: it takes away its interested finality, the gratuitousness of its affirmation, the stiffness of its commination; for the banal invitation (*buy*), it substitutes the spectacle of a world where it is *natural* to buy Astra or Gervais; the commercial motivation is thus found not so much masked as *doubled* by a much broader representation, since it puts the reader in communication with the great human themes, the very ones which have always identified pleasure with a perfusion of being, or the excellence of an object with the purity of gold. By its double message, the connoted language of advertising reintroduces the dream into the humanity of the purchasers: the dream: *i.e.*, no doubt, a certain alienation (that of competitive society), but also a certain truth (that of poetry).

Here, in effect, it is the denoted message (which is also the signifier of the advertising signified) which possesses, so to speak, the human responsibility of advertising: if it is "good," advertising enriches; if it is "bad," advertising degrades. But what does it mean to be "good" or "bad," for an advertising message? To evoke the effectiveness of a slogan is not to provide an answer, for the paths of this effectiveness remain uncertain: a slogan can "seduce" without convincing, and nonetheless lead to purchase by that seduction alone; keeping to the linguistic level of the message, we can say that the "good" advertising message is the one that condenses in itself the richest rhetoric and attains with precision (often by a single word) the great oneiric themes of humanity, thus performing that great liberation of images (or by images) which defines poetry itself. In other words, the criteria of advertising language are those of poetry: rhetorical figures, metaphors, puns, all those ancestral signs, which are *double* signs, broaden language in the direction of latent signifieds and thereby give the person who receives them the power of an experience of totality. In a word, the more duplicity an advertising sentence contains, or, to avoid a contradiction in terms, the more multiple it is, the better it fulfills its function as a connoted message; let an ice cream make us "melt with pleasure" and we have united, in an economical utterance, the literal representation of a substance which melts (and whose excellence depends on its rhythm of melting) and the great anthropological theme of annihilation by pleasure; let cooking be golden and we have, condensed, the idea of an inestimable value and a crisp substance. The excellence of the advertising signifier thus depends on the power, which we must know how to impart to it, of *linking* its reader with the greatest quantity of "world" possible: the world, *i.e.*: experience of very old images, obscure and profound sensations of the body, poetically named by generations, wisdom of the relations of man and nature, patient accession of humanity to an intelligence of things through the one incontestably human power: language.

Thus, by the semantic analysis of the advertising message, we can understand that what "justifies" a language is not its submission to "Art" or to "Truth," but quite the contrary its duplicity; or better still: that this (technical) duplicity is not at all incompatible with the frankness of language, for this frankness concerns not the *content of the assertions*, but the declared character of the semantic systems engaged in the message; in the case of advertising, the second signified (the product) is always exposed unprotected by a frank system, *i.e.*, one which reveals its duplicity, for this *obvious* system is not a *simple* system. As a matter of fact, by the articulation of the two messages, advertising language (when it is "successful") opens us to a spoken representation of the world which the world has been practicing for a very long time and which is "narrative": all advertising *says* the product but *tells* something else; this is why we must classify it among those great aliments of psychic nutrition (according to R. Ruyer's phrase) which for us include literature, performances, movies, sports, the press, Fashion; by swathing the product in advertising language, mankind gives it *meaning* and thereby transforms its simple use into an experience of the mind.

*Les Cahiers de la publicité*, 1963

# Semantics of the Object

I should like to offer some reflections on the object in our civilization, which is commonly known as a technological civilization; I should like to place these reflections in the context of an inquiry which is being carried out at the present time in several countries, under the name of semiology or the science of signs. Semiology or, as it is more usually called in English, *semiotics*, was postulated some fifty years ago by the great Genevan linguist Ferdinand de Saussure, who had foreseen that linguistics would eventually be only one department of a much more general science of signs, which he called, specifically, semiology. Now, this semiological project has received, in recent years, a currency, a new power, because other sciences, other subsidiary disciplines have undergone a considerable development, in particular information theory, structural linguistics, formal logic, and certain investigations in anthropology; all these inquiries have helped to focus the preoccupations of a semiological discipline which would study how humanity gives meaning to things. Till now, one science has studied how humanity gives meaning to articulated sounds: this is linguistics. But how does humanity give meaning to the things which are not sounds? It is this exploration which now remains before the investigators. If it has not yet made decisive steps, this is for several reasons; first of all, because we have studied, on this level, only extremely rudimentary codes, which have no sociological interest, for instance the highway code; then because everything which signifies in the world is always more or less mixed up with language: we never have signifying systems of objects in the pure state; language always intervenes, as a relay, notably in image systems, as titles, captions, articles, which is why it is not fair to say that we live exclusively in a civilization of the image. Hence it is in this general context of a semiological inquiry that I should like to offer some rapid and summary reflections on the way in which objects can signify in the contemporary world. And here I must specify at once that I am granting a very strong sense to the word *signify*; we must not confuse *signify* with *communicate*: *to signify* means that objects carry not only information, in which case they would communicate, but also constitute structured systems of signs, *i.e.*, essentially systems of differences, of oppositions and of contrasts.

And first of all, how shall we define objects (before seeing how they can signify)? The dictionaries give vague definitions: the object is what is presented to sight, it is what is thought in relation to the subject who thinks, in short, as most dictionaries say, the object is *something*, a definition which teaches us nothing, unless we try to see what the connotations of the word *object* are. For my part, I see two major groups of connotations; first of all an initial group constituted by what I should call the object's existential connotations. The object very quickly assumes in our eyes the appearance or the existence of a thing which is non-human and which persists in existing, somewhat *against* us; in this perspective, there are many developments, many literary treatments of the object: in Sartre's *Nausea*, some famous pages are devoted to this stubbornness the object has in being external to man, in existing outside man, provoking a sentiment of nausea in the narrator confronting the tree trunks in a city park, or his own hand. In another style, Ionesco's plays afford us a kind of extraordinary proliferation of objects: objects invade man, who cannot protect himself, and who is, in a sense, smothered by them. There is also a more esthetic treatment of the object, presented as harboring a kind of essence to be reconstituted, and it is this treatment that we find either in painters of still lifes, or in the cinema among certain directors whose style consists precisely in reflecting on the object (I am thinking of Bresson); in what is commonly called the New Novel, there is also a particular treatment of the object, precisely described in its strict appearance. In this direction, we see then that there is continuously a kind of breaking loose on the part of the object toward the infinitely subjective; and thereby, ultimately, all these works tend to show that the object develops for humanity a kind of absurdity, and that it has, one might say, the meaning of a non-meaning; it is there to signify that it has no meaning; hence, even in such a perspective, we find ourselves in a more or less semantic climate. There is also another group of connotations, on which I shall rely for the continuation of my remarks: these are the object's "technological" connotations. The object is here defined as what is fabricated or produced; it is of finite substance, standardized, formed, and normalized, *i.e.*, subject to norms of fabrication and of quality; the object is then above all defined as an element of consumption: a certain notion of the object is reproduced in thousands of examples in the world, in millions of copies: a telephone, a watch, a trinket, a plate, an article of furniture, a pen—these are really what we commonly call objects; the object no longer breaks away toward the infinitely subjective, but toward the infinitely social. It is from this latter conception of the object that I should like to proceed.

Ordinarily, we define the object as "something used for something." Consequently the object is at first glance entirely absorbed in a finality of use, in what is called a function. And, thereby, there is, we spontaneously feel, a kind of transitivity of the object: the object serves man to act upon the world, to modify the world, to be in the world in an active fashion; the object is a kind of mediator between action and man. We might point out here, moreover, that there is virtually never an object *for nothing*; of course there are objects presented under the form of useless trinkets, but these trin-

kets always have an esthetic finality. The paradox I want to point
out is that these objects which always have, in principle, a function,
a utility, a purpose, we believe we experience as pure instruments,
whereas in reality they carry other things, they are also something
else: they function as the vehicle of meaning: in other words, the
object effectively serves some purpose, but it also serves to communicate information; we might sum it up by saying that there is
always a meaning which overflows the object's use. Can we imagine
an object more functional than a telephone? Yet the appearance
of a telephone always has a meaning independent of its function:
a white telephone always transmits a certain notion of luxury or of
femininity; there are bureaucratic telephones, there are old-fash-
ioned telephones which transmit the notion of a certain period
(1925); in short, the telephone itself is susceptible of belonging to
a system of objects-as-signs; similarly, a pen necessarily parades a
certain sense of wealth, of simplicity, of seriousness, of whimsicality,
etc.; the plates we eat on always have a meaning, as well, and when
they do not, when they feign to have none, then precisely they
end up by having the meaning of having no meaning. Consequently, there is no object which escapes meaning.

When is this kind of semantization of the object produced? When
does the object's signification begin? I would be tempted to answer
that it occurs as soon as the object is produced and consumed by
a human society, as soon as it is fabricated, normalized; here, historical examples abound; for example, we know that the soldiers
of the ancient Roman Republic would throw a blanket over their
shoulders against the rain, the wind, the cold; at that moment, of
course, the garment-as-object did not yet exist; it had no name, it
had no meaning; it was reduced to a pure use; but, from the day
when blankets were slit, when they were mass-produced, when they
were given a standardized form, thereby it became necessary to give
them a name, and this unnamed garment became the poncho or
"*penule*"; at that moment, this miscellaneous covering became the
vehicle of a meaning, "militariness." All objects which belong to
a society have a meaning; to find objects without meaning, we must

imagine objects which are altogether improvised; now, to tell the truth, no such things can be found; a famous page of Lévi-Strauss's *The Savage Mind* tells us that *bricolage*, the invention of the object by a *bricoleur*, by an amateur, is itself the seeking-out and the imposition of a meaning upon the object; in order to find absolutely improvised objects, we should have to proceed to completely asocial states; we can imagine that a tramp, for example, improvising foot-wear out of newspaper, produces a perfectly "free" object; but even this is not so—very quickly, this newspaper will become precisely the *sign* of the bum. In short, the function of an object always becomes, at the very least, the sign of that function: there are never objects, in our society, without a kind of functional supplement, a slight emphasis which makes the objects (at least) always signify themselves. For example, for all my real needs to telephone and to have, for that reason, a telephone on my desk, all the same in the eyes of certain persons who come to see me, who do not know me well, this telephone functions as a sign, the sign of the fact that I am a man who needs to have contacts in his profession; and even this glass of water, which I have really used because I was really thirsty—in spite of everything, I can do nothing about the fact that it functions as the very sign of the lecturer.

Like any sign, the object is at the intersection of two coordinates, two definitions. The first of the coordinates is what I should call a symbolic one: every object has, so to speak, a metaphorical depth, it refers to a *signified*; the object always has at least one signified. Here I have a series of images: these are images borrowed from advertising: you see that here there is a lamp and immediately understand that this lamp signifies evening, or more exactly, the nocturnal; if you have an advertisement for Italian pasta (I am speaking of a French advertisement), it is obvious that the Italian tricolor (green, white, and red) functions as a sign of a certain Italianness; hence, the first coordinate, the symbolic coordinate, is constituted by the fact that every object is at least the signifier of a signified. The second coordinate is what I should call the coor-dinate of classification, or the taxonomic coordinate (taxonomy is

the science of classifications); we do not live without having within ourselves, more or less consciously, a certain classification of
objects, which is imposed upon us or suggested by our society. These
classifications of objects are very important in big business, or heavy
industry, where we must know how to classify all the pieces, or all
the nuts and bolts and screws of a machine in the shops, and hence
where we must adopt criteria of classification; there is another order
of phenomena in which the classification of objects is very important, and this is a very everyday order: it is the department store;
in the department store, there is also a certain notion of the classification of objects, and this idea, of course, is not gratuitous, it
involves a certain responsibility; another example of the importance
of the classification of objects is the encyclopedia; as soon as we
want to make an encyclopedia, without determining to classify
words according to alphabetical order, we are indeed obliged to
adopt a classification of objects.

Having thus asserted that the object is always a sign, defined by
two coordinates, a deep symbolic coordinate, and an extended
coordinate of classification, I should like to say a few words concerning the semantic system of objects strictly so-called; these will
be prospective remarks, for our research remains to be made in any
serious fashion. There is in fact a very great obstacle to studying
the meaning of objects, and this obstacle I shall call the obstacle
of the obvious: if we are to study the meaning of objects, we must
give ourselves a sort of shock of detachment, in order to objectivize
the object, to structure its signification: to do this, there is a means
which every semanticist of the object can use; it is to resort to an
order of representations in which the object is presented in a simultaneously spectacular, rhetorical, and intentional fashion, which
is advertising, the cinema, or even the theatre. For the objects
dealt with by the theatre, I shall point out that we have precious
indications, of an extremely dense intelligence, in Brecht's commentaries on a certain number of productions; the most famous one
concerns the production of *Mother Courage*, in which Brecht explains the long and complicated treatment that had to be imposed

upon certain objects used in the production to make them signify a certain concept; for the law of the theatre is that it is not sufficient that the object represented be real, its meaning must also be somehow detached from reality: it is not enough to offer the public a really worn peddler-woman's jacket in order for it to signify wear-and-tear; you must invent, as a director, the signs of wear-and-tear.

If then we were to revert to these kinds of rather artificial "corpus," however precious, such as the theatre, the cinema, and advertising, we might then isolate, in the object represented, certain signifiers and signifieds. The signifiers of the object are of course material units, like all the signifiers of any system of signs, *i.e.*, colors, shapes, attributes, accessories. I shall indicate here two main states of the signifier, in mounting order of complexity.

First of all a purely symbolic state; this is what happens, as I have already said, when a signifier, *i.e.*, an object, refers to a single signified; this is the case of great anthropologic symbols, such as the cross, for example, or the crescent, and it is likely that humanity here possesses a sort of finite reservoir of great symbolic objects, an anthropological or at least a broadly historical reservoir which therefore concerns a sort of science or, in any case, a discipline which we might call *symbolics*; this symbolics has been, in general, carefully studied for past societies, in the works of art through which it functions, but do we really study it or even prepare ourselves to study it, in our present-day society? We have reason to ask what remains of these great symbols in a technological society like our own; have these great symbols vanished, have they been transformed, are they hidden? These are questions which we might raise. I am thinking, for example, of an ad sometimes seen on French highways. This is an ad for a brand of trucks; it is a rather interesting example, because the ad writer who devised this poster has produced a poor ad, precisely because he has not thought the problem through in terms of signs; seeking to indicate that the trucks last a very long time, he has represented the palm of a hand with a sort of cross over it; for the adman, it was a matter of indicating the truck's lifeline; but I am convinced that according to the rules of symbolics, a cross over the hand is perceived as a symbol of death: even in the prosaic order of advertising, the organization of this very ancient symbolics must be explored.

Another case of simple relation—we are still in the symbolic relation between object and signified—is the case of all the *displaced* relations: by this I mean that an object perceived in its entirety, or, in advertising, given in its entirety, nonetheless signifies by only one of its attributes. I have a number of examples here: an orange, though represented entire, will signify only the quality of *juicy* and *thirst-quenching*: it is *juicy* which is signified by the representation of the object, not the whole object: hence there is a displacement of the sign. When we represent a beer, it is not essentially beer which constitutes the message, it is the fact that it is cold: here too is a displacement. It is what we might call a displacement no longer by metaphor, but by metonymy, *i.e.*, by a skidding of meaning. These metonymic significations are extremely frequent in the world of objects; it is a mechanism that is certainly very important, for the signifying element is then perceptible—we receive it in a perfectly clear fashion—and yet in some sense drowned, naturalized in what we might call the *Dasein* of the object. Hence we arrive at a sort of paradoxical definition of the object: an orange is, in the emphatic mode of advertising, *the juicy plus the orange*; the orange is always there as a natural object to sustain one of its qualities which becomes its sign.

After the purely symbolic relation, we must examine all the significations attached to collections of objects, to organized pluralities of objects; these are cases in which meaning is born not from an object, but from an intelligible assemblage of objects: meaning is in some sense extended. We must avoid comparing the object to the word in linguistics, and the collection of objects to the sentence; that would be an inexact comparison, for the isolated object is already a sentence; this is a question which the linguists have now elucidated: the question of *word-sentences*; when you see a revolver in the cinema, the revolver is not the equivalent of the word in relation to a larger group; the revolver is already in itself a sentence, obviously a very simple sentence, whose linguistic equivalent would be: *here is a revolver*. In other words, the object is never—in the world we live in—an element of a nomenclature. The signifying collections of objects are numerous, notably in advertising. Here is the man who reads in the evening: there are in this image four or five signifying objects which combine to put across a single total meaning, that of relaxation, of repose: there is the lamp, there is the comfort of the heavy wool sweater, there is the leather armchair, there is the newspaper; the newspaper is not a book; it is not so serious, it is a diversion: all this means that we can drink some coffee, peacefully, in the evening, without any trouble. These assemblages of objects are *syntagms*, *i.e.*, extended fragments of signs. The syntax of objects is of course an extremely elementary syntax. When objects are put together, we cannot attribute to them coordinations as complicated as in human language. In reality the objects—whether these are the objects of the image or the real objects of a room, or of a street—are linked only by a single form of connection, which is parataxis, *i.e.*, the pure and simple juxtaposition of elements. This kind of parataxis of objects is extremely frequent in life: it is the system to which are subject, for example, all the pieces of furniture in a room. The furnishing of a room achieves a final meaning (a "style") solely by the juxtaposition of elements. Here is an example: it concerns an ad for a brand of tea; hence we must signify not England, for things are more subtle than that, but Englishness, or Britishness, *i.e.*, a sort of rhetorical identity of the English: hence we have here, by a scrupulously composed syntagm, the shutters of colonial houses, the costume of the man, his moustache, the typical British enthusiasm for the navy and horseback riding, which is here in these bottled ships, in these bronze horses, and finally we read quite spontaneously in this image, solely by the juxtaposition of a certain number of objects, an extremely strong signified, which is precisely that Englishness of which I was speaking.

What are the signifieds of these systems of objects, what is the information transmitted by the objects? Here we can present only an ambiguous answer, for the signifieds of objects depend a great deal not on the emitter of the message, but on the receiver, *i.e.*, on the reader of the object. As a matter of fact, the object is polysemous, *i.e.*, it readily offers itself to several readings of meaning; in the presence of an object, there are almost always several readings possible, and this not only between one reader and the next, but also, sometimes, within one and the same reader. In other words, each of us has in himself, so to speak, several lexicons, several reservoirs of reading, depending on the kinds of knowledge, the cultural levels he possesses. All degrees of knowledge, of culture, and of situation are possible, facing an object and a collection of objects. We can even imagine that, facing an object or a collection of objects, we might have a strictly individual reading, by which we invest what might be called our own *psyche* in the spectacle of the object: we know that the object can produce in us readings of a psychoanalytic level. This does not weaken the systematic, the codified nature of the object. We know that even if we descend into the depths of the individual psyche, we do not thereby escape meaning. If we give the Rorschach test to thousands of subjects, we arrive at a very strict typology of responses: the more we imagine we descend into the depths of individual reaction, the more we identify meanings that are actually simple and codified: at whatever level we occupy, in this operation of reading the object, we discover that meaning always traverses humanity and the object through and through.

Are there objects outside meaning, *i.e.*, limit cases? I do not think so. A non-signifying object, once it is assumed by a society— and I do not see how it could not be—functions at least as the sign of the insignificant, it signifies itself as non-signifying. This is a case which we can observe at the cinema: we can find directors whose entire art consists in suggesting, for the very motifs of the argument, insignificant objects; the unexpected object itself is not outside meaning; we must seek the meaning: there are objects before which we ask: *what is it?* This is a slightly traumatic form, but such anxiety finally does not last, the objects furnish in and of themselves a certain reply, and thereby a certain satisfaction. In a general fashion, in our society, there are no objects which do not end by supplying a meaning and rejoining that great code of objects in which we live.

We have "operated" a sort of ideal decomposition of the object. In a first phase (all this being purely operational), we have remarked that the object always presents itself to us as useful, functional: it is only a use, a mediator between humanity and the world: the telephone serves to telephone, the orange to be eaten. Then, in a second phase, we have seen that in reality, the function always sustains a meaning. The telephone indicates a certain mode of activity in the world, the orange signifies vitamins, vitamin-rich juice. Now, we know that meaning is a process not of action, but of equivalences; in other words, meaning does not have a transitive value; meaning is in some sense inert, motionless; hence we can say that there is in the object a sort of struggle between the activity of its function and the inactivity of its signification. Meaning deactivates the object, renders it intransitive, assigns it a frozen place in what we might call a *tableau vivant* of the human image-repertoire. These two phases, to my understanding, are not adequate in order to explain the object's trajectory: I should add, personally, a third: this is the moment when a sort of return-movement occurs which will restore the object from sign to function; in a somewhat special manner, however. As it happens, objects do not give us that meaning which they have in a frank, declared manner. When we read a highway sign, we receive an absolutely frank message; this message does not play at being a non-message, it really gives itself out as a message. Similarly when we read printed letters, we are aware of perceiving a message. Conversely, the object which suggests a meaning nonetheless always remains in our eyes a functional object: the object always seems functional, at the very moment when we read it as a sign. We think that a raincoat serves to protect us from the rain, even if we read it as the *sign* of an atmospheric situation. This last transformation of the sign into a utopic, unreal function (Fashion can propose raincoats which could not protect us from the rain at all) is, I believe, a major ideological phenomenon, especially in our society. Meaning is always a phenomenon of culture, a product of culture; now, in our society, this phenomenon of culture is constantly naturalized, reconverted into nature by speech, which makes us believe in a purely transitive situation of the object. We believe we are in a practical world of uses, of functions, of total domestication of the object, and in reality we are also, by objects, in a world of meanings, of reasons, of alibis: function gives birth to the sign, but this sign is reconverted into the spectacle of a function. I believe it is precisely this conversion of culture into pseudo-nature which can define the ideology of our society.

Colloquium at the Cini Foundation in Venice, 1964

# Semiology and Urbanism

The subject of this discussion concerns a certain number of the problems of urban semiology.

But I must add that anyone who wants to sketch a semiotics of the city must be at once a semiologist (a specialist in signs), a geographer, an historian, an urbanist, an architect, and probably a psychoanalyst. Since it is obvious that this is not my case—as a matter of fact, I am none of all this except, barely, a semiologist—the reflections I shall present to you are those of an amateur, in the etymological sense of the word: an amateur of signs, one who loves signs, an amateur of cities, one who loves the city. For I love both the city and signs. And this double love (which is probably, as a matter of fact, only one) impels me to believe, perhaps with a certain presumption, in the possibility of a semiotics of the city. On what conditions or rather with what precautions and what preliminaries will an urban semiotics be possible?

This is the theme of the reflections I shall present. I should like first of all to remind you of a very familar thing which will serve as a point of departure: human space in general (and not only urban space) has always been a signifying space. Scientific geography and especially modern cartography can be considered as a kind of obliteration, a censorship objectivity has imposed upon signification (an objectivity which is a form like any other of the image-repertoire). And, before speaking of the city, I should like to recall several phenomena of the cultural history of the West, more specifically of Greek antiquity: the human habitat, the "oekoumène," as we can glimpse it through the first maps of the Greek geographers: Anaximander, Hecataeus, or through the mental cartography of a man like Herodotus, constitutes a veritable discourse, with its symmetries, its oppositions of sites, with its syntax and its paradigms. A map of the world by Herodotus, graphically realized, is constructed like a language, like a sentence, like a poem, on oppositions: hot countries and cold countries, known and unknown countries; then on the opposition between men on the one hand, and monsters and chimeras on the other, etc.

If we turn from geographical space to urban space, strictly speaking, I shall remind you that the notion of *Isonomy*, created for sixth-century Athens by a man like Cleisthenes, is a truly structural conception by which the center alone is privileged, since all the citizens have relations with it which are at the same time symmetrical and reversible.[1] At this period, the conception of the city was exclusively a signifying one, for the utilitarian conception of an urban distribution based on functions and usages, which incontestably prevails in our day, will appear much later on. I wanted to point out this historical relativism in the conception of signifying spaces.

Finally, it is in a recent past that a structuralist like Lévi-Strauss has produced, in *Tristes Tropiques*, a form of urban semiology, even if on a reduced scale, apropos of a Bororo village whose space he has studied according to an essentially semantic approach.

It is strange that, parallel to these strongly signifying conceptions of inhabited space, the theoretical elaborations of the urbanists have not hitherto granted, if I am not mistaken, anything but a

---

[1] On Cleisthenes and Isonomy, cf. P. Leveque and P. Vidal-Naquet, *Clisthène l'Athénien*, Paris: Macula, 1983.

very reduced status to problems of signification.[2] Of course, there are exceptions; several writers have discussed the city in terms of signification. One of the authors who has best expressed this essentially signifying nature of urban space is, I believe, Victor Hugo. In *Notre-Dame de Paris*, Hugo has written a very fine chapter, of an extremely subtle intelligence, "This will kill that"; *this*, which is to say the book, *that*, which is to say the monument. By expressing himself thus, Hugo gives evidence of a rather modern way of conceiving the monument and the city, actually as a writing, as an inscription of man in space. This chapter of Hugo's is devoted to the rivalry between two modes of writing, writing in stone and writing on paper. Moreover, this theme can find its current version in the remarks on writing by a philosopher like Jacques Derrida. Among present-day urbanists, signification is virtually unmentioned: one name stands out, therefore, that of the American Kevin Lynch, who seems to be closest to these problems of urban semantics insofar as he is concerned with conceiving the city in the very terms of the perceiving consciousness, *i.e.*, of identifying the image of the city in the readers of that city. But in reality, Lynch's researches, from the semantic point of view, remain quite ambiguous: on the one hand, there is a whole vocabulary of signification in his work (for example, he grants a good deal of attention to the *readability* of the city, and this is a very important notion for us) and, as a good semanticist, he has the sense of *discrete units*: he has tried to rediscover in urban space the discontinuous units which, within limits, somewhat resemble phonemes and semantemes. He calls these units paths, enclosures, districts, intersections, points of reference. These are categories of units which might readily become semantic categories. But, on the other hand, despite this vocabulary, Lynch has a conception of the city which remains more gestaltist than structural.

Aside from those authors who explicitly entertain the notion of a semantics of the city, we note a growing consciousness of the

---

[2] Cf. F. Choay, *L'Urbanisme: utopie et réalités*, Paris: Éd. du Seuil, 1965.

functions of symbols in urban space. In several studies of urbanism based on quantitative estimations and on motivation-research, we see appearing—in spite of everything, even if this is only for memory's sake—the purely qualitative motif of symbolization frequently used even today to explain other phenomena. We find for example in urbanism a relatively common technique: simulation; now, the technique of simulation leads, even if it is used in a rather narrow and empirical spirit, to a more thorough investigation of the concept of *model*, which is a structural or at the very least a pre-structuralist concept.

At another stage of these studies in urbanism, the demand for signification appears. We gradually discover that there exists a kind of contradiction between signification and another order of phenomena, and that consequently signification possesses an irreducible specificity. For instance, certain urbanists, or certain of those investigators who are studying urban planning, are obliged to note that, in certain cases, there exists a conflict between the functionalism of a part of the city, let us say of a neighborhood or a district, and what I should call its semantic content (its semantic power). Hence they have noted with a certain ingenuousness (but perhaps we must begin with ingenuousness) that Rome presents a permanent conflict between the functional necessities of modern life and the semantic burden communicated to the city by its history. And this conflict between signification and function constitutes the despair of the urbanists. There also exists a conflict between signification and reason, or at least between signification and that calculating reason which wants all the elements of a city to be uniformly recuperated by planning, whereas it is increasingly obvious that a city is a fabric formed not of equal elements whose functions can be inventoried, but of strong elements and of neutral elements, or else, as linguistics tells us, of marked elements and non-marked elements (we know that the opposition between the sign and the absence of sign, between the measurable degree and zero degree, constitutes one of the major processes in the elaboration of signification). From all evidence, each city possesses this kind of rhythm;

Kevin Lynch has noted as much: there exists in every city, from the moment when it is truly inhabited by man, and made by him, that basic rhythm of signification which is opposition, alternation and juxtaposition of marked and non-marked elements. Lastly, there exists an ultimate conflict between signification and reality itself, at least between signification and that reality of objective geography, the reality of maps. Investigations made by psycho-sociologists have shown that, for example, two neighborhoods are contiguous if we rely on the map, *i.e.*, on "reality," on objectivity, whereas, from the moment they receive two different significations, they are radically split in the image of the city: signification is experienced in complete opposition to objective data.

The city is a discourse, and this discourse is actually a language: the city speaks to its inhabitants, we speak our city, the city where we are, simply by inhabiting it, by traversing it, by looking at it. Yet, the problem is to extract an expression like "language of the city" from the purely metaphorical stage. It is metaphorically very easy to speak of *the language of the city* as we speak of the language of the cinema or of the language of flowers. The real scientific leap will be achieved when we can speak of the language of the city without metaphor. And we can say that this is precisely what happened to Freud when he first spoke of the language of dreams, emptying this expression of its metaphorical meaning in order to give it a real meaning. We too, we must confront this problem: how to shift from metaphor to analysis when we speak of the language of the city? Once again, it is to the specialists in the urban phenomenon that I am referring, for even if they are quite remote from these problems of urban semantics, they have nonetheless already noted (I am quoting the results of one investigation) that "the usable data in the social sciences offer a form poorly adapted to an integration into models." Indeed, if we have difficulty inserting into a model the urban data supplied us by psychology, sociology, geography, demography, this is precisely because we lack a final technique, that of symbols. Consequently, we need a new scientific energy in order to transform such data, to shift from

metaphor to the description of signification, and it is here that
semiology (in the broadest sense of the word) may by a still un-
predictable development afford us some assistance. It is not my
intention to evoke here the procedures for discovering an urban
semiology. It is likely that such procedures would consist in dis-
sociating the urban text into units, then in distributing these units
into formal classes, and, thirdly, in finding the rules of combination
and of transformation for these units and for these models. I shall
confine myself to three observations which have no direct relation
with the city but which might usefully orient us toward an urban
semiology, insofar as they draw up a balance sheet for current
semiology and take account of the fact that, in recent years, the
semiological "landscape" is no longer the same.

The first observation is that "symbolism" (which must be understood as a general discourse concerning signification) is no longer
conceived nowadays, at least as a general rule, as a regular correspondence between signifiers and signifieds. In other words, one
notion of semantics which was fundamental some years ago has
become outdated; this is the lexicon notion, *i.e.*, that of a set of
lists of corresponding signifieds and signifiers. This erosion of the
notion of lexicon is to be found in many sectors of research. First
of all, there is the distributive semantics of Chomsky's disciples,
such as Katz and Fodor, who have launched an attack in force
against the lexicon. If we turn from the realm of linguistics to that
of literary criticism, we see that the thematic criticism which has
prevailed for some fifteen or twenty years, at least in France, and
which has formed the essential part of the studies which we know
as the new criticism, is nowadays limited, remodeled to the detriment of the signifieds which that criticism proposed to decipher.
In the realm of psychoanalysis, finally, we can no longer speak of
a term-to-term symbolism; this is obviously the dead part of Freud's
work: a psychoanalytic lexicon is no longer conceivable. All this
has cast a certain discredit on the word "symbol," for this term has
always (till today) suggested that the signifying relation was based
on the signified, on the presence of the signified. Personally, I use

the word "symbol" as referring to a syntagmatic and/or paradigmatic but no longer semantic signifying organization: we must make a very clear distinction between the semantic bearing of the symbol and the syntagmatic or paradigmatic nature of this same symbol.

Similarly it would be an absurd undertaking to attempt to elaborate a lexicon of the significations of the city by putting sites, neighborhoods, functions on one side, and significations on the other, or rather by putting on one side the sites articulated as signifiers and on the other the functions articulated as signifieds. The list of the functions that a city's neighborhoods can assume has been known for a long time; there are by and large some thirty functions for a neighborhood (at least for a neighborhood of the center-city: a zone which has been closely studied from the sociological point of view). This list can of course be completed, enriched, refined, but it will constitute only an extremely elementary level for semiological analysis, a level which will probably have to be revised subsequently: not only because of the weight and pressure exerted by history, but because, precisely, the signifieds are like mythical beings, of an extreme imprecision, and because at a certain moment they always become the signifiers of *something else*: the signifieds pass, the signifiers remain. The hunt for the signified can therefore constitute only a provisional undertaking. The role of the signified, when we manage to isolate it, is only to afford us a sort of testimony as to a specific state of the signifying distribution. Further, we must note that we attribute an ever-growing importance to the *empty signified*, to the empty site of the signified. In other words, the elements are understood as signifiers more by their own correlative position than by their content. Thus Tokyo, which is one of the most intricate urban complexes imaginable from the semantic point of view, nonetheless possesses a sort of center. But this center, occupied by the imperial palace which is surrounded by a deep moat and hidden by verdure, is experienced as an empty center. As a more general rule, the studies made of the urban core of different cities have shown that the central point of the center of the city (every city possesses a center), which we call the "solid core," does not constitute the culminating point of any particular activity, but a kind of empty "heart" of the community's image of the center. Here too we have a somehow empty place which is necessary to the organization of the rest of the city.

The second remark is that symbolism must be defined essentially as the world of signifiers, of correlations, and above all of correlations which can never be imprisoned in a full signification, in a final signification. Henceforth, from the point of view of descriptive technique, the distribution of elements, *i.e.*, of signifiers, "exhausts" semantic discovery. This is true for the Chomskian semantics of Katz and Fodor and even for the analyses of Lévi-Strauss which are based on the clarification of a relation which is no longer analogical but homological (this is a demonstration made in his book on totemism, one rarely cited). Hence we discover that, if we want to produce the semiology of the city, we must intensify, more meticulously, the signifying division. For this, I appeal to my experience as an amateur of cities. We know that, in certain cities, there exist certain spaces which present a very extended specialization of functions; this is true, for example, of the Oriental *souk* where one street is reserved for the tanners and another exclusively for the silversmiths; in Tokyo, certain parts of the same neighborhood are quite homogeneous from the functional point of view: we find there only bars or snack bars or places of entertainment. Yet we must go beyond this first aspect and not limit the semantic description of the city to this unit; we must try to dissociate microstructures in the same way we can isolate tiny sentence fragments within a long period; hence we must get into the habit of making a very extended analysis which will lead to these microstructures, and conversely we must accustom ourselves to a broader analysis, which will lead to macrostructures. We all know that Tokyo is a polynuclear city; it possesses several cores around five or six centers; we must learn to differentiate semantically these centers, which moreover are indicated by railroad stations. In other terms, even in this domain, the best model for the semantic study of the city will be furnished, I believe, at least at the start, by the sentence of discourse. And here we rediscover Victor Hugo's old intuition: the city is a writing; the man who moves about in the city, *i.e.*, the city's user (which is what we all are, users of the city), is a sort of reader who, according to his obligations and his movements, samples fragments of the utterance in order to actualize them in secret. When we move about in a city, we are all in the situation of the reader of Queneau's *100,000 Million Poems*, where we can find a different poem by changing a single verse; unknown to us, we are something like that avant-garde reader when we are in a city.

Lastly, the third observation is that nowadays semiology never posits the existence of a definitive signified. Which means that the signifieds are always signifiers for others, and reciprocally. In reality, in any cultural or even psychological complex, we find ourselves confronted with infinite chains of metaphors whose signified is always recessive or itself becoming a signifier. This structure is beginning to be explored, as you know, in Lacan's psychoanalysis, and also in the study of writing, where it is postulated if it is not actually explored. If we apply these notions to the city, we shall doubtless be led to emphasize a dimension which I must say I have never seen cited, at least never clearly, in the studies and investigations of urbanism. This dimension I should call the *erotic* dimension. The eroticism of the city is the teaching which we can derive from the infinitely metaphorical nature of urban discourse. I am using this word *eroticism* in its broadest sense: it would be absurd to identify the eroticism of a city merely with the neighborhood reserved for such pleasures, for the concept of the place of pleasure is one of the stubbornest mystifications of urban functionalism; it is a functional and not a semantic notion; I am using eroticism or *sociality* here without differentiation. The city, essentially and semantically, is the site of our encounter with the other, and it is for this reason that the center is the gathering point of any city; the center-city is instituted above all by the young, the adolescent. When the latter express their image of the city, they always tend to limit, to concentrate, to condense the center; the

center-city is experienced as the exchange-site of social activities
and I should almost say of erotic activities in the broad sense of
the term. Still better, the center-city is always experienced as the
space in which certain subversive forces act and are encountered,
forces of rupture, ludic forces. Play is a theme which is very often
underlined in the investigations of the center; in France there is a
series of investigations concerning the attraction exerted by Paris
upon its suburbs, and through these investigations it has been observed that for the periphery Paris as a center was always experienced
semantically as the privileged site where the other is and where we
ourselves are the other, as the site where one plays. On the contrary,
everything which is not the center is precisely what is not ludic
space, everything which is not alterity: family, residence, identity.
Naturally, especially in terms of the city, we would have to investigate the metaphorical chain, the chain which substitutes for Eros.
We must especially investigate, among the major categories, other
great habits of humanity, for example food and shopping, which
are actually erotic activities in a consumer society. I refer once
again to the example of Tokyo: the great railway stations which
are the points of reference of the main neighborhoods are also great
department stores. And it is certain that the Japanese railroad
station, the station-as-shop, has a unique signification and that this
signification is erotic: purchase or encounter. Then we would have
to explore the deep images of the urban elements. For example,
many investigations have emphasized the imaginary function of the
*watercourse* which, in any city, is experienced as a river, a canal,
a body of water. There is a relation between the road and the
watercourse, and we know that the cities which offer most resistance
to signification, and which moreover often present difficulties of
adaptation for their inhabitants, are precisely the cities lacking
water, the cities without seaside, without a body of water, without
a lake, without a river, without a watercourse; all these cities offer
difficulties of life, of legibility.

  To conclude, I should like to say merely this: in the observations
I have just made, I have not approached the problem of method-

ology. Why? Because, if we seek to undertake a semiology of the city, the best approach, in my opinion, as indeed for any semantic enterprise, will be a certain ingenuity on the reader's part. It will require many of us to attempt to decipher the city where we are, beginning, if necessary, with a personal report. Mustering all these readings of various categories of readers (for we have a complete range of readers, from the sedentary to the foreigner), we would thereby elaborate the language of the city. This is why I shall say that the most important thing is not so much to multiply investigations or functional studies of the city as to multiply the readings of the city, of which, unfortunately, till now, only the writers have given us some examples.

Starting from these readings, from this reconstitution of a language or of a code of the city, we might orient ourselves toward means of a more scientific nature: investigation of units, syntax, etc., but always remembering that we must never try to fix and render rigid the signifieds of the units discovered, for historically these signifieds are extremely imprecise, challengeable, and unmanageable.

Every city is somewhat constructed, created by us in the image of the galley *Argo* of which each piece was no longer an original one, yet which still remained the ship *Argo*, *i.e.*, a group of readily legible and identifiable significations. In this attempt at a semantic approach to the city, we must try to understand the interplay of signs, to understand that any city is a structure but that we must never attempt and never hope to fill that structure.

For the city is a poem, as has often been said and as Hugo put it better than anyone, but not a classical poem, not a poem centered on a subject. It is a poem which deploys the signifier, and it is this deployment which the semiology of the city must ultimately attempt to grasp and to make sing.

Colloquium at the University of Naples, 1967

# Semiology and Medicine

You know that the word *semiology*, in the meaning it now has in the human sciences, was proposed by Saussure in his *Cours de linguistique générale*, some fifty years ago, as a general science of signs, a science which did not yet exist but of which linguistics was later to be only a department. When the semiology proposed by Saussure and subsequently developed by others has constituted the object of international colloquiums, the word has been formally examined, and it has been suggested that it be replaced by the word *semiotics*—and this for a reason which specifically interests us here: in order to avoid the confusion between a semiology of linguistic origin and medical semiology: this is why an effort has been made to designate non-medical semiology by the term semiotics. I believe that this was a somewhat futile fear, or precaution, because the word "semiology" in the post-linguistic sense has already taken root in our intellectual vocabulary, and it is always somewhat dangerous and somewhat futile to go into reverse in the use of words once they have passed into the language; our Littré cites "*sémiologie*" (I might observe in this regard that "*séméiologie*" is occasionally used by some physicians but, in any linguistic orthodoxy, this is an error, for the diphthong *ei* is always rendered in French by *i*: hence it is "*sémiologie*" which is correct, not "*séméiologie*") as a medical term; this term, Littré asserts, refers to that part of medicine which deals with the signs of diseases; but Littré also cites "*sémiotique*"; as a matter of fact, we find *"sémiotique"* in sixteenth-century texts, in Ambroise Paré, and much later, in medical books from the early nineteenth century. I might observe that the word "*sémiotique*," in Littré's own period, also had another meaning than the medical one; it could designate the art of maneuvering troops by indicating their movements to them by signs and not by voice; hence what was involved, even then, was a science of signs which is not that of articulated language.

Obviously, between general semiology and medical semiology, there is not only an identity of the word, but also systematic correspondences, correspondences of systems, of structures; there is even, perhaps, an identity of *ideological* implications, in the broadest sense of the word, around the very notion of *sign*, which appears ever more frequently as a historical notion, linked to a certain type of civilization (our own). This last point has been dealt with by Michel Foucault, who has discussed the medical sign in his book *Birth of the Clinic*; I shall leave this point aside, first of all because, in fact, it has been discussed by Foucault, and because the philosophical investigation of the sign would exceed the context of our discussion, which is to shed some light on the relations between the medical sign and the linguistic sign. I shall therefore confine myself to the problem of the systematic correspondences between the two semiologies.

I find this problem very interesting indeed, and I was hoping to be able, though not a physician, to grasp with some ease certain principles of medical semiology in the books which bear this title; these books have afforded me no help whatever because they are strictly technical, outside the range of my reading, and also because they involve no conceptualization of semiology nor any theory of the science of medical signs. Hence I shall be obliged to posit, quite summarily, a sort of naïve and, I may even say, primitive framework—that of the rudimentary correspondences between the two semiologies—until I can in fact generate by this text the testimony of physicians.

I shall group these observations around several concepts in a very simple fashion; first of all the concept of *sign* itself. I believe it is good, as Foucault has said and as a relatively recent medical dictionary confirms, to distinguish *symptoms* from *signs*, and to oppose them to each other. What is the symptom, from a semiotic point of view? According to Foucault, it is the form in which the disease presents itself; one medical dictionary says: "Symptom: particular phenomenon provoked in the organism by the state of disease"; in the past *objective symptoms* were acknowledged, discovered by the physician, and *subjective symptoms*, indicated by the patient. If this definition is retained—and I believe it is ultimately important to do so—the symptom would be the apparent reality, or the real appearance; let us call it the *phenomenal*; but a phenomenal which in fact has as yet nothing semiological, nothing semantic about it. The symptom would be the morbid phenomenon in its objectivity and in its discontinuity; this is why we can speak, as is done quite commonly in the discourse of nineteenth-century physicians, of the obscurity and the confusion of symptoms; which does not mean the obscurity of signs, but on the contrary the obscurity of the morbid phenomena which do not yet reach the nature of signs. This definition is of importance because, if it is correct, it means that the word "symptom" has not immediately involved the idea of signification, contrary to the word's connotation when it is taken in its metaphoric sense—in effect, when we speak of "symptom" metaphorically, we are already attaching a semantic idea to the word. We believe that the symptom is something to be deciphered, whereas in fact it seems that medically, the idea of a symptom does not immediately involve the idea of a deciphering, of a legible system, of a discoverable signified; it is actually no more than the crude fact available to a deciphering labor, before this labor has begun. If we want to pursue the analogy with the categories of semiotics or of general linguistics, we might say that the symptom corresponds to what Hjelmslev called the substance of the signifier, *i.e.*, the signifier as substance, as matter which has not yet been segmented into signifying units.

Confronting the symptom, the sign which belongs to the definition of medical semiology would actually be the symptom added to, supplemented by the physician's organizing consciousness; Foucault has insisted on this point: the sign is the symptom insofar as it takes place within a description; it is an explicit product of language insofar as it participates in the elaboration of the clinical picture of the physician's discourse; the physician would then be the one who transforms, by the mediation of language—I believe this point is essential—the symptom into a sign. If this definition holds, it means that we have then passed from the phenomenal realm to the semantic. At this point, two observations: the medical sign, by means of certain operations of which we shall speak in a moment, obviously refers to a signified; it is for this reason that it is a sign; there is a signified or, in any case, for several signs it is possible to postulate a signified; this signified is nosographic, it is the named disease which is given through the sign or signs; consequently we are indeed dealing, in the medical context, with an entirely orthodox sign from the point of view of composition, *i.e.*, with a kind of two-faced unit, of which one hidden face, still to be discovered and to be named, is by and large the disease, and one exteriorized face, materialized, eventually fragmented into several signifieds, is to be constructed, interpreted, given a syntax, etc. A second observation: the sign, as opposed to the symptom, belongs to the field of the intelligible: by shifting from symptom to sign, the medical sign compels a mastery of time, a mastery of the disease as duration; here we recognize the very principle of Hippocratic medicine; to the very degree that it is constituted in order to master the time of the disease, the medical sign has a triple value, or a triple function; it is anamnestic, it says what has happened; it is prognostic, it says what will happen; and it is diagnostic, it says what is happening. The medical sign would therefore be comparable to the strictly structural elements of the sentence, *i.e.*, to the syntactical elements which link the signifiers, which structure

them in the gradual unfolding of the meaning; I am not thinking
only of verbs, but of the sentence's syntagmatic temporality which
depends on its syntactic part, of the fact that a preposition announces (like a sort of project) another element of the sentence
which will be taken up later on: we can say that in a sentence,
syntax is this power to dominate time—the actual time of the
sentence and not only the time of reality. In other words, the sign
denounces, it defines or it pronounces, but it also announces; hence
I shall say that if the symptom corresponds to the *substance* of the
signifier, the sign belongs very broadly to the *form* of the signifier
or in any case implies the form of the signifier. So much for the
notions of symptom and of sign.

Another cardinal notion of general semiology is the notion of
system. The system is the field of the sign's correlations. I shall
note a very commonplace opposition in semiology, that of the
paradigmatic and the syntagmatic; the paradigmatic is the level of
virtual oppositions between a sign and its various neighbors, between a phenomenon and its virtual neighbors; for instance *p* and
*b* are in the paradigmatic relation, since in passing from *b* to *p* we
perform a change of meaning, since, at least in French, "*boisson*"
(drink) does not have the same meaning as "*poisson*" (fish); it is
the level of the virtual opposition between two elements of which
only one is actualized in the word or phrase being used. A paradigmatics of the medical sign (I don't know if it exists or if it is
perceived as such) would consist in opposing the medical signs
among themselves, insofar as such an opposition would involve a
change in the disease; hence we would inventory the medical signs
insofar as each of them is in opposition to another sign, such an
opposition involving a change of the signified, *i.e.*, of the reading
of the disease. Further, we should ideally be able to simplify or
reduce this opposition between two signs to the presence or absence
of an element, *i.e.*, to the interplay of the marked and the unmarked. We know that in phonology we have finally been able to
reduce all the signifying oppositions of languages to kinds of alter-

native interplays of which one term is marked, the other not; the marked term possesses a feature which is lacking in the unmarked term. Can we imagine that in medical semiology, it is possible to classify signs by reducing them to the presence/absence of a feature, in certain contexts of course—this is the question we would have to raise to solve the problem of medical paradigmatics. It is immediately apparent, to an outsider, that in medicine the sign, if we want to determine it by the absence of a feature, requires, in order to signify, its site, *i.e.*, a corporeal space. The sign signifies according to a certain space of the body, unless we can imagine a class of medical signs without sites, *i.e.*, of which the whole body would be the site, as for example fever. We then see that medical semiology, and in this it would be distinguished from the mechanism of language, requires, for the sign to perform its signifying function, a sort of corporeal support, a particularized site, which is not the case in language, where the phonematic sound is not supported by a substance which would be independent of it.

As for syntagmatics—*i.e.*, the extended group of signs or the fasciculation of signs, several signs being read at the same time throughout the body or successively throughout time—it is obvious that this is the essential part of medical semiology: here we recognize the same movement and the same hierarchy as in linguistics and in general semiology, where what seems most important, finally, is not the paradigmatic, although this may be actually what has been discovered first, but the syntagmatic; it is, under the name of syntax, the part of linguistics which is the most developed, the most studied, whereas the semantic itself is not only retarded but even, at present, at a certain impasse. Medical syntagmatics would therefore be the functioning of the sign by a combinatory operation. Let us add, here too, several observations. First of all, a question: does there exist, in medicine, such a thing as a pure sign? By which I mean: does there exist, in the general clinical picture of diseases, a sign, for instance, which in and of itself suffices to reveal, to *name* a signified, *i.e.*, a disease to the exclusion of any combination with other signs? I presume there does, for it seems to me that we see

such a thing precisely insofar as we attribute certain typical signs
to certain physicians who have discovered them; perhaps, at such
a moment, we mean that we are in the presence of that typical
sign which, in and of itself, can ultimately signify the actual specificity of a disease? Then this unique, sufficient sign would be the
equivalent of sentence-words in language, of interjections, etc. But
it is obvious that the ordinary regime is, I presume, the concurrence
of signs, i.e., the combinative operation or syntax of signs, implying
time as a space of reading, i.e., the diachrony of the appearance of
signs, this being of course very important. At the beginning of the
nineteenth century, for example, Cabanis had perfectly formulated
this combinatory nature of medical signs by saying that, in the
pathological condition, there is always only a small number of
principal phenomena, all the others resulting from their mixture
and from their different degrees of intensity, the order in which
they appear, their respective importance, their various relations,
sufficing to generate all the varieties of diseases. This is the typical
definition of a process: the power of the combinative operation
which, with only a few reduced elements, gives the results of the
reading. It seems to me that a stable and repeated configuration of
the same medical signs might be called, precisely, the *syndrome*,
which would then be, linguistically, the equivalent of what is called
the fixed syntagm, i.e., the group of stereotyped words which keeps
returning conglomerated in the same way in various sentences, and
which, consequently, though itself composed, strictly speaking, of
several words—two, three, or four—presents absolutely the same
functional value as a single word. This is, or at least this was, we
know, one of the great problems of linguistics: how to treat at once
systematically, theoretically, and practically—in a word, opera-
tionally—the fixed syntagms? When, for example, we say *pomme
de terre* (potato), our way of speaking raises problems; it is obvious
that *pomme de terre* is in fact one word, though it is concretized in
three terms; but it is a word which raises difficulties, notably when
we deal with the problem of machine translation, since we cannot
formally treat it as a single word. Saussure had clearly seen the

theoretical difficulty raised by the fixed syntagms, insofar as they tend to constitute intermediary states between the purely paradigmatic and the syntagmatic, since it is syntagmatic elements, a sequence of words, which finally have a paradigmatic value. Here then perhaps is what would constitute the syndrome: the act of reading the configuration of signs, *i.e.*, the apprehension of a certain number of medical signs as a signifying, stable, regular, legal configuration, one referring to a signified which is always the same. Now, this is precisely what diagnosis is: an act of reading a configuration of signs; the dictionary says "act by which the physician, grouping the morbid symptoms presented by the patient, connects them to a disease having its place in the nosological context."

Here a new question arises, to which I cannot, unfortunately, give an answer, for lack of medical knowledge: how might we define linguistically, structurally, the difficulties or the errors of diagnosis? It is certainly possible to give a structural definition of the difficulties encountered by the physician in reading a sign or signs, in being wrong about the signs. But at what precise moment of the combinative operation does the risk of difficulties or of errors occur? It would be very interesting, from the viewpoint of a systematics of signs, to manage to clarify this (not to mention the interest which the solution of this problem might offer the patient!).

One or two observations, now, around the notion of the signified. Of course the syntagmatic configuration of medical signs, of articulated signs, refers to a signified. This medical signified is a site, a location in the nosographic context. The physician connects all these morbid symptoms, *i.e.*, the signs, to a disease having its place within the nosological context. The site of the nosological context is then quite simply a name, it is the disease as name. At least this was the case in an absolutely indisputable fashion in the early days of the clinic. This is precisely what Foucault has revealed, by showing the role of language in the birth of the clinic; actually, to read a disease is to give it a name; and from that moment—it is here moreover that matters become rather subtle—there is a kind of

perfect reversibility, which is that of language itself, a dizzying
reversibility between the signifier and the signified; the disease is
defined as a name, it is defined as a concurrence of signs: but the
concurrence of signs is oriented and fulfilled only within the name
of the disease, there is an infinite circuit. The diagnostic reading,
i.e., the reading of medical signs, seems to conclude by naming:
the medical signified exists only when named; here we recognize
the critique of the sign made nowadays by certain philosophers: we
can manipulate the signifieds of a sign or signs only by naming
these signifieds, but, by this very act of nomination, we reconvert
the signified into a signifier. The signified becomes a signifier in its
turn, and this is a proposition which, as a matter of fact, has
structured the whole modification of the semiological landscape for
some time—let us say the last four or five years—insofar as we now
understand better, without yet seeing all the consequences, that
the critique of meaning is infinite and that the retreat of the signifieds is in some sense interminable; theoretically, we can never
halt a sign at a final signified; the only halt we can give a sign in
its reading is a halt which comes from practice, but not from the
semiological system itself. Let us take two examples. In medicine,
what halts this kind of retreat or conversion of the signified into
signifier, is medical practice, the fact that once the signified is
apprehended as the name of the disease, we then convert the semiological system into a therapeutic problem, we try to cure the
disease and, consequently, at that very moment, we escape this
kind of dizzying circuit of signifier and signified by the operational,
by the intrusion of the operational which is a venture outside meaning. In linguistics, it is the same thing; in a dictionary, each signifier
is defined by other signifiers, i.e., a word is defined by other words;
but, if we want to define these other words, we must still resort to
other words, and we can never halt the circuit of signifier and
signified; theoretically, systematically, a dictionary is an impossible
object, it is a dizzying object and in some sense a demoniac one.
Yet dictionaries are useful and are workable, precisely because, at
a certain moment, we halt the infinite critique by the intrusion of

the operational, *i.e.*, we simply stop at a definition and make use of it for tasks of a practical or operational type.

I also wonder, apropos of this problem of the signified, if there are not limit-cases in medical semiology, *i.e.*, if we cannot find signs which refer in some sense only to themselves. By accident, I came across a disease which would be a kind of progressive pigmentary dermatosis; now, if I have understood properly, in this disease, which is signified by tiny spots on the skin, these spots refer to nothing other than to themselves; they would necessitate, consequently, no critique of reading or of exploration or of interpretation; the disease would be the sign itself. Perhaps we might philosophize concerning the phenomenon that skin diseases can invariably be reduced to a disease of signs. If such a hypothesis as I am making here as to certain medical signs were approximately true, it would be the equivalent of what in linguistics we call autonymy—*i.e.*, the demonstration of the sign by itself.

In conclusion, I should like to raise the problem of language in an interrogative manner. It seems that in clinical space (but once again, I repeat that I have interrogated this space through Foucault's book, *i.e.*, at a probably archeological period of the clinic), disease is the field of a veritable language, since there is a substance, the symptom, and a form, the sign (signifier/signified); a reductive combinative operation; a nominal signified, as in the dictionaries; and a reading, the diagnosis, which moreover, as in the case of languages, requires an apprenticeship. The last question is whether such an order of signs is actually a language; this is the question of *double articulation*, since it seems effectively established that human articulated language is essentially defined by this double articulation, *i.e.*, by the fact that there are primary units which are significant units, each of which has a meaning (these are, by and large, the words): and that each of these significant units in its turn can be decomposed into distinctive units, *i.e.*, into phonemes, each element of which no longer has a meaning; it is because there is this double articulation that languages can be of an incredible richness with very few elements; that with an average of some thirty phonemes per language, we can construct dictionaries of a hundred thousand words.

Hence, we might ask if the medical language, too, is subject to a double articulation. I shall say, in a certain sense, that it is, since there are distinctive and insignificant units, signs which, in and of themselves, do not manage to signify, which are combined into signifying units, and since, like the phonemes, each sign can participate in several syndromes; I shall take as an example a kind of diagnosis made about a hundred and fifty years ago, through the four following signs: muscular weakness, which could belong to hydropsy; lividity of complexion, which could belong to what was called the obstructions; spots on the body, which could belong to smallpox; and swelling of the gums, which could be provoked by accumulations of tartar; now, if you detach these signs from a certain complex, in which they exist, and if you gather them together, you produce another disease which is scurvy, *i.e.*, you actually have certain signs which belong to several diseases, and it is solely their grouping which produces a morbid specificity; this would be, in fact, the very schema of double articulation.

The final question we may now ask, and which is really a question of a philosophical, ideological order, would be whether linguistics, and consequently the semiology of recent years, does not belong to a certain history of the sign, to a certain ideology of the sign. For if the semiological nature of the field of diseases—and this is Foucault's hypothesis—corresponds to a certain history, then the predominance of the notion of the sign, the *culture* of the notion of the sign, would correspond to a certain ideological phase of our civilization. But, at such a moment, how could it happen that there was an agreement between a positivist science and an ideological science, such as hermeneutics? Actually, there is, in the very terms of the nineteenth-century clinic, a medical hermeneutics. Can a positivist science be identified with a hermeneutics, which is after all engaged in a certain ideological vision of the world? As a matter of fact, the exercise of a positivist science, such as medicine, need not exclude the possibility that there continue to circulate within it certain "mythic schemas," since medical semiology does correspond quite closesly to a certain schema of an animistic type: disease is in fact made intelligible as a person who is first of all in the body's secret, under the skin, if I may say so, and who emits signs, messages, which the physician must receive and interpret rather like a deciphering soothsayer: this is, in reality, a divination, a mantic art. There remains the final question: is today's medicine as yet truly semiological?

In *Les Sciences de la folie*, Mouton, 1972

# ANALYSES

# The Structural Analysis of Narrative

## Apropos of Acts 10-11

### The vision of Cornelius in Caesarea

10 There was in Caesarea a man called Cornelius, a centurion of the Italica cohort. He and the whole of his household were devout and God-fearing, and he gave generously to Jewish causes and prayed constantly to God.

One day at about the ninth hour he had a vision in which he distinctly saw the angel of God come into his house and call out to him, "Cornelius!" He stared at the vision in terror and exclaimed, "What is it, Lord?" "Your offering of prayers and alms," the angel answered, "has been accepted by God. Now you must send someone to Jaffa and fetch a man called Simon, known as Peter, who is lodging with Simon the tanner whose house is by the sea." When the angel who said this had gone, Cornelius called two of the slaves and a devout soldier of his staff, told them what had happened, and sent them off to Jaffa.

### The vision of Peter in Jaffa

Next day, while they were still on their journey and had only a short distance to go before reaching Jaffa, Peter went to the housetop at about the sixth hour to pray. He felt hungry and was looking forward to his meal, but before it was ready he fell into a trance and saw heaven thrown open and something like a big sheet being let down to earth by its four corners; it contained every possible sort of animal and bird, walking, crawling or flying ones. A voice then said to him, "Now, Peter; kill and eat!" But Peter answered, "Certainly not, Lord; I have never yet eaten anything profane or unclean." Again, a second time, the voice spoke to him, "What God has made clean, you have no right to call profane." This was repeated three times, and then suddenly the container was drawn up to heaven again.

Peter was still worrying over the meaning of the vision he had seen, when the men sent by Cornelius arrived. They had asked where Simon's house was and they were now standing at the door, calling out to know if the Simon known as Peter was lodging there. Peter's mind was still on the vision and the Spirit had to tell him, "Some men have come to see you. Hurry down, and do not hesitate about going back with them; it was I who told them to come." Peter went down and said to them, "I am the man you are looking for; why have you come?" They said, "The centurion Cornelius, who is an upright and God-fearing man, highly regarded by the entire Jewish people, was directed by a holy angel to send for you and bring you to his house and listen to what you have to say." So Peter asked them in and gave them lodging.

Next day, he was ready to go off with them, accompanied by some of the brothers from Jaffa. They reached Caesarea the following day, and Cornelius was waiting for them. He had asked his relations and close friends to be there, and as Peter reached the house Cornelius went out to meet him, knelt at his feet and prostrated himself. But Peter helped him up. "Stand up," he said, "I am only a man after all!" Talking together they went in to meet all the people assembled there, and Peter said to them, "You know it is forbidden for Jews to mix with people of another race and visit them, but God has made it clear to me that I must not call anyone profane or unclean. That is why I made no objection to coming when I was sent for; but I should like to know exactly why you sent for me." Cornelius replied, "Three days ago I was praying in my house at the ninth hour, when I suddenly saw a man in front of me in shining robes. He said, 'Cornelius, your prayer has been heard and your alms have been accepted as a sacrifice in the sight of God; so now you must send to Jaffa and fetch Simon known as Peter who is lodging in the house of Simon the tanner, by the sea.' So I sent for you at once, and you have been kind enough to come. Here we all are, assembled in front of you to hear what message God has given you for us."

### Peter's address at the house of Cornelius

Then Peter addressed them: "The truth I have now come to realize," he said, "is that God does not have favorites, but that anybody of any nationality who fears God and does what is right is acceptable to him.

"It is true, God sent his word to the people of Israel, and it was to them that the good news of peace was brought by Jesus Christ—but Jesus Christ is Lord of all men. You must have heard about the recent happenings in Judaea, about Jesus of Nazareth and how he began in Galilee, after John had been preaching baptism. God had anointed him with the Holy Spirit and with power, and because God was with him, Jesus went about doing good and curing all who had fallen into the power of the devil. Now I, and those with me, can witness to everything he did throughout the countryside of Judea and in Jerusalem itself: and also to the fact that they killed him by hanging him on a tree, yet three days afterwards God raised him to life and allowed him to be seen, not by the whole people but only by certain witnesses God had chosen beforehand. Now we are those witnesses—we have eaten and drunk with him after his resurrection from the dead—and he has ordered us to proclaim this to his people and to tell them that God has appointed him to judge everyone, alive or dead. It is to him that all the prophets bear this witness: that all who believe in Jesus will have their sins forgiven through his name."

### The coming of the Spirit upon the pagans

While Peter was still speaking the Holy Spirit came down on all the listeners. Jewish believers who had accompanied Peter were all astonished that the gifts of the Holy Spirit should be poured out on the pagans too, since they could hear them speaking strange languages and proclaiming the greatness of God. Peter himself then said, "Could anyone refuse the water of baptism to these people, now they have received the Holy Spirit just as much as we have?" He then gave orders for them to be baptized in the name of Jesus Christ. Afterwards they begged him to stay on for some days.

### Peter's narrative in Jerusalem

11 The apostles and the brothers in Judaea heard that the pagans too had accepted the word of God, and when Peter came up to Jerusalem the Jews criticized him and said, "So you have been visiting the uncircumcised and eating with them, have you?" Peter in reply gave them the details point by point: "One day, when I was in the town of Jaffa," he began, "I fell into a trance as I was praying and had a vision of something like a big sheet being let down from heaven by its four corners. This sheet reached the ground quite close to me. I watched it intently and saw all sorts of animals and wild beasts—everything possible that could walk, crawl or fly. Then I heard a voice that said to me, 'Now, Peter; kill and eat!' But I answered: 'Certainly not, Lord; nothing profane or unclean has ever crossed my lips.' And a second time the voice spoke from heaven, 'What God has made clean, you have no right to call profane.' This was repeated three times, before the whole of it was drawn up to heaven again.

"Just at that moment, three men stopped outside the house where we were staying; they had been sent from Caesarea to fetch me, and the Spirit told me to have no hesitation about going back with them. The six brothers here came with me as well, and we entered the man's house. He told us he had seen an angel standing in his house who said, 'Send to Jaffa and fetch Simon known as Peter; he has a message for you that will save you and your entire household.'

"I had scarcely begun to speak when the Holy Spirit came down on them in the same way as it came on us at the beginning, and I remembered that the Lord had said, 'John baptized with water, but you will be baptized with the Holy Spirit.' I realized then that God was giving them the identical thing he gave to us when we believed in the Lord Jesus Christ; and who was I to stand in God's way?"

This account satisfied them, and they gave glory to God. "God," they said, "can evidently grant even the pagans the repentance that leads to life."*

* The Jerusalem Bible (Doubleday), 1966.

My task is to present what is already commonly called the Structural Analysis of Narrative. It must be admitted that the name outstrips the thing. What it is possible to call by such a name at present is a collective research, it is not yet a science nor even, strictly speaking, a discipline; calling it a discipline would imply that the Structural Analysis of Narrative is being taught, and this is not yet the case. The first word of this presentation must therefore be a warning: there is not, at present, a science of narrative (even if we were to give the word "science" an extremely broad meaning); there does not exist, at present, a "diegetology." I should like to make this clear and try to forestall certain disappointments.

## Origin of the Structural Analysis of Narrative

This origin is, if not confused, at least "undetermined." We may think of it as quite remote, if we trace the state of mind which presides over the analysis of narrative and of texts back to Aristotle's *Poetics* and *Rhetoric*; closer at hand, if we refer to Aristotle's classical posterity, to the theoreticians of genres; much more recent, even very recent, but more specific, if we consider that it can be traced in its present form to the work of those men we call the Russian Formalists, some of whose works have been translated into French by Tzvetan Todorov. This Russian Formalism (and its diversity concerns us here) included poets, literary critics, linguists, folklorists who investigated, during the early 1920s, the forms of the literary work; the group was then dispersed by cultural Stalinism and migrated abroad, notably through the linguistic group of Prague. The spirit of this Russian Formalist research passed, essentially, into the work of the great contemporary linguist Roman Jakobson.

Methodologically (and no longer historically), the origin of the Structural Analysis of Narrative is, of course, the recent development of what is called structural linguistics. Based on this linguistics, there has been a "poetic" extension, as a result of Jakobson's research, in the direction of the study of the poetic message or the literary message; and there has been an anthropological extension as a result of Lévi-Strauss's studies of myth and his continuation of the work of one of the most important Russian Formalists for the study of narrative, Vladimir Propp, the folklorist. At present, research in this realm is being pursued, in France, within the Centre d'Études des Communications de Masse, at the École Pratique des Hautes Études, and in the semio-linguistic group of my friend and colleague Greimas. This type of analysis is beginning to penetrate academic teaching, notably at Vincennes; abroad, isolated researchers are working in this direction, chiefly in Russia, the United States, and Germany. I shall indicate some of the efforts to coordinate this research: in France, the appearance of a *Revue de Poétique* (in the Jakobsonian sense of the word, of course), directed by Todorov and Genette; in Italy, an annual colloquium on the Analysis of Narrative at Urbino; and finally an International Association of Semiology (*i.e.*, of the science of significations) has just been created, on a broad scale; it already has its review, called *Semiotica*, which will frequently investigate problems of the Analysis of Narrative.

However, at present this research is subject to a certain dispersion, and this dispersion is in a sense constitutive of the investigation itself—at least that is how I see it. First of all, this research remains individual, not out of individualism, but because what is involved is an enterprise of *finesse*: work on the meaning or meanings of the text (for that is the Structural Analysis of Narrative) cannot be intersected by a phenomenological departure: there is no machine for reading meaning; of course there are translating machines; but these, if they can transform denoted meanings, literal meanings, obviously have no grasp of secondary meanings, of the connoted, associative level of a text; at the outset there must still be an individual operation of reading, and the notion of a "team" on this level, remains, I believe, quite illusory; the Structural Analysis of Narrative cannot be treated, as a discipline, like biology nor even like sociology: there is no canonical account possible, one investigator cannot quite speak in another's name. Further, this individual research is, on the level of each researcher, *in process*: each investigator has his own history; it can vary, especially because the history of the environing structuralism is an accelerated history: concepts change rapidly, divergences soon become pronounced, polemics suddenly turn acrimonious, and all this has an obvious influence on research.

Finally, I shall take the liberty of saying, because it is what I truly believe: since we are studying a cultural language, to wit the language of narrative, analysis is immediately sensitive (and we must be clear about this) to its ideological implications. At present, what passes for "the" structuralist enterprise is a notion actually quite sociological and quite fabricated, insofar as it is seen as a united school. This is not at all the case. As for French structuralism, in any event, there are profound ideological divergences between the various representative figures who have been crammed in the same structuralist pigeonhole, for instance between Lévi-Strauss, Derrida, Lacan, or Althusser; there is accordingly a structuralist fractionalism, and if we were to situate it (and it is not my intention to do so here), it would crystallize, I believe, around the notion of "Science."

I have said this to forestall disappointment and to limit confidence in a scientific method which is barely a method and certainly not a science. Before turning to the text from the Acts of the Apostles which is our concern, I should like to offer three general principles which might, I think, be recognized by all those concerned today with the Structural Analysis of Narrative. To them I shall add some remarks on the subject of the operational arrangements of the analysis as well.

# I  GENERAL PRINCIPLES
# AND ARRANGEMENTS OF THE ANALYSIS

## 1.  Principle of formalization

This principle, which might also be called a *principle of abstraction*, derives from the Saussurian opposition of *language* and *speech*. We consider that each narrative (let us recall that in the world and in the history of the world, and the history of entire nations of the earth, the number of narratives produced by humanity is incalculable), each narrative in this apparently heteroclite mass of narratives, is the *speech*, in the Saussurian sense, the message of a general language of narrative. This language of narrative is obviously identifiable beyond language proper, beyond what the linguists study. The linguistics of national languages (in which narratives are written) stops at the sentence, which is the ultimate unit a linguist can "attack." Beyond the sentence, the structure no longer concerns linguistics proper; it concerns a second linguistics, a translinguistics which is the site of the analysis of narrative: after the sentence, there where several sentences are set together. What happens then? We do not yet know; we thought we knew for a very long time, and it was Aristotelian or Ciceronian rhetoric which informed us on the matter; but the concepts of that rhetoric are obsolete, for they were chiefly normative; however, classical rhetoric, though in decline, has not yet been replaced. The linguists themselves have not ventured to undertake such a task; Benveniste has given a few indications, as always extremely penetrating, on this subject; there are also certain Americans who have been concerned with speech-analysis; but this linguistics remains to be constructed. And the analysis of narrative, the language of narrative, belongs, at least postulatively, to such future translinguistics.

One practical impact of this principle of abstraction, in whose name we are trying to establish a language of narrative, is that we cannot and do not desire to analyze a text in itself. This must be said, since I shall be discussing a single text: I am embarrassed to do so because the attitude of the classic analyst of narrative is not to concern himself with an isolated text; on this point there is a fundamental difference between the Structural Analysis of Narrative and what is traditionally called *explication de textes*. For us, a text is speech which refers to language, a message which refers to a code, a performance which refers to a competence—all these words being the words of linguists. The Structural Analysis of Narrative is fundamentally, constitutively *comparative*: it seeks forms, not a content. When I speak of the text of the Acts, it will not be to explicate this text, it will be to confront this text as an investigator who unites certain materials in order to construct a grammar; for this, the linguist is obliged to unite sentences, a *corpus* of sentences. The analyst of narrative has exactly the same task, he must unite narratives, a *corpus* of narratives, in order to attempt to extract from them a structure.

## 2. Principle of pertinence

This second principle has its origin in phonology. As opposed to phonetics phonology seeks not to study the intrinsic quality of each sound emitted within a language, the physical and acoustical quality of the sound, but to establish the differences of sounds of a language, insofar as these differences of sounds refer to differences of meaning, and only so far: this is the principle of pertinence; we try to find differences of form attested to by differences of content; these differences are pertinent or non-pertinent features. I should like to propose here a clarification, an example, and a kind of warning.

A *clarification*, first of all, as to the word *meaning*: in the analysis of narrative, we do not attempt to find signifieds which I shall call *full* signifieds, lexical signifieds, meanings in the usual acceptation of the word. We call "meaning" any type of intratextual or extra-textual correlation, *i.e.*, any feature of narrative which refers to another moment of the narrative or to another site of the culture necessary in order to read the narrative: all types of anaphora, of cataphora, in short of "diaphora" (if I may be permitted this word), all linkages, all paradigmatic and syntagmatic correlations, all the phenomena of signification and also the phenomena of distribution. I repeat: meaning, therefore, is not a *full signified*, such as I might find in a dictionary, even a dictionary of Narrative; it is essentially a correlation, or the term of a correlation, a correlate, or a connotation. Meaning, for me (this is how I envision it in research), is essentially a *citation*, the departure of a code, what permits us to postulate a code and what implies a code, even if this code (I shall return to this) is not or cannot be reconstituted.

Next, an *example*: for the Structural Analysis of Narrative, at least for me (though this is arguable), the problems of translation are not systematically pertinent. So, in the case of the narrative of the visions of Cornelius and of Peter, the problems of translation concern the analysis only within certain limits: only if the differences of translation involve a structural modification, *i.e.*, the alteration of a group of functions or of a sequence. I should like to give one example:

The King James version of Acts 10:2:

A devout man [referring to Cornelius], and one that feared God with all his house, which gave much alms to the people, and prayed to God alway.

The Jerusalem Bible version of the same passage:

He and the whole of his household were devout and God-fearing, and he gave generously to Jewish causes and prayed constantly to God.

One can say that the two passages reveal entirely different syntactical structures, many differences in vocabulary. Yet in the present case, this does not at all affect the distribution of codes and functions, because the structural sense of the passage is exactly the same in either translation. What is involved is a signified of psychological or characterical or even, more specifically, of evangelical type, since the Gospel uses a certain entirely coded paradigm, which is a three-term opposition: the circumcised / the uncircumcised / the "God-fearing"; these terms form the third category, which is neutral (if I may be permitted this linguistic term) and which is precisely at the center of our text: it is the paradigm which is pertinent, not the sentences in which it is dressed.

On the other hand, if we compare at other points the King James version with the Jerusalem Bible, structural differences appear: in the Jerusalem Bible, the angel does not say what Cornelius should ask Peter, after having sent for him; in the King James (verse 6): "he shall tell thee what thou oughtest to do": on the one hand, absence, on the other, presence. I insist on the fact that the difference of the two versions has a structural value, because the sequence of the angel's injunction is modified: in the earlier translation, the content of the angel's injunction is specified, there is a kind of desire to make homogeneous what is announced (Peter's mission, a mission of speech) and what will happen: *Peter will make a speech*; I do not know the origin of this version, nor am I concerned with it; what I see is that the King James version rationalizes the structure of the message, while, in the Jerusalem Bible, the angel's version not being specified, it remains void, and thereby makes emphatic Cornelius's obedience, who sends for Peter "blindly" and without knowing why; in the later translation, absence functions as a feature which operates a certain suspense, which reinforces and makes emphatic the suspense of the narrative, which was not the case in the King James version—less narrative, less dramatic, and more rational.

Lastly, a precaution and a *warning*: we must be suspicious of the *naturalness* of the notations. In analyzing a text, we must constantly react against the impression of obviousness, against the it-goes-without-saying aspect of what is written. Every statement, however trivial and normal it appears, must be evaluated in terms of structure by a mental test of commutation. Confronting a statement, a sentence-fragment, we must always think of what would happen if the feature were not noted or if it were different. The good analyst of narrative must have a sort of imagination of the *counter-text*, an imagination of the aberration of the text, of what is narratively scandalous; he must be sensitive to the notion of logical, narrative "scandal"; thereby we shall be emboldened to assume the often very banal, tedious, and obvious character of the analysis.

### 3.  Principle of plurality

The Structural Analysis of Narrative (at least as I conceive of it) does not seek to establish "the" meaning of the text, it does not even seek to establish "a" meaning of the text; it differs fundamentally from philological analysis, for it aims at tracing what I shall call the geometric site, the site of meanings, the site of the possible meanings of the text. Just as a language is a possibility of words (a language is the possible site of a certain number of words, actually of an infinite number), so what the analyst wants to establish in the language of narrative is the possible site of meanings, or again the plurality of meaning, or meaning as plurality. When we say that the analyst seeks or defines meaning as a possibility, this is not a tendency or an option of a liberal sort; for me, in any case, there is no question of liberally determining the truth's conditions of possibility, no question of a philological agnosticism; I am not considering the *possibility of meaning* as a sort of indulgent and liberal preamble to a *certain meaning*; for me, the meaning is not a possibility, it is not *one* possible thing, it is *the very being of the possible*, it is the being of plurality (and not one or two or several possibilities).

In these conditions, structural analysis cannot be a method of interpretation; it does not seek to interpret the text, to propose the probable meaning of the text; it does not follow an anagogical path toward the truth of the text, toward its deep structure, toward its secret; and consequently it differs fundamentally from what is called literary criticism, which is an interpretive criticism, of the Marxist or the psychoanalytic type. The structural analysis of the text is different from these criticisms, because it does not seek the secret of the text: for it, all the text's roots are in the air; it does not have to unearth these roots in order to find *the main one*. Of course if, in a text, there is one meaning, a monosemy, if there is an anagogical process, which is precisely the case with our text from the Acts, we shall treat this anagogy as a code of the text, among the other codes, and given as such by the text.

## 4. Operational arrangements

I prefer this expression to the more intimidating one of *method*, for I am not sure we possess a method; but there are a certain number of operational arrangements in the investigation which must be mentioned. It seems to me (this is a personal position and not inalterable) that, if we work on a single text (previous to the comparative work of which I have spoken and which is the very goal of classical Structural Analysis), we must anticipate three operations.

1. *Segmentation* of the text, *i.e.*, of the material signifier. This segmentation can, in my opinion, be entirely arbitrary; in a certain state of the investigation, there is no disadvantage to this arbitrariness. It is a way of making a grid of the text which provides the fragments of the statement on which one is going to work. Now, precisely, for the New Testament, and indeed for the whole Bible, this work is already done, since the Bible is segmented into verses (in the case of the Koran, into suras). The verse is an excellent working unit of meaning; since it is a question of *creaming* (or skimming) the text, the correlations or apertures of the verse-sieve are of an excellent dimension. It would moreover greatly interest me to know where the segmentation into verses comes from; if it is linked to the citational nature of the Word, what are the exact links, the structural links, between the citational nature of the Biblical speech and the verse. For other tests, I have proposed calling these speech fragments on which we work "lexias," units of reading. For us, a verse is a lexia.

2. *Inventory* of the codes which are cited in the text: inventory, collection, harvest, or as I have just said, creaming-off. Lexia after lexia, verse after verse, we try to inventory the meanings, in the acceptation I have given, the correlations or code-departures present in this speech fragment. I shall return to this, since I am going to be working on several verses.

3. *Coordination*: to establish the correlations of units, of identified functions which are often separated, superimposed, mingled, or even braided, since a text, as the word's very etymology says, is a fabric, a braid of correlates, which can be separated from each other by the insertion of other correlates, which belong to other groups. There are two main types of correlations: internal and external. For those internal to the text, here is an example: if we are told that the angel appears, *appearance* is a term whose correlate is inevitably *disappearance*. This is an intratextual correlation, since *appearance* and *disappearance* are in the same narrative. It would be, strictly speaking, a narrative scandal if the angel did not disappear. Hence we must note the sequence *appear/disappear*, because that is what readability is: that the presence of certain elements be *necessary*. There are also external correlations: a feature of discourse can refer to a diacritical, suprasegmental totality superior to the text; it can refer to the total character of a person, or to the total atmosphere of a place, or to an anagogic meaning, as here in our text, *i.e.*, the integration of the Gentiles into the Church. A feature can even refer to other texts: this is intertextuality, a notion recently proposed by Julia Kristeva.[1] It implies that a feature of discourse *refers* to another text, in the almost infinite sense of that word; for we must not confuse the sources of a text (which are merely the minor version of this phenomenon of citation) with citation, which is a kind of illimitable reference to an infinite text, the cultural text of humanity. This is particularly valid for literary texts, which are woven of extremely varied stereotypes, and where, consequently, the phenomenon of reference, of citation, to an anterior or ambient culture is very frequent. In what is called inter-textuality, we must include texts which come *after*: the sources of a text are not only *before* it, they are also *after* it. This is the point of view so convincingly adopted by Lévi-Strauss when he says that the Freudian version of the Oedipus myth belongs to the Oedipus

---

[1] Julia Kristeva, *Sèmeiotikè*, Paris: Éd. du Seuil, 1969.

myth: if we read Sophocles, we must read Sophocles as a citation of Freud; and Freud as a citation of Sophocles.


## II  STRUCTURAL PROBLEMS PRESENT IN THE TEXT OF ACTS

I now proceed to the text, Acts 10; I am afraid the disappointment will begin, since we are going to enter into the concrete and since, after these grand principles, our harvest risks seeming thin indeed. I shall not analyze the text step by step, as I ought to do; I ask you simply to suppose this: I am a researcher, I am doing research in the structural analysis of narrative: I have decided to analyze perhaps 100 or 200 or 300 narratives; among these narratives, there is, for one reason or another, the narrative of Cornelius's vision; here is the work I am doing and which I do not privilege in any way. Normally, this would take several days: I would go through the narrative verse after verse, lexia after lexia, and I would *cream off* all the meanings, all the possible codes, which takes a certain amount of time, because the imagination of correlation is not immediate. A correlation is searched out, is worked out; hence it takes some time and some patience; I shall not be doing that work here, but I shall make use of the narrative from Acts in order to raise three main structural problems, present in my opinion in this text.


## 1.  The problem of the codes

I have said that the meanings were code-departures, citations of codes; if we compare our text to a literary text (I have just been working at some length on a *nouvelle* by Balzac), it is obvious that the codes are not numerous here and of a certain poverty. Their richness would probably show up better on the scale of the New Testament in its entirety. I shall attempt an identification of the codes, as I see them (I may forget some) in the first verses (verses

1 to 3), and I shall set aside the case of the two most important codes invested in the text.

1. *"There was in Caesarea a man called Cornelius, a centurion of the Italica cohort."* In this sentence, I see four codes. And first of all the formula "There was," which culturally refers (I am not speaking here in terms of Biblical exegesis, but in a more general fashion) to a code which I shall call the *narrative code*: this narrative which begins by "there was" refers to all inaugurations of narrative. A brief digression here to say that the problem of the inauguration of discourse is an important one, which has been clearly seen and carefully treated, on the pragmatic level, by ancient and classical rhetoric: that rhetoric has laid down extremely specific rules for beginning the discourse. In my opinion, these rules are attached to the sentiment that there is in humanity a native aphasia, that it is difficult to speak, that there is perhaps nothing to say, and that, consequently, there is required a whole group of protocols and rules to find *what* to say: *invenire quid dicas*. The inauguration is a perilous zone of discourse: the beginning of speech is a difficult action; it is the emergence from silence. In reality, there is no reason to begin *here* rather than *there*. Language is an infinite structure, and I believe that it is this sentiment of the infinity of language which is present in all the inauguration-rites of speech. In the oldest, pre-Homeric epics, the bard, the recitant, began the narrative by saying, according to a ritual formula: "I take up the story at this point . . ."; he indicated thereby that he was conscious of the arbitrariness of his point of entry; to begin is to enter into an infinity quite arbitrarily. Hence narrative-inaugurations are important to study, and this has not yet been done. I have several times suggested to students that they take as a thesis subject the first sentences of novels: this is a fine subject; as yet my suggestion has not been followed, but I know that this work is being done in Germany, where there has even been a publication on the beginnings of novels. From the point of view of structural analysis, it would be fascinating to know what implicit information is contained in a

beginning, since this site of discourse is preceded by no information whatever.

2.   *"in Caesarea . . ."* This is a *topographic code*, relative to the systematic organization of places in the narrative. In this topographic code, there are doubtless rules of association (rules of the *probable*), there is a narrative functionality of places: here we find a paradigm, a significant opposition between Caesarea and Jaffa. The distance between the two cities must correspond to a distance in time: a typically structural problem, since it is a problem of concordance, of concomitance, according to a certain logic (moreover, one still to be explored), but which is at first glance the logic of *probability*. This topographic code is to be found at other points in the text. The topographic code is obviously a cultural code: Caesarea and Jaffa—this implies a certain knowledge on the reader's part, even if the reader is supposed to possess this knowledge quite naturally. Further: if we include in the language of narrative the way in which we, in our situation as modern readers, receive the narrative, we identify here all the Oriental connotations of the word Caesarea, everything we put into the word Caesarea, because of what we have *read* subsequently, in Racine or in other authors.

Another observation relative to the topographic code: in verse 9, we have a feature of this code: *"Peter went to the housetop."* The topographic citation here has a very powerful function within the narrative, since it justifies the fact that Peter does not hear the arrival of the men sent by Cornelius, so that consequently notification by the angel is necessary: *"Some men have come to see you."* The topographical feature becomes a narrative function. I take advantage of this to raise an important problem of *literary* narrative: the theme of the housetop is both a term of the topographic code, *i.e.*, of a cultural code which refers to a habitat where there are houses with roof-terraces, and a term of what I shall call the *actional code*, the code of actions, of sequences of actions: here, the intervention of the angel; further, we might readily connect this notation to the symbolic field, insofar as the rooftop is a high place and consequently implies an ascensional symbolism, if the elevation is coupled with other terms of the text. Thus, the notation of the rooftop corresponds to three different codes: topographic, actional, symbolic. Now, the characteristic of narrative, in a sense one of its fundamental laws, is that the three codes are given in an *undecidable* fashion: we cannot decide if there is one prevalent code, and this undecidability, in my opinion, constitutes the narrative, for it defines the performance of the teller. "To tell a story well," according to classical readability, is to manage to keep us from deciding among two or more codes, is to propose a sort of turnstile by which one code can always present itself as the natural alibi of the other, by which one code naturalizes the other. In other words, what is necessary to the story, what puts itself under the instance of discourse, seems determined by reality, by the referent, by nature.

3.   "A man called Cornelius . . ." Here there is a code which I shall call *onomastic* since it is the code of proper names. Recent analyses have renewed the problem of the proper name, which moreover had never been really raised by linguistics. These analyses are those of Jakobson on the one hand, and of Lévi-Strauss on the other, who in *Structural Anthropology* (1958), has dedicated a chapter to the problems of classifying proper names. On the level of the text, the investigation will not lead very far, but in the perspective of a grammar of narrative, the onomastic code is obviously a very important one.

4.   "A centurion of the Italica cohort": this is, quite banally, the *historical code* which implies a historical knowledge, or, if we are concerned with a reader contemporary with the referent, an assumption of political, social, and administrative information. It is a cultural code.

5.   "He and the whole of his household were devout and God-fearing, and he gave generously to Jewish causes and prayed constantly to God." There is here what I call a *semic code*. The seme, in linguistics, is

a unit of the signified, not of the signifier. I call *semic code* the group of signifieds of connotation, in the current meaning of the term; the connotation can be characterial, if we read the text psychologically (we will then have a characterial signified of Cornelius, referring to his psychological character), or merely structural, if we read the text anagogically, the category of "God-fearing" not having a psychological value, but a strictly relational value in the distribution of the partners of the Gospel, as I have said.

6.    There is also a *rhetorical code* in this verse, because it is built on a rhetorical schema, to wit: there is a general proposition, a signified: piety, which is coined in two "*exempla*," as classical rhetoric would say: generosity and prayer.

7.    "*He had a vision in which he distinctly saw . . .*" Here we have one of the terms of an extremely important code, to which I shall return and which I am provisionally calling the *actional code*, or code of sequences of actions. The action here is "to see in a vision." We shall return to this problem later on.

8.    "*At about the ninth hour . . .*" This is the *chronological code*; there are several citations from it in the text; we shall make the same remark as for the topographic code: this code is linked to problems of probability and verisimilitude; the Spirit regulates the synchronism of the two visions: the chronological code has a structural importance, since, from the narrative point of view, the two visions must coincide. For the study of the novel, this chronological code is obviously very important; and we must further recall that Lévi-Strauss has studied chronology as a code apropos of the problems of historical dates.

9.    "*A vision . . . in which he saw the angel of God come into his house and call out to him, 'Cornelius!' . . .*" I here identify the presence of a code which I shall call, after Jakobson's classification, the *phatic code* (from the Greek word *phasis*: speech). As a matter of fact,

Jakobson has distinguished six functions of language, and among these, the phatic function or group of features of enunciation by which one assures, maintains, or renews a contact with the interlocutor. These are, then, language features which have no content as message, but play a role of renewed interpellation. (The best example is the telephonic word "Hello" which opens contact and often maintains it: it is a feature of the phatic code.) The features of interpellation thus derive from this phatic code; it is a sort of generalized vocative; later on, we shall classify within this code an indication such as "this was repeated three times." For we can interpret the notation as a feature of redundance, of insistence, of communication between the angel and Peter, between the Spirit and Peter: feature of the phatic code.

10.  It is possible to see later on, in the "*big sheet let down to earth*," a citation from the *symbolic field* (I prefer to say symbolic field rather than symbolic code), to wit the organization of signifiers according to an ascensional symbolism. The symbolic meaning is obviously important: the text organizes, on the level of the narrative and through an elaboration of signifiers, the account of a transgression; and, if this transgression is to be analyzed in symbolic terms, it is because it is a transgression linked to the human body. From this point of view, this is a remarkable text, since the two transgressions studied and recommended in the text are both corporeal. One concerns food, and the other circumcision. and these two strictly corporeal, hence symbolic (in the psychoanalytic sense of the term) transgressions are explicitly united by the text, since alimentary transgression serves as an introduction or, if one may say so, as an *exemplum* for the transgression of the law of exclusion by circumcision. A symbolic description would not retain, moreover, the hierarchy I have just posited between the two transgressions. This logical hierarchy is given by the analogy of the text, it is the meaning which the text itself has sought to give its narrative; but if we wanted to "interpret" the text symbolically, we would not have to place the alimentary transgression *before* the religious one, we would

have to try to discern what general *form* of transgression there is behind the text's anagogic construction.

11. As for the *anagogic code* I have just mentioned, it is the system to which all the features which specifically articulate *the* meaning of the text refer, for the text here articulates and announces its own meaning—which is not always the case. In the current literary text, there is no anagogic code: the text does not utter its deep meaning, its secret meaning, and it is moreover because it does not do so that criticism has been able to seize upon it. Several times over, citations derive from the anagogic code, as for example when Peter tries to explain to himself the meaning of the vision he has just had; or else the discussion of meaning, the assurance by meaning within the community of Jerusalem. Hence the anagogical meaning is given by the text: it is the integration of the Uncircumcised into the Church. Perhaps we should attach to this code all the features which allude to the problem of hospitality: they would also belong to this anagogic code.

12. A last important code is the *metalinguistic code*: this word designates a language which speaks of another language. If, for instance, I am writing a grammar of the French language, I produce a metalanguage, since I am speaking a language (to wit, my grammar) about a language which is French. Hence the metalanguage is a language which speaks of another language or whose referent is a language or a discourse. Now, what is interesting here, is that the metalinguistic episodes are important and numerous: they are the four or five summaries which constitute the text. A summary or résumé is a metalinguistic episode, a feature of the metalinguistic code: there is a narrative referent, a language referent: Cornelius's vision, Peter's vision, the two visions, the story of Christ . . ., here are four narrative referents; then there are the metalinguistic repetitions, depending on the different recipients.

—the envoys summarize to Peter the order given to Cornelius;

—Cornelius summarizes his vision to Peter;

—Peter summarizes his vision to Cornelius;

—Peter summarizes the two visions to the community of Jerusalem;

—finally, the story of Christ is summarized by Peter to Cornelius.
I shall return to this code. But now I should like to speak of two
other important problems, which correspond to two particular or
isolated codes in the text.


## 2.   The code of actions

This code refers to the organization of actions undertaken or
undergone by the agents present in the narration; it is an important
code since it covers everything which, in a text, seems to us properly
and immediately narrative, to wit the relation of *what happens*,
ordinarily presented according to a logic at once causal and temporal. This level immediately received the attention of analysts.
Propp established the major "functions" of the folktale, *i.e.*, the
constant, regular actions which we find with few variations in almost
all the narratives of Russian folklore; his schema (postulating the
sequence of some thirty actions) has been adopted and corrected
by Lévi-Strauss, Greimas, and Bremond. We can say that today
the "logic" of narrative actions is conceived in several fashions,
related and yet different. Propp sees the sequence of narrative actions as alogical; for him, it is a constant, regular sequence, but
without content. Lévi-Strauss and Greimas have postulated that
these sequences must be given a paradigmatic structure and recon-
structed as successions of oppositions; here in fact, for example, the
initial victory (of the letter) is set in opposition to its (final) defeat:
a median term neutralizes them temporarily: confrontation. Bremond, for his part, has sought to reconstitute a logic of the alter-
natives of actions, each "situation" being "resolvable" in one
fashion or another and each solution engendering a new alternative.
Personally, I incline toward the notion of a sort of cultural logic
which owes nothing to any mental datum, even on an anthropological level; for me, the sequences of narrative actions are encased

in a logical appearance which comes solely from the *already-written*: in a word, from the stereotype.

This said, and in whatever fashion they are to be structured, here for example are two sequences of actions present in our text.

*a.* An elementary sequence, with two centers, of the type *Question/Answer*: Peter's question to the envoys/envoys' answer; Peter's demand for an explanation to Cornelius/Cornelius's answer. The same schema can be complicated without losing its structure: disturbing information/demand for enlightenment formulated by the community/explanation given by Peter/reassurance of the community. We may note that it is insofar as such sequences are quite banal that they are interesting; for their very banality attests to the fact that what is involved is a quasi-universal constraint, or again: a grammatical rule of narrative.

*b.* A developed sequence, with several centers: this is the *Search* (for Peter by Cornelius's envoys): to set out/to seek/to arrive in a place/to ask/to obtain/to bring back. Some of the terms are *substitutable* (in other narratives): *to bring back* can elsewhere be replaced by *to renounce, to abandon*, etc.

The sequences of actions, constituted according to a logico-temporal structure, are presented throughout the narrative according to a complicated order: two terms of the same sequence can be separated by the appearance of terms belonging to other sequences; this interlacing of sequences forms the *braid* of the narrative (let us not forget that etymologically *text* means a weaving). Here the interlacing is relatively simple: there is a certain *simpleness* of the narrative, and this simpleness derives from the pure and simple juxtaposition of the sequences (they are not crisscrossed or intricated). Further, a term from one sequence can in and of itself represent a subsequence (what the cyberneticians call a *bit*); the sequence of the angel includes four terms: to enter/to be seen/to communicate/to depart; one of these four terms, communication,

constitutes an *order* (a command) which is itself coined in secondary terms (to interpellate/to demand/reason for the choice/
content of the interpellation/execution); there is in a sense a *proxy*
of a sequence of actions by a term responsible for representing that
sequence in another sequence of actions: *greet/answer*; this fragment
of a sequence represents a certain meaning ("I, too, am a man").

These few indications form the sketch of analytical operations
to which we must subject the actional level of a narrative. This
analysis can be a thankless task, for the sequences give an impression
of *obviousness* and their identification seems trivial; hence we must
always realize that this very triviality, by constituting the *normality*
of our narratives, requires the study of a crucial phenomenon concerning which we have little illumination: why is a narrative *readable*? What are the conditions of a text's *readability*? What are its
limits? How, why does a story seem to us *endowed with meaning*?
Confronting normal sequences (such as the sequences of our narrative) we must always think of the possibility of logically scandalous
sequences, either by their extravagance or by the absence of a term:
thereby appears the grammar of the *readable*.


### 3.   The metalinguistic code

The last problem I want to extract from this text from the Acts
relates to what I have called the metalinguistic code. The metalinguistic occurs, as we have said, when a language speaks of another
language. This is the case of the summary or résumé, which is a
metalinguistic act, since it is a discourse which has for referent
another discourse. Now, in our text, there are four intertextual
resumes and, further, a résumé exterior to the text, since it refers
to the entire Gospel, to wit the life of Christ.

—the vision of Cornelius is repeated, summarized by Cornelius's
envoys to Peter, and by Cornelius himself to Peter;

—Peter's vision is summarized by Peter to Cornelius;

—the two visions are summarized by Peter to the community of
Jerusalem;

—finally the story of Christ is summarized, one might say, by Peter to Cornelius and to Cornelius's friends.

1. *The summary.* If, confronting this text, I were in a perspective of general research, I should classify it under the rubric of the problem of the summary, of the organization of the metalinguistic structure of narratives. Linguistically, the summary is a citation without its letter, a citation of content (not of form), a statement which refers to another statement, but whose reference, no longer being literal, involves a labor of structuration. What is interesting is that a résumé structures an anterior language, which is moreover already structured. The referent here is already a *narrative* (and not "reality"): what Peter summarizes to the community of Jerusalem is only in appearance reality; in fact, it is what we have already learned by a kind of zero narrative, which is the narrative of the performer of the text, to wit, apparently, Luke. Consequently, what would interest us from the point of view of the problematics of the summary, is to understand if there is really a hiatus between the *princeps* narrative, the zero narrative, and its referent, the supposedly real material of the narrative. Is there really a kind of prenarrative, which would be reality, the absolute referent; and then a narrative, which would be that of Luke; and then the narrative of the active participants, numbering them: narrative 1, 2, 3, 4, etc.? As a matter of fact, from the narrative of Acts, *i.e.*, from Luke's narrative to the supposed reality, we should say today that there is simply the relation of one *text* to another *text*. This is one of the crucial ideological problems which are raised, less perhaps in research than in groups concerned about the commitment of writing; it is the problem of the final signified: does a text possess in some way a final signified? And by scouring a text clean of its structures do we arrive, at a certain moment, at a final signified which, in the case of the realistic novel, would be "reality"?

Jacques Derrida's philosophical investigation has taken up in a revolutionary fashion this problem of the final signified, postulating that there is never ultimately, in the world, anything but the writing of a writing: a writing always finally refers to another writing, and the prospect of the signs is in a sense infinite. Consequently to describe systems of meaning by postulating a final signified is to side against the very nature of meaning. This reflection is today neither within my purpose nor my competence; but the realm which brings us together here, to wit Scripture, is a privileged domain for this problem, because, on the one hand, theologically, it is certain that a final signified is postulated: the metaphysical definition or the semantic definition of theology is to postulate the Last Signified; and because, on the other hand, the very notion of Scripture, the fact that the Bible is called Scripture, Writing, would orient us toward a more ambiguous comprehension of the problems, as if effectively, and theologically too, the base, the *princeps*, were still a Writing, and always a Writing.

2. *Catalysis*. In any case, this problem of the disconnection of the signifiers through summaries which seem to be projected in mirrors, is very important for a modern theory of literature. Our text is exceptionally dense in disconnections, in summaries, which are spaced out as if we were looking into a set of mirrors. There is a fascinating structural problem here which has not yet been carefully studied: this is the problem of what is called *catalysis*; in a narrative, there are several levels of necessity; the summaries show what one can remove or add: since a story hangs together through its summary, this means that we can "fill" this story; whence this term of *catalysis*; one can say that the story without its résumé, the integral story, is a sort of catalytic stage of a résumé state; there is a relation of filling between an empty structure and a full structure, and this movement is interesting to study, because it illustrates the play of structure. A narrative, on a certain level, is like a sentence. A sentence can be catalyzed, in principle, to infinity. I no longer recall which American linguist (Chomsky or someone of his school) has said as much, which is philosophically very fine: "We never speak anything but a single sentence, which only death comes to interrupt . . ." The structure of the sentence is such that you can

always add words, epithets, adjectives, subordinate clauses, or other main clauses, and never alter the structure of the sentence. Ultimately, if we today grant so much importance to language, it is because language, as it is now described, gives us the example of an object at once structured and infinite: there is in language the experience of an *infinite* structure (in the mathematical sense of the word); and the sentence is the very example of this: you can fill a sentence indefinitely; and, if you stop your sentences, if you close them, which has always been the great problem of rhetoric (as is testified to by the notions of *period*, of *clause*, which are operators of closure), it is solely under the pressure of contingences, because of breath, of memory, of fatigue, but never because of structure: no structural law compels you to close the sentence, and you can open it structurally to infinity. The problem of the résumé or summary is the same, shifted to the level of the narrative. The résumé proves that a story is in some sense endless: you can fill it to infinity; then why stop it at this particular moment? This is one of the problems which the analysis of narrative should permit us to approach.

3.   *The diagrammatic structure.* Further, in relation to our text, the disconnection of the summaries and their multiplicity (there are five summaries for a small extent of text) imply that there is for each summary a new circuit of destination. In other words, to multiply the summaries means to multiply the destinations of the message. This text from Acts, structurally—and I shall even be naive enough to say, phenomenologically—this text appears to be the privileged site of an intense multiplication, diffusion, dissemination, refraction of messages.

The same thing can be said on four successive levels; for instance the angel's order to Cornelius is spoken as an order given, as an order executed, as the narrative of that execution, and as a summary of the narrative of that execution; and the recipients obviously relay each other: the Spirit communicates to Peter and to Cornelius,

Peter communicates to Cornelius, Cornelius communicates to Peter, then Peter to the community of Jerusalem, and finally to us the readers. It has been said that most narratives are narratives of a quest, of a search in which a subject desires or searches for an object (this is the case of the narratives of miracles). In my opinion, and this is the structural originality of this text, its mainspring is not the quest, but communication, "trans-mission": the characters of the narrative are not actors but agents of transmission, agents of communication and diffusion. This is interesting: we see in a concrete and I should like to say "technical" fashion that the text presents what I should call a *diagrammatic* structure, in relation to its content. A diagram is a proportional analogy (which is moreover pleonastic, since *analogia* in Greek means *proportion*); it is not a figurative copy (it suffices to recall the diagrams in demography, in sociology, in economics); it is a form which has been illuminated by Jakobson: in the activity of language, the diagram is important, because at every moment language produces diagrammatic figures: it cannot literally copy (according to a complete *mimesis*) a content by a form, because there is no common measure between the content and the linguistic form; but what it can do is to produce diagrammatic figures; the example given by Jakobson is famous: the poetic diagram (for poetry is the site of the diagram) is the electoral slogan of General Eisenhower, when he was a candidate for the presidency: *I like Ike*; this is a diagram since the word *Ike* is enveloped in the affection of the word *like*. There is a diagrammatic relation between the sentence *I like Ike* and the content, to wit that General Eisenhower was enveloped by the love of his electors.

This diagrammatic structure is what we have in our text, for the text's content—and it is not we who are inventing it, since, once again, we are concerned with a text which I shall call anagogic, which gives its meaning itself—this content is the possibility of the diffusion of baptism. And the diagram is the diffusion of narrative by multiplication of summaries; in other words, there is a kind of diagrammatic refraction around the notion of limitless, vulgarized communication. Ultimately, what the narrative enacts diagrammatically is this idea of *limitlessness*. The fact that in so little space there should be four summaries of the same episode constitutes a diagrammatic image of the limitless character of grace. The theory of this "non-limit" is given by a narrative which enacts the "non-limit" of the summary. Consequently the "subject" of the text is the very idea of message; for structural analysis, this text has for its subject the message, it is a functionalization of language, of communication; moreover this is a theme of Pentecost (this is alluded to in the text). The subject is the communication and the diffusion of messages and languages. Structurally, as we have seen, the content of what Cornelius must ask Peter is not uttered: the angel does not say to Cornelius why he must send messengers in search of Peter. And now we apprehend the structural meaning of this absence, which I mentioned at the beginning: it is because, as a matter of fact, the message is its very form, it is its destination. Ultimately, what Cornelius must ask of Peter is not a veritable content, it is the communication with Peter. The content of the message is therefore the message itself; the destination of the message, *i.e.*, the Uncircumcised—*that* is the very content of the message.

These indications will no doubt seem *withdrawn* in relation to the text. My excuse is that the goal of the investigation, of the research, is not the explication or interpretation of a text, but the interrogation of this text (among others) with a view to the reconstitution of a general language of narrative. Obliged to speak about a text, and about only one, I could neither speak of the Structural Analysis of Narrative in general, nor structure this text in detail: I have sought a compromise, with all the disappointments which such a decision may involve; I have proceeded to a work of partial recension; I have sketched the structural dossier of a text, but for this work to find its whole meaning, one would have to unite this dossier with others, to pour this text into the immense corpus of the world's narratives.

1969; in *Exégèse et Herméneutique* (Éd. du Seuil), 1971

# Wrestling with the Angel: Textual Analysis of Genesis 32:23-33

---

²³That same night he rose, and taking his two wives and his two slave-girls and his eleven children he crossed the ford of the Jabbok. ²⁴He took them and sent them across the stream and sent all his possessions over too. ²⁵And Jacob was left alone.

And there was one that wrestled with him until daybreak ²⁶who, seeing that he could not master him, struck him in the socket of his hip, and Jacob's hip was dislocated as he wrestled with him. ²⁷He said, "Let me go, for day is breaking." But Jacob answered, "I will not let you go unless you bless me." ²⁸He then asked, "What is your name?" "Jacob," he replied. ²⁹He said, "Your name shall no longer be Jacob, but Israel, because you have been strong against God, you shall prevail against men." ³⁰Jacob then made this request, "I beg you, tell me your name," but he replied, "Why do you ask my name?" And he blessed him there.

³¹Jacob named the place Peniel, "Because I have seen God face to face," he said, "and I have survived". The sun rose as he left Peniel, limping because of his hip. ³²That is the reason why to this day the Israelites do not eat the sciatic nerve which is in the socket of the hip; because he had struck Jacob in the socket of the hip on the sciatic nerve. *

---

* The Jerusalem Bible (Doubleday), 1966.

The particulars—or the precautions—which will serve as an introduction to our analysis will in fact be largely negative. First of all, I must acknowledge that I shall not be providing any preliminary account of the principles, the perspectives, and the problems of the structural analysis of narrative: that analysis is certainly not a science, nor even a discipline (it is not taught), but in the context of the nascent semiology, it is an area of research which is beginning to be well known, to the point where one would risk an impression of redundance by offering its prolegomena on the occasion of each new analysis.[1] Furthermore, the structural analysis presented here will be anything but a pure one; of course I shall refer in essentials to the principles common to all the semiologists concerned with narrative, and even, in conclusion, shall show how our text sustains a very classical, even canonical structural analysis; this orthodox inquiry (from the point of view of the structural analysis of narrative) will be all the more justified in that we are dealing here with a mythic narrative which may have entered writing (Scripture) by an oral tradition; but I shall occasionally permit myself (and perhaps continuously, in an underhanded way) to orient my investigation toward an analysis with which I am more comfortable, Textual Analysis ("textual" is used here in reference to the present theory of the *text*, which is to be understood as a signifying production and not at all as a philological object, custodian of the Letter); this textual analysis seeks to "see" the text in its difference—which does not mean in its ineffable individuality, for such difference is "woven" in the known codes; for this analysis, the text is caught in an *open* network, which is the very infinity of language, itself structured without closure; textual analysis seeks to say, no longer where the text *comes from* (historical criticism), nor even *how* it is made (structural analysis), but how it is unmade, how it explodes, disseminates: according to what coded avenues it *goes*. Finally, a last precaution, in order to forestall any disappointment: there will be no question in the text which follows of a methodological con-

---

[1] See the preceding essay.

frontation between structural or textual analysis and Biblical exegesis: I should have no competence there whatever.[2] I shall confine
myself to analyzing the text of Genesis 32 (traditionally known as
"Jacob Wrestles with the Angel"), as if I were in the first stage of
an investigation (which is indeed the case): it is not a "result" I
offer here, nor even a "method" (which would be too ambitious
and would imply a "scientific" view of the text I do not have), but
simply a "way of proceeding."

## 1. Sequential analysis

Structural analysis includes by and large three types—or three
objects—of analysis, or, to put it differently, involves three tasks:
1. to proceed to the inventory and classification of the "psychological," biographical, characterial, social attributes of the characters involved in the narrative (age, sex, external qualities, social
situation or rank, etc.); structurally, this is the instance of *indices*
(notations, of infinitely varied expression, which serve to transmit
a signified—for example "nervousness," "grace," "power"—which
the analyst names in his metalanguage, it being understood that
the metalinguistic term may very well not figure directly in the
text, which will never use "nervousness" or "grace," etc.: this is
the case here); if we establish a homology between the narrative
and the (linguistic) sentence, the *index* corresponds to the adjective,
to the *epithet* (which, let us not forget, was once a figure of rhetoric):
this is what we might call *indicial analysis*; 2. to proceed to the
inventory and classification of the *functions* of the characters: what
they do according to their narrative status, their quality as subject
of a constant action: the Sender, the Seeker, the Emissary, etc.;
at the level of the sentence, this would correspond to the *present
participle*: it is the *actantial analysis* of which A. J. Greimas was the
first to offer a theory; 3. to proceed to the inventory and classifi-

[2] I want to express my gratitude to Jean Alexandre, whose exegetic, linguistic, socio-
historical competence and whose openness of mind have helped me understand the text
here analyzed; many of his ideas will appear in this analysis; only the fear of having distorted
them keeps me from acknowledging them on each occasion.

cation of *actions*: this is the level of *verbs*; these narrative actions
are organized, as we know, in sequences, in series apparently organized according to a pseudo-logical schema (such logic is purely
empirical, cultural, and results from an experience which may be
ancestral, but not from reasoning): this is *sequential analysis*.

Our text lends itself, if briefly, to indicial analysis. The combat
which is staged can be read as an index of Jacob's strength (attested
in other episodes of the chronicle of this hero); the index leads
toward an anagogical meaning, which is the (invincible) strength
of God's Chosen. Actantial analysis is also possible; but since our
text is essentially composed of actions which are apparently contingent, it would be better to proceed directly to a sequential (or
actional) analysis of the episode, merely adding in conclusion a few
remarks on the actantial. We shall divide the text (and I believe
this is not forcing matters) into three sequences: 1. the Crossing;
2. the Wrestling; 3. the Namings.

1.   *The Crossing* (vv. 23–25). Let us immediately give the sequential schema of this episode; this is a double schema, or at the
very least, one may say, "strabismic" (what is at stake will be
immediately apparent):

| | | | |
|---|---|---|---|
| I | rising | collecting | cross |
| | 23 | 23 | 23 |
| II | collecting | sending across | remaining alone |
| | 24 | 24 | 25 |

Let us note at once that structurally, *rising* is a simple *operator of
beginning*; we might say, as a short cut, that by *rising* we are to
understand not only that Jacob gets under way, but also that *the
discourse gets under way*; the beginning of a narrative, of a discourse,
of a text, is a very sensitive place: *where to begin?* The *said* must be
wrenched away from the *not-said*: whence a whole rhetoric of beginning *markers*. Yet the most important thing is that the two
sequences (or subsequences) seem in a state of redundance (this

may be habitual in the discourse of that time: a piece of information is given and repeated; but our rule is reading, not the historical, philological determination of the text: we are not reading the text in its "truth," but in its "production"—which is not its "determination"); paradoxically, moreover (for usually redundance serves to homogenize, to clarify, and to strengthen a message), when we read it after two thousand years of Aristotelian rationalism (since Aristotle is the principal theoretician of classical narrative), the redundance of the two subsequences creates an abrasion, a grating of readability. The sequential schema can in fact be read in two ways: *a.* Jacob himself crosses the ford—if need be after having made several such trips—and therefore the wrestling occurs on the left bank of the stream (he is coming from the North), after having *definitively crossed over*; in this case, *sending across* is to be read: *crossing, oneself*; *b.* Jacob sends across but does not cross, himself; he wrestles on the right bank of the Jabbok *before crossing*, in a rearguard position. Let us not look for a *true* interpretation (our very hesitation will perhaps seem ridiculous in the eyes of the exegetes); let us acknowledge rather two different pressures of readability: *a.* if Jacob remains alone *before* having crossed the Jabbok, we are led to a "folkloristic" reading of the episode; indeed the mythic reference is overwhelming here, one that desires a trial by combat (for example, with a dragon or the genius of the river) be imposed upon the hero before he overcomes the obstacle, *i.e.*, *so that*, being victorious, he can overcome it; *b.* if, on the contrary, Jacob (and his tribe) having crossed, he remains alone on the right side of the stream (that of the country where he wants to go), the crossing is without structural finality; on the other hand, it acquires a religious finality: if Jacob is alone, it is not in order to regulate and obtain the crossing, it is to *mark himself* by solitude (this is the familiar *setting apart* of the chosen of God). A historical circumstance here augments the undecidability of the two interpretations: the question for Jacob is to return home, to enter the land of Canaan: crossing the Jordan would then be more understandable than crossing the Jabbok; we find ourselves, in short, confronting the crossing of a neutral site; this crossing is "strong" if Jacob must make it against the genius of the place; it is indifferent if what matters is Jacob's solitude, his mark; but perhaps we have here the mingled vestige of two stories, or at least of two narrative instances: one, the more "archaic" (in the simple stylistic sense of the term), makes the crossing itself a test; the other, more "realistic," gives a "geographical" expression to Jacob's journey by mentioning the places he passes through (without attaching a mythic value to them).

If we project back onto this double sequence what occurs subsequently, to wit the Wrestling and the Naming, the double reading continues, coherent to the end, in each of its two versions; let us consider the diagram again:

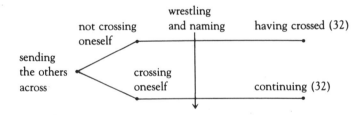

If the Combat separates the "not crossing" and the "having crossed" (folkloristic, mythic reading), the mutation of Names corresponds to the very project of every etymological saga; if, on the contrary, the Combat is merely a halt between a position of immobility (of meditation, of election) and a continuing movement, the mutation of the Name has the value of a spiritual renaissance (of "baptism"). We can summarize all this by saying that, in this first episode, there is sequential readability but cultural ambiguity. The theologian would no doubt be distressed by this indecision; the exegete would acknowledge it, hoping that some element, factual or argumentative, would allow him to bring it to an end; the textual analyst, it must be said, if I may judge by my own impression, will savor this sort of *friction* between two intelligibilities.

2.   *The Combat* (vv. 25–30). Here again, for this second episode,

we must start from an indetermination (I am not saying: a doubt) of readability—we know that textual analysis is based on *reading* rather than on the objective structure of the text, which is more the concern of structural analysis. This indetermination has to do with the interchangeable character of the pronouns which refer to the two partners of the wrestling match: a style which a purist would call *confused*, but whose vagueness no doubt raised no difficulty for Hebrew syntax. Who is "one"? Remaining on the level of v. 26, is this "one" who does not manage to overcome Jacob, or Jacob who cannot manage to overcome this "one"? Is the "he" of "he could not master him" (26) the same as the "he" of "he said" (27)? Doubtless it is all eventually clarified, but this requires a kind of retroactive reasoning, of the syllogistic type: You have defeated God. Now, he who speaks to you is the one whom you have defeated. Hence he who speaks to you is God. The identification of the partners is oblique, the readability is *deviated* (whence occasional commentaries which verge on misapprehension; this one for instance: "He wrestles with the Angel of the Lord and, defeated, obtains thereby the certainty that God is with him").

Structurally, this amphibology, even if it is subsequently illuminated, is not without significance; it is not, in our opinion (which, I repeat, is that of a contemporary reader), a simple awkwardness of expression due to a crude, archaizing style; it is linked to a paradoxical structure of the combat (paradoxical with regard to the stereotype of mythical combats). In order to appreciate the paradox in its structural *finesse*, let us imagine for a moment an endoxical (and no longer paradoxical) reading of the episode: A wrestles with B, but does not manage to defeat him; in order to gain the victory at all costs, A then resorts to an exceptional technique, whether this is an illegal and even forbidden hold (the forearm chop in our wrestling matches) or a hold which, remaining legal, supposes a secret knowledge, a "ploy" (as was the maneuver of Guy de Jarnac, who in 1547 defeated his opponent by an unlooked-for hold); such a hold, generally said to be "decisive" *in the very logic of narrative*, accords victory to the wrestler who uses it: the mark of which this hold is structurally the object cannot be reconciled with its ineffectiveness: it *must*, by the god of narrative, succeed. Now, it is the contrary which occurs here: the decisive hold fails; A, who has employed it, is not the victor: this is the structural paradox. The sequence then takes an unexpected course:

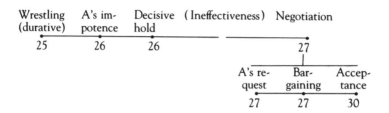

It will be noted that A (it is of little consequence, from the structural point of view, whether this is *one*, *a man*, *God*, or *the Angel*) is not, strictly speaking, defeated, but *checked*; for this check to be regarded as a defeat, there must be the addition of a *time limit*: this is daybreak ("for day is breaking," 27); this notation takes up from v. 25 ("until daybreak"), but this time in the explicit context of a mythic structure: the theme of the combat by night is structurally justified by the fact that at a certain moment, foreseen ahead of time (as is the sunrise, and as is the length of a boxing match), the rules of the combat will no longer be valid: the structural play will cease, the supernatural play as well (the "demons" withdraw at dawn). We thereby see that it is in a "regular" combat that the sequence establishes an unexpected readability, a logical surprise: the one who possesses the knowledge, the secret, the special hold, is nonetheless defeated. In other words, the sequence itself, entirely actional, entirely anecdotal as it is, has its function to *unbalance* the opponents in the combat, not only by the unexpected victory of one over the other, but above all (let us note the *formal* delicacy of this surprise) by the illogical, *inverted* character of this victory; in other words (and we recognize here an eminently structural term, familiar to linguists) the struggle, as it is inverted in its unexpected outcome, *marks* one of the combatants: the weaker defeats the stronger, *in exchange for which* he is marked (on the hip).

It is plausible (but here we depart somewhat from pure structural analysis and approach textual analysis, which is a vision *without barriers* of meanings) to fill this schema of the mark (of the imbalance) by contents of an ethnological type. The structural meaning of the episode, let us once more recall, is as follows: a situation of balance (the struggle at its outset)—such a situation is necessary for any marking: the Ignatian ascesis, for example, has for its function to establish the *indifference* of the will, which permits the divine mark, choice, election—is disturbed by the undue victory of one of the combatants: there is an inversion of the mark, there is a counter-mark. Then let us turn to the family configuration: traditionally, the line of brothers is in principle balanced (they are all located on the same level in relation to the parents); equigeniture is normally unbalanced by the right of primogeniture: the oldest is marked; now, in the story of Jacob, there is an inversion of mark, there is a counter-mark: it is the youngest who supplants the oldest (Genesis 27:36), taking his older brother by the heel to turn time backward: it is the youngest, Jacob, who marks himself. Jacob having just been marked in his struggle with God, we can say in a sense that A (God) is the substitute of the oldest Brother, who is once again defeated by the youngest: the conflict with Esau is *displaced* (every symbol is a *displacement*; if the "struggle with the Angel" is symbolic, it is because it has displaced something). The commentary—for which I am inadequately equipped—would no doubt have to enlarge, here, the interpretation of this *inversion of the mark*: by placing it either in a historico-economic field—Esau is the eponym of the Edomites; there were economic links between the Edomites and the Israelites; perhaps what has been figured here is an overthrow of the alliance, the inception of a new league of interests?—or in the symbolic field (in the psychoanalytic sense of *symbolic*)—the Old Testament seems to be the world less of the Fathers than of the Enemy Brothers: the elder are ousted in favor of the younger; Freud has pointed out in the myth of the Enemy

Brothers the narcissistic theme of *the smallest difference*: the blow on the hip, on that thin tendon—is that not just such a *smallest difference*? Whatever the case, in this universe, God marks the youngest, he acts as a counter-nature: his (structural) function is to constitute a *counter-marker*.

To be done with this extremely rich episode of the Struggle, of the Mark, I should like to make a semiologist's observation. We have just seen that in the binary opposition of combatants, which is perhaps the binary of the Enemy Brothers, the younger is marked both by the inversion of the expected relation of forces and by a bodily sign, lameness (which cannot fail to remind us of Oedipus, the Swollen Foot, the Lame One). Now, the mark is a creator of meaning; in the phonological representation of language, the "equality" of the paradigm is unbalanced to the benefit of a marked element, by the presence of a feature which remains absent from its correlative and oppositional term: by marking Jacob (Israel), God (or Narrative) permits an anagogic development of meaning: he creates the formal conditions for the functioning of a new "language," of which Israel's election is the "message," God is a logothete, Jacob is here a "morpheme" of the new language.

3.  *The Namings or Mutations* (vv. 28–33). The object of the last sequence is the exchange of names, *i.e.*, the promotion of a new status, of new powers; Naming is obviously linked to Blessing: to bless (to receive the homage of a kneeling suppliant) and to name are a suzerain's actions. There are two namings:

| I | Request for name, from God to Jacob | Jacob's answer | Result: Mutation |
|---|---|---|---|
| | 28 | 28 | 29 |

| II | Request for name, from Jacob to God | Indirect answer | (Result: Decision) |
|---|---|---|---|
| | 30 | 30 | ( ) |

Mutation: Peniel
(31)

The mutation concerns Names; but as a matter of fact, it is the entire episode which functions as *the creation of a multiple trace*: in

Jacob's body, in the status of the Brothers, in Jacob's name, in the name of the place, in eating (the creation of an alimentary taboo: the whole story can also be interpreted *a minimo* as the mythic foundation of a taboo). The three sequences we have analyzed are homological: in all three there is a question of a *crossing*: of the place, of the parental line, of the name, of the alimentary rite: all this remaining very close to a language activity, to a transgression of the rules of meaning.

Such is the sequential (or actional) analysis of our episode. We have attempted, as is evident, to remain on the level of structure, *i.e.*, of the systematic correlation of the terms denoting an action; if we have happened to mention certain possible meanings, this has not been in order to discuss the probability of these meanings, but rather to show how structure "disseminates" contents—which each reading can deal with on its own. Our object is not the philological or historical document, custodian of a truth to be found, but the text's *signifying* volume.

## 2. Structural analysis

The structural analysis of narrative having already been partially constituted (by Propp, Lévi-Strauss, Greimas, Bremond), I should like, in closing—and perhaps more modestly—to confront our text with two practices of structural analysis, in order to show the interest of these practices—though my own work is oriented in a somewhat different direction[3]—: Greimas's actantial analysis and Propp's functional analysis.

1. *Actantial analysis.* The actantial grid conceived by Greimas[4]—to be employed, as its creator himself has said, with discretion and flexibility—distributes the characters, the actors of a narrative, into

---

[3] My work on Balzac's *Sarrasine* (*S/Z*, Paris: Éd. du Seuil, 1970; English trans., New York: Hill & Wang, 1975) belongs more to textual than to structural analysis.

[4] See especially A. J. Greimas, *Sémantique structurale*, Paris: Larousse, 1966, and *Du sens*, Paris: Éd. du Seuil, 1970.

six formal classes of actants, defined by what they do according to their status and not by what they are psychologically (the actant can unite several characters, but also a single character can unite several actants; a character can also be represented by an inanimate entity). The Struggle with the Angel constitutes a familiar episode of mythic narratives: the overcoming of an obstacle, the Ordeal. At the level of this episode (since, for the whole chronicle of Jacob, this might be different), the actants are "filled" as follows: Jacob is the *Subject* (subject of the demand, of the search, of the action); the *Object* of this same demand, search, action) is the crossing of the guarded, forbidden place, the stream, the Jabbok; the *Sender*, who puts into circulation the stake of the search (to wit, the crossing of the stream), is obviously God; the *Receiver* is again Jacob (two actants are here present in one and the same figure); the *Opponent* (the one or ones who hamper the Subject in his search) is God himself (it is he who, in mythic terms, guards the crossing); the *Helper* (the one or ones who assist the Subject) is Jacob, who helps himself by his own strength, which is legendary (an indicial feature, as we have seen).

The paradox, or at least the anomic character, of the formula is immediately apparent: that the subject be identified with the receiver is banal enough: that the subject be his own helper is rarer; this usually happens in "voluntarist" narratives and novels; but that the sender be the opponent is extremely rare; there is only one type of narrative which can stage this paradoxical formula: narratives which relate a blackmail; of course, if the opponent were merely the (temporary) custodian of the stake, there would be nothing extraordinary about it: it is the opponent's role to defend the ownership of the object which the hero seeks to conquer: as in the case of the dragon which guards a crossing; but here, as in any blackmail, God, at the same time that he guards the stream, dispenses the mark, the privilege. As we see, the actantial formula of our text is far from being conciliatory: it is structurally very audacious—which corresponds to the "scandal" represented by God's defeat.

2. *Functional analysis*. As we know, Propp was the first[5] to have established the structure of the folktale by dividing it up into *functions*,[6] or narrative actions; according to Propp, the functions are stable elements, their number is limited (to about thirty), their concatenation is always the same, even if certain functions are occasionally missing from one narrative or another. Now, it so happens—as we shall see below—that our text honors quite perfectly a portion of the functional schema revealed by Propp: this author could not have conceived of a more convincing application of his discovery.

In a preparatory section of the folktale as analyzed by Propp, there must be an instance of the Hero's absence; and this is just what occurs in the chronicle of Jacob: Isaac sends Jacob far from his country, to Laban (Genesis 28:2,5). Our episode actually begins with no. 15 of Propp's narrative functions; we shall therefore encode it in the following manner, showing at each stage the impressive parallelism between Propp's schema and the Genesis narrative:

| *Propp & the folktale* | *Genesis* |
|---|---|
| 15. Transfer from one place to another (by birds, horses, boats, etc.). | Setting out from the North, from the Aramaeans, from Laban's house, Jacob journeys home to his father (29:1, Jacob sets out). |
| 16. Combat of the Hero against the Enemy. | This is our sequence of the Combat (32:25–28). |
| 17. Marking of the Hero (usually a mark on his body, but in other cases, merely the gift of a jewel, of a ring). | Jacob is marked on the hip (32:27). |

[5] Vladimir Propp, *Morphologie du conte*, Paris: Éd. du Seuil, 1970.

[6] The word "function" is unfortunately ambiguous in all cases; we used it initially to define the actantial analysis which assesses a character by his role in the action (which is precisely his "function"); in Propp's terminology, there is a displacement from the character to the action itself, apprehended as it is *linked* to the actions surrounding it.

18. Victory of the Hero, defeat of the    Jacob's victory (32:26).
      Enemy.

19. Liquidation of disaster or of some lack:    After having succeeded in crossing
      the disaster or the lack had been pos-    Peniel (32:32), Jacob reaches She-
      ited in the hero's initial absence: this    chem in Canaan (33:18).
      absence is done away with.

There are other points of parallelism. In Propp's function 14, the Hero receives a magical object; for Jacob, this talisman is doubtless the blessing he tricks his blind father into giving him (Genesis 27). Further, Propp's function 29 stages the Hero's transfiguration (for example, the Beast is transformed into a handsome nobleman); this transfiguration seems to be present in the change of Name (Genesis 32:29) and the rebirth it implies. No doubt the narrative model assigns God the role of the Enemy (his *structural* role: no question of a psychological role): in our episode of Genesis can be read a veritable stereotype of the folktale: the difficult crossing of a ford guarded by a hostile genius of the place. Another analogy with the tale is that in both cases the motivations of the characters (their reasons for acting) are not indicated: the ellipsis of notations is not a phenomenon of style, it is a structural, pertinent characteristic of the narration. Structural analysis, in the strict sense of the term, would therefore conclude that Wrestling with the Angel is a true fairy tale—since, according to Propp, all fairy tales belong to the same structure, the one he has described.

As we see, what might be called the structural exploitation of our episode is quite possible: it is even indispensable. Yet I shall say, in conclusion, that what most interests me in this famous passage is not the "folklore" model, but the frictions, the breaks, the discontinuities of readability, the juxtaposition of narrative entities which manage to escape an explicit logical articulation: we are dealing here (at least, for me, this is the relish of the reading) with a sort of *metonymic montage*: the themes (Crossing, Struggle, Naming, Alimentary Rite) are *combined* and not "developed." This abruptness, this asyndetic character of the narrative is well expressed by Hosea (12:3): "In the very womb he supplanted his brother, in maturity he wrestled against God. He wrestled with the Angel and beat him." Metonymic logic, as we know, is that of the unconscious. It is therefore perhaps in this direction that we should continue our research, *i.e.*, I repeat, the *reading* of the text, its dissemination, not its truth. Of course, we then risk weakening the economico-historical range of the episode (it certainly exists, on the level of the exchanges of tribes and of the problems of power); but it also reinforces the symbolic explosion of the text (which is not necessarily of a religious order). The problem, at least the one I raise for myself, is in effect not to reduce the Text to a signified, whatever it may be (historical, economic, folkloric, or kerygmatic), but to keep its signifying power open.

In *Analyse structurale et Exégèse biblique*
(Labor et Fides), 1972

# Textual Analysis of a Tale by Edgar Allan Poe

## THE TEXTUAL ANALYSIS

Structural analysis of narrative is in the process of its own elaboration. All our investigations have one and the same scientific origin: semiology, or the science of significations; but they already reveal among themselves (and this is a good thing) divergences, according to the critical scrutiny each brings to bear on the scientific status of semiology, *i.e.*, on its own discourse. These (constructive) divergences can be unified within two major tendencies: according to the first, analysis, confronting all the world's narratives, attempts to establish a *narrative model*, obviously a formal one, a structure or a grammar of Narrative, from which (once elaborated) each particular narrative will be analyzed in terms of its departures; according to the second tendency, the narrative is immediately subsumed (at least when it lends itself to being so) within the notion of "Text," space, process of significations under way, in a word *signifying process* (*signifiance*: a word to which we shall return), which is observed not as a finite, closed-off product, but as a production in the process of being made, "grafted" onto other texts, other codes (it is the *intertextual*), articulated thus in terms of society, of History, not according to determinist paths, but to citational ones. Hence, in a certain way, we must distinguish *structural analysis* from *textual analysis*,[1] though we are not prepared to declare them to be antagonistic: structural analysis, strictly speaking, is chiefly applied to oral narrative (to myth); textual analysis, which we shall attempt to perform in the following pages, applies exclusively to written narrative.

Textual analysis does not attempt to *describe* the structure of a work; it is not a matter of recording a structure, but rather of producing a mobile structuration of the text (a structuration which shifts from reader to reader down through History), of staying within the signifying volume of the work, within its *signifying process*. Textual analysis does not seek to know by what the text is determined (collected as the final term of a causality), but rather how the text explodes and scatters. Hence we shall take a narrative text, a tale, and shall read it, as slowly as will be necessary, stopping as often as we must (*deliberation* is a crucial dimension of our work), trying to locate and to classify *without rigor* not all the meanings of the text (which would be impossible, for the text is open *ad infinitum*: no reader, no subject, no science can exhaust the text), but the forms, the codes which make meanings possible. We shall locate the *avenues* of meaning. Our goal is not to find *the* meaning, nor even *a* meaning of the text, and our work is not related to a literary criticism of the hermeneutic type (which attempts to interpret the text according to the truth it regards as hidden within it), as is for instance Marxist or psychoanalytic criticism. Our goal is ultimately to conceive, to imagine, to experience the plurality of the text, the open-endedness of its *signifying process*. The stake of this work is therefore not limited, evidently, to the academic handling of the text (albeit overtly methodological), nor even to literature in general; it borders on a theory, a

---

[1] I have attempted the textual analysis of a whole narrative (which cannot be undertaken here for reasons of space) in my book S/Z (1970).

practice, a choice which are caught up in the battle between men and signs.

In order to proceed to the textual analysis of a narrative, we shall follow a certain number of operational procedures (let us say, a certain number of elementary rules of manipulation, rather than methodological principles: that phrase would be too ambitious and above all ideologically questionable, insofar as "method" too frequently postulates a positivistic result). We shall reduce these procedures to four briefly described accounts, preferring to let the theory function within the analysis of the text itself. For the time being, we shall say only what is necessary in order to *begin* as quickly as possible the analysis of the tale we have chosen.

1.  We shall segment the text I am proposing for our study into contiguous and generally very short fragments (a sentence, a phrase, at most a group of three or four sentences); we shall number these fragments starting from 1 (for some ten pages, there are 150 of them). These segments are units of reading, which is why I have proposed calling them *lexias*.[2] A lexia is obviously a textual signifier; but since our goal here is not to observe signifiers (our goal is not stylistic) but meanings, our segmentation need not be theoretically founded (being in *discourse* and not in *language*, we must not expect to find an easily perceived homology between signifier and signified; we do not know how one corresponds to the other, and consequently we must be willing to segment the signifier without being guided by the underlying segmentation of the signified). In short, the segmentation of the narrative text into lexias is purely empirical, dictated by a concern for convenience: the lexia is an arbitrary product, it is simply a segment within which we observe the distribution of meanings; what surgeons would call an operational field: the useful lexia is the one in which only one, two, or three meanings occur (superimposed within the *volume* of the text fragment).

---

[2] For a closer analysis of the notion of *lexia*, as for the operational procedures which follow, I am obliged to refer to *S/Z*.

2.   For each lexia, we shall observe the meanings which are
generated by it. By *meaning*, we obviously understand not the meanings of the words or of the groups of words which the dictionary
and grammar, in short the knowledge of our language, would account for adequately. We understand, rather, the *connotations* of
the lexia, the secondary meanings. These connotative meanings
may be *associations* (for instance, the physical description of a character, extending over several sentences, may have only one signified
of connotation, that character's "nervousness," though the word
does not figure on the level of denotation); they may also be *relations*, resulting from the juxtaposition of two sometimes quite
diverse places in the text (an action begun here can be completed
much farther on). Our lexias will be, we may say, the finest possible
sieves, by which we shall "skim off" the meanings, the connotations.

3.   Our analysis will be gradual: we shall proceed step by step
through the text, at least postulatively, since, for reasons of space,
we shall be able to give only two fragments of analysis here. This
means that we shall not aim at treating the large (rhetorical) masses
of the text; we shall not construct a map of the text, and we shall
not be tracing its thematics; in a word, we shall not be doing an
*explication de texte*, unless we give the word "explication" its etymological meaning, unless we *unfold* the text, the layering of the
text. We shall allow our analysis to follow the text *as read*; quite
simply, this reading will be *filmed in slow motion*. This way of proceeding is theoretically important: it signifies that we do not aim
at reconstituting the text's structure, but at following its structuration, and that we regard the structuration of reading as more
important than that of composition (a rhetorical and classical notion).

4.   Finally, we shall not be unduly concerned if, in our account,
we "forget" some meanings. Forgetting meaning is in a sense part
of reading: what matters to us is to show certain *departures*, not

arrivals, of meaning (actually, what is meaning but a departure?). What establishes the text is not an internal, closed, accountable structure, but the *opening* of the text into other texts, other codes, other signs; what makes the text is the intertextual. We are beginning to glimpse (through other sciences) that research must gradually become familiar with the conjunction of two notions which for a very long time were regarded as contradictory: the notion of structure and the notion of combinative infinity; the reconciliation of these two postulations is now forced upon us because language, which we are getting to know better, is both infinite and structured.

These remarks are, I believe, sufficient for us to begin the analysis of the text (we must always yield to the text's impatience, never forgetting, whatever the imperatives of our study, that the *pleasure* of the text is our law). The text chosen is a short narrative by Edgar Allan Poe, "The Facts in the Case of M. Valdemar," which I have read in Baudelaire's translation: *La Vérité sur le cas de M. Valdemar.* My choice—at least consciously, for perhaps it is really my unconscious which has made the choice—has been dictated by two didactic considerations: I needed a very short text in order to be able to master entirely its signifying surface (the sequence of lexias), and one that was symbolically very dense, so that the text analyzed might touch us continuously, beyond any particularism: who would not be touched by a text whose declared "subject" is death?

I must add, in all frankness, that in analyzing the signifying process of a text, we shall deliberately refrain from considering certain problems; we shall not speak of the author, Poe, nor of the literary history to which he belongs; we shall not take into account the fact that our work will be performed upon a translation: we shall take the text as is, as we read it, without concerning ourselves to know if, in a university, it is the province of students of American literature rather than of students of French or of philosophers. This does not necessarily mean that these problems will not pass into our analysis; on the contrary, they will, quite literally, *pass*: the analysis is a *crossing* of the text; these problems can be located as cultural *citations*, as departures of codes, not as determinations.

One last word, perhaps by way of exorcism: the text we are about to analyze is neither lyrical nor political, it speaks neither of love nor of society, it speaks of death. Which is to say that we must lift one form of censorship: the form which is attached to the *sinister*. We shall do so by convincing ourselves that any censorship stands for all the rest: to speak of death outside any religion is to lift both the religious ban and the rationalist one.

## ANALYSIS OF LEXIAS 1 TO 17

**(1)**   *The Facts in the Case of M. Valdemar*

**(2)**   Of course I shall not pretend to consider it any matter for wonder, that the extraordinary case of M. Valdemar has excited discussion. It would have been a miracle had it not—especially under the circumstances. **(3)**   Through the desire of all parties concerned, to keep the affair from the public, at least for the present, or until we had further opportunities for investigation—through our endeavors to effect this— **(4)**   a garbled or exaggerated account made its way into society, and became the source of many unpleasant misrepresentations, and, very naturally, of a great deal of disbelief.

**(5)**   It is now rendered necessary that I give the *facts*—as far as I comprehend them myself. **(6)**   They are, succinctly, these:

**(7)**   My attention, for the last three years, had been repeatedly drawn to the subject of Mesmerism; **(8)**   and, about nine months ago, it occurred to me, quite suddenly, that in the series of experiments made hitherto, **(9)**   there had been a very remarkable and most unaccountable omission: **(10)**—no person had as yet been mesmerized *in articulo mortis*. **(11)**   It remained to be seen, **(12)**   first, whether in such condition, there existed in the patient any susceptibility to the magnetic influence; **(13)**   secondly, whether, if any existed, it was impaired or increased by the condition; **(14)**   thirdly, to what extent, or for how long a period, the encroachments of Death might be arrested by the process. **(15)**   There were other points to be ascertained, **(16)**   but these most excited my curiosity, (17)—the last in especial, from the immensely important character of its consequences.

(1)   *"The Facts in* [la vérité sur—*the truth about*—in Baudelaire's translation] *the Case of M. Valdemar"*
The function of titles has not been properly studied, at least from a structural point of view. What can be immediately said is that society, for commercial motives, needing to assimilate the text to a product, to a commodity, requires *markers*: the title's function is to mark the beginning of the text, *i.e.*, to constitute the text as a commodity. Thus every title has several simultaneous meanings, of which at least two are: 1. what it utters, linked to the contingency of what follows it; 2. the announcement itself that a piece of literature will follow (*i.e.*, in fact, a commodity); in other words, the title always has a double function: as utterance and as deixis.

   *a.*   To announce a truth is to stipulate that there is an enigma. The posing (or position) of the enigma results (on the level of signifiers): from the word *truth*; from the word *case* (what is exceptional, hence marked, hence signifying, and consequently whose meaning must be found); from the definite article *the* (there is only one truth, hence all the work of the text is to pass through this strait gate); from the cataphoric form implied by the title: what follows will effect what is announced, the solution of the enigma is already announced; it will be noted that the English says: *"The facts in the case . . ."*: the signified sought by Poe is of an empirical order, that sought by the French translator (Baudelaire) is hermeneutic: the truth then refers to the exact facts, but also perhaps to their meaning. Be that as it may, we shall code this first meaning of the lexia: *Enigma, position* (the *Enigma* is the general name of a code, its *position* is merely one of its terms).

   *b.*   the truth could be spoken without being announced, without any reference being made to the word. If we speak of what we are going to say, if we double the language into two layers, the first of which tops the second, we are in fact resorting to a metalanguage. Here, then, is the presence of the *metalinguistic* code.

c.   This metalinguistic announcement has an *aperitive* function: the reader's appetite is to be whetted (a procedure akin to "suspense"). The narrative is a commodity, whose proposition is preceded by a sales pitch. This *appetizer* is a term of the narrative code (rhetoric of narration).

d.   A proper name must always be carefully examined, for it is, so to speak, the prince of signifiers; its connotations are rich, social, and symbolic. We may read in the name *Valdemar* at least the two following connotations: 1. presence of a socio-ethnic code: is this a German name? Slavic? In any case, not Anglo-Saxon; this little enigma, here formulated implicitly, will be solved in no. 19 (Valdemar is a Pole); 2. "Valdemar" is "vale of the sea"; the oceanic abyss, the submarine depths, a theme dear to Poe: the gulf refers to what is doubly outside nature, underwater and underground. Hence there is here, from the analytical viewpoint, the trace of two codes: a socio-ethnic code and a (or the) symbolic code (we shall return to these codes a little later).

e.   Saying "M(*onsieur*) Valdemar" is not the same thing as saying "Valdemar." In many tales, Poe uses simple first names (Ligeia, Eleonora, Morella). The presence of this *Monsieur* involves an effect of social reality, of the historically real: the hero is socialized, he belongs to a specific society, in which he is provided with a civil status. Hence we must note: social code.

**(2)**   *Of course I shall not pretend to consider it any matter for wonder, that the extraordinary case of M. Valdemar has excited discussion. It would have been a miracle had it not—especially under the circumstances.*

a.   The obvious function of this sentence (and those immediately following) is to arouse the reader's expectations, and this is why they are apparently insignificant: what we want is the solution to the enigma posed in the title (the "truth"), but even the exposition of this enigma is delayed. Hence we must code: delay in posing (in the position of) the enigma.

*b.* Same connotation as in (1) *c*: the reader's appetite is to be whetted (narrative code).

*c.* The word *extraordinary* is ambiguous: it refers to what departs from the norm, but not necessarily from nature (if the case remains "medical"), but it can also refer to what is supernatural, to what has become a transgression (this is the "fantastic"—the "extraordinary"—element in Poe's tales). The word's ambiguity is significant here: the story will be a horrible one (outside the limits of nature) and yet one covered by a scientific alibi (connoted here by "discussion," a scientist's word). This combination is in fact cultural: the mixture of the strange and the scientific reached its apogee in that part of the nineteenth century to which Poe belongs: people were concerned to make scientific observations of the supernatural (magnetism, spiritualism, telepathy, etc.); the supernatural assumes the rationalistic, scientific alibi; this is the *cri du coeur* of that positivistic age: if only we could believe *scientifically* in immortality! This cultural code, which we shall here, for simplicity's sake, call a scientific code, will have great importance throughout the narrative.

(3) *Through the desire of all parties concerned, to keep the affair from the public, at least for the present, or until we had further opportunities for investigation—through our endeavors to effect this—*

*a.* The same scientific code, continued by the word "investigation" (also a detective word: we know the success of the detective novel in the second half of the nineteenth century, starting (precisely) with Poe: the important thing here, ideologically and structurally, is the conjunction of the code of the detective enigma and the code of science—of scientific discourse—which proves that structural analysis can readily cooperate with ideological analysis).

*b.* The motives of the secret are not divulged; they may proceed from two different codes, present together in our reading (to read is also to imagine, in silence, what is unspoken): 1. the scientific-deontological code: Poe and the doctors, out of professional discretion, are reluctant to make public a phenomenon which has no scientific explanation; 2. the symbolic code: there is a taboo on "living Death": it is not spoken of because it is horrible. It should be said at once (though we must return to it subsequently and insistently) that these two codes are *undecidable* (we cannot choose one over the other), and it is this very undecidability which constitutes the good narrative.

c. From the point of view of narrative *actions* (this is the first one we have encountered), a sequence is initiated here: "to keep hidden" logically (or pseudo-logically) implies certain consequent operations (for instance: to disclose). Hence we must posit here the first term of an actional sequence: *to keep hidden*, and we shall discover what follows it later on.

**(4)** *a garbled or exaggerated account made its way into society, and became the source of many unpleasant misrepresentations, and, very naturally, of a great deal of disbelief.*

a. The demand for truth, *i.e.*, the enigma, has already been posited twice (by the word "truth" and by the expression "extraordinary case"). Here the enigma is posited a third time (to posit an enigma, in structural terms, means to utter: *there is an enigma*), by alleging the error to which it has given rise: the error, posited here, retroactively justifies, by anaphora, the title (*"La vérité sur . . ."*). The redundancy enforced on the *posing* (*position*) of the enigma (that there is an enigma is repeated in several ways) has an aperitive value: the reader is to be excited, and customers procured for the narrative.

b. In the actional sequence "to hide," a second term appears: it is the effect of secrecy, distortion, mistaken opinion, accusation of mystification.

**(5)** *It is now rendered necessary that I give the facts—as far as I comprehend them myself.*

a. The emphasis on "the facts" assumes the intrication of two codes, between which, as in (3) *b.*, it is impossible to decide: 1. the law, scientific deontology, subjugates the scientist, the observer of *fact*; the opposition fact/rumor is an old mythic theme; invoked in a fiction (and invoked emphatically, by a word in italics), the *fact* has as its structural function (for the real bearing of this artifice fools no one) to authenticate the story, not to make the reader believe it really happened, but to pursue the discourse of the real, and not that of fable. *Fact* is then caught up in a paradigm in which it is opposed to *mystification* (Poe admitted in a letter that the story of M. Valdemar was a pure mystification: *it is a mere hoax*). The code which structures the reference to fact is then the scientific code we are already familiar with; 2. however, any more or less ceremonial recourse to Fact can also be regarded as the symptom of the subject's difficulties with the symbolic; to argue aggressively in favor of "Facts alone," to insist on the triumph of the referent, is to cast suspicion on signification, to mutilate reality's symbolic supplement. It is an act of censorship against the signifier which *displaces* fact, it is a rejection of the *other scene*, that of the unconscious. By rejecting the symbolic supplement, the narrator assumes an imaginary role, that of the scientist (even if he does so, in our eyes, by a narrative trick); the lexia's signified is then the *asymbolism* of the subject of the utterance: *I* passes itself off as asymbolic; the denial of the symbolic obviously belongs to the symbolic code itself.

*b.*   The actional sequence "to hide" develops: the third term expresses the necessity of correcting the distortion noted in (4) *b.*; this correction is equivalent to: *wanting to disclose* (what was hidden). This narrative sequence "to hide" obviously constitutes an excitation for the narrative; in a sense, it justifies the narrative, and thereby emphasizes its *value* (its *value-for*), making it into a commodity: I tell the story, says the narrator, *in exchange* for an insistence on a counter-distortion, for truth (we are in a civilization where truth is a value, *i.e.*, a commodity). It is always interesting to try to identify a narrative's *value-for*: in exchange for what is the story told? In the *Arabian Nights*, each story is worth one day's survival. Here we are warned that the story of M. Valdemar *has the value of* truth (presented first as a counter-distortion).

*c.*   The *I* appears explicitly in the French for the first time—it was already present in the *we* of "our endeavors" (3). The utterance includes, in fact, three *I*'s, *i.e.*, three imaginary roles (to say *I* is to enter the image-repertoire): 1. a narrator-*I*, an artist, whose motive is the search for effect; to this *I* corresponds a *you* which is that of the literary reader, the one who reads "a fantastic tale by the great writer Edgar Allan Poe"; 2. a witness-*I*, who is empowered to bear witness concerning a scientific experiment; the corresponding *you* is that of a jury of scientists, of serious public opinion, of the scientific reader; 3. an actor-*I*, the experimenter who will magnetize Valdemar; here the *you* is Valdemar himself; in these last two cases, the motive of the imaginary role is the "truth." We have here the three terms of a code which we shall call, temporarily perhaps, the code of *communication*. Among these three roles there is doubtless another language, that of the unconscious, which is uttered neither *in* science, nor *in* literature; but this language, which is literally the language of *interdiction*, does not say *I*: our grammar, with its three persons, is never directly that of the unconscious.

(6)   *They are, succinctly, these:*
    *a.*   To announce *what follows* derives from the metalanguage (and from the rhetorical code); it is the signpost marking the start of a story within the story.
    *b.*   *Succinctly* involves three mixed and undecidable connotations: 1. "Don't worry, this won't take too long": in the narrative code, this is the *phatic* mode (identified by Jakobson), whose function is to attract attention, to maintain contact; 2. "This will be short because I shall keep to the facts"; this is the scientific code, which permits expressing the scientist's "asceticism," the superiority of the factual instance over that of discourse; 3. to pride oneself on speaking briefly is, in a sense, to lay a claim against speech, to limit the *supplement* of discourse, *i.e.*, the symbolic; it is to speak the code of the asymbolic.

(7)   *My attention, for the last three years, had been repeatedly drawn to the subject of Mesmerism;*

*a.* In any narrative, the *chronological code* must be closely observed; here, in this code ("the last three years"), two values are
combined; the first is naïve, as it were; we note one of the temporal
elements of the experiment which is to be conducted: the time of
its preparation; the second has no diegetic, operational function
(as is shown by the commutation test; if the narrator had said *seven
years* instead of *three*, this would have had no effect on the story);
hence this is altogether a matter of what we have called *effet de
réel*: the number rhetorically connotes the truth of *fact*: what is
*precise* is reputedly *real* (an illusion, moreover, since there exists a
well-known delirium of figures). We note that linguistically the
word *last* is a "shifter": it refers to the situation of the speaker in
time; it therefore reinforces the *presence* of the testimony to follow.

*b.* Here begins a long actional sequence, or at least a sequence
rich in terms; its objects is the starting-up of an experiment (we
are under the alibi of experimental science); this starting-up, structurally, is not the experiment itself; it is an experimental *program*.
This sequence stands in fact for the *formulation* of the enigma, which
has already been posited several times over ("there is an enigma"),
but which has not yet been formulated. In order not to burden the
account of the analysis, we shall code the "Program" separately,
granting that the entire sequence, by proxy, stands for a term of
the code of the Enigma. In this "Program" sequence, we have here
the first term: positing of the scientific field of the experiment,
magnetism.

*c.* The reference to magnetism is taken from a cultural code,
one very insistent in this part of the nineteenth century. Following
Mesmer (in English, "magnetism" can be called "Mesmerism") and
the Marquis Armand de Puységur, who had discovered that magnetism could induce somnambulism, the number of magnetizers and
magnetism societies had increased in France (around 1820); in
1829, a painless excision of a tumor could be effected under hypnosis; in 1845, the year of our tale, Braid, in Manchester, codified
hypnotism by inducing nervous fatigue by contemplation of a shiny
object; in 1850, at the Mesmeric Hospital in Calcutta, painless

childbirth was achieved. We know that Charcot subsequently classified hypnotic states and related hypnosis to hysteria (1882), but
that subsequently hysteria vanished as a clinical entity from our
hospitals (from the moment it was no longer observed). The year
1845 marks the peak of scientific illusion: a physiological reality of
hypnosis was acknowledged (though Poe, adducing Valdemar's
"nervousness," may suggest the subject's hysterical predisposition).

d. Thematically, magnetism connotes (at least in this period)
a notion of *fluid*: there is a *passage* of something from one subject
to another; there is an inter-diction (an interdiction) between the
narrator and Valdemar: this is the code of communication.

(8)   *and, about nine months ago, it occurred to me, quite suddenly,
that in the series of experiments made hitherto,*

a.   The chronological code (*nine months*) calls for the same observations as those made in (7) *a.*

b.   Here is the second term of the "Program" sequence: a realm
has been selected in (7) *b.*, magnetism; it is now segmented; a
specific problem will be isolated.

(9)   *there had been a very remarkable and most unaccountable omission:*

a.   The structure of the "Program" continues to be articulated:
here is the third term: the experiment which has not yet been
performed—and hence, for any scientist concerned with research,
which must be performed.

b.   This experimental gap is not a simple "omission," or at least
this omission is highly significant: it is quite simply the omission
of Death; there has been a taboo (which will be lifted, in the deepest
horror); the connotation belongs to the symbolic code.

(10)   *—no person had as yet been mesmerized* in articulo mortis.

a.   Fourth term of the "Program" sequence: the contents of the
gap (there is obviously a falling off in the relation between the

assertion of the gap and its definition in the rhetorical code: to announce/to specify).

*b.* Latin (*in articulo mortis*), a juridical and medical language, produces an effect of scientificity (scientific code), but also, by means of a euphemism (saying in a little-known language something one dares not say in ordinary language), designates a taboo (symbolic code). It seems clear that, in Death, what is essentially taboo is the passage, the threshold, "dying" itself; life and death are relatively classified states, they enter, moreover, into a paradigmatic opposition, they are accommodated by meaning, which always pacifies; but the transition between the two states, or more exactly, as will be the case here, their *encroachment*, balks meaning, engenders horror: an antithesis, a classification is transgressed.

**(11)** *It remained to be seen,*

The detail of the "program" is announced (rhetorical code and "Program" actional sequence).

**(12)** *first, whether in such condition, there existed in the patient any susceptibility to the magnetic influence;*

*a.* In the "Program" sequence, this is the first coining of the announcement made in (11): a first problem to be elucidated.

*b.* This Problem I itself titles an organized sequence (or a subsequence of the "Program"); here we have its first term: the formulation of the problem; its object is the very *being* of magnetic communication: does it exist, yes or no? (The affirmative answer will be given in (78): the great textual distance which separates the question from its answer is specific to narrative structure: it authorizes and even obliges the careful construction of the sequences, each one of which is a thread braided into the neighboring ones.)

**(13)** *secondly, whether, if any existed, it was impaired or increased by the condition;*

*a.* In the "Program" sequence, the second problem takes its place here (it will be noted that Problem II is linked to Problem I by an implicative logic: *if yes . . ., then*; if no, the whole story would collapse; hence the alternative, *according to the instance of the discourse*, is rigged).

*b.* Second subsequence of "Program": this is Problem II: the first problem concerned the being of the phenomenon; the second concerns its *measurement* (all this is quite "scientific"); the answer to the question will be given in (82); receptivity is increased: *In such experiments with this patient, I had never perfectly succeeded before . . . but to my astonishment . . .*

**(14)** *thirdly, to what extent, or for how long a period, the encroachments of Death might be arrested by the process.*

*a.* This is Problem III posited by the "Program."

*b.* This Problem III is, like the others, formulated—this formulation will be emphatically repeated in (17); the formulation implies two subquestions: 1. how far does hypnosis permit life to encroach upon death? The answer is given in (110): *up to and including language*; 2. for how long? To this question there will be no direct answer given: the encroachment of life upon death (the survival of the hypnotized corpse) will cease after seven months, but it will be by the arbitrary intervention of the experimenter. Hence we may assume: to infinity, or at least indefinitely within the limits of observation.

**(15)** *There were other points to be ascertained,*

The "Program" mentions other problems possible to raise apropos of the experiment envisaged, in a general form. The sentence is equivalent to *et cetera*. Valéry once said that in nature there was no *et cetera*; we may add: nor in the unconscious. As a matter of fact, the *et cetera* belongs only to *faked* discourse: on the one hand, it seems to play the scientific game of the great program of experimentation, it is an operator of the pseudo-real; on the other, by dodging the other problems, it reinforces the meaning of the questions already articulated: the strong symbolic has been uttered, the rest is, under the instance of the discourse, no more than a pretense.

**(16)**   *but these most excited my curiosity,*
   In the "Program," there is a question of a general recall of the three problems (the "recall" or the "résumé," like the "announcement," are terms of the rhetorical code).

**(17)**   *—the last in especial, from the immensely important character of its consequences.*
   *a.*   An emphasis (term of the rhetorical code) is given to Problem III.
   *b.*   Again two undecidable codes: 1. scientifically, the stake is the retreat of a biological datum, death; 2. symbolically, it is the transgression of meaning which sets Life in opposition to Death.

## ACTIONAL ANALYSIS OF LEXIAS 18 TO 102

Among all the connotations we have encountered, or at least identified, in this first part of Poe's tale, some could be defined as the gradual terms of sequences of narrative actions; we shall return in conclusion to the different codes which have been brought to light by the analysis, including precisely the actional code. Until we have this theoretical explanation, we can isolate these sequences of actions and make use of them in order to account with less difficulty (yet keeping a structural bearing in our enterprise) for the sequence of the story. In effect, it will be understood, it is not possible to analyze minutely (and even less, exhaustively: textual analysis is never, and never attempts to be, exhaustive) Poe's entire tale: it would take too long; we intend however to take up the textual analysis again with regard to several lexias at the work's culminating point (lexias 103–110). To join the fragment we have analyzed to the one we shall analyze, *on the level of intelligibility*, it will suffice to indicate the main actional sequences which begin and develop (but do not necessarily conclude) between lexia 18 and lexia 102. We cannot, for lack of space, give Poe's text which separates our two fragments, nor the numeration of the intervening lexias; we give only the actional sequences (moreover without even being able to note their details term by term), to the detriment of other codes, which are more numerous and certainly more interesting, essentially because these sequences constitute, by definition, the *anecdotic* armature of the story (I shall make a slight exception for the chronological code, indicating, by an initial or final notation, the moment of the narrative where the outset of each sequence is located).

I.   *Program:* the sequence has begun and been largely developed in the fragment analyzed. The problems raised by the projected experiment are known. The sequence continues and closes with the choice of the subject (of the patient) necessary to the experiment: this will be M. Valdemar (the positing of the program is located nine months before the moment of the narration).

II.   *Magnetization* (or rather, if this clumsy neologism may be indulged: magnetizability). Before selecting M. Valdemar for the subject of the experiment, P. has tested his magnetic receptibility; it exists, but the results are nonetheless disappointing: M. Valdemar's obedience involves resistance. The sequence lists the terms of this test, anterior to the decision to conduct the experiment and of which the chronological situation is not specified.

III.   *Medical death:* the actional sequences are generally extended, intertwined with other sequences. By informing us of M. Valdemar's poor health and the fatal prognosis offered by the doctors, the narrative commences a very long sequence which runs throughout the story and ends only with the final lexia (150), with the liquefaction of M. Valdemar's corpse. Its episodes are numerous, interrupted, yet *scientifically* logical: poor health, diagnosis, death sentence, deterioration, agony, mortification (physiological signs of death)—it is at this moment in the sequence that our second textual analysis will be placed—disintegration, liquefaction.

IV. *Contract:* P. offers to hypnotize M. Valdemar when he reaches the threshold of death (since he knows he is doomed) and M. Valdemar agrees; there is a contract between the subject and the experimenter: conditions, proposition, acceptance, agreements, decision to perform the experiment, official record in the presence of doctors (this last point constituted as a subsequence).

V. *Catalepsy* (seven months before the moment of narration, a Saturday at 7:55): M. Valdemar's last moments having come, and the experimenter having been informed by the patient himself, P. begins the hypnosis *in articulo mortis*, according to the Program and the Contract. This sequence can be entitled *Catalepsy*; it includes, among other terms: magnetic passes, the subject's resistance, signs of a cataleptic state, verification by the experimenter, verification by the doctors (the actions of this sequence occupy three hours: it is 10:55).

VI. *Interrogation I* (Sunday, 3 A.M.): P. interrogates M. Valdemar under hypnosis on four occasions; it is pertinent to identify each interrogative sequence by the answer given by the hypnotized subject. To the first interrogation, the answer is: *Yes—asleep now* (the interrogative sequences canonically include the announcement of the question, the question, the delay or the resistance to answer, and the answer).

VII. *Interrogation II:* this interrogation follows shortly after the first. M. Valdemar then answers: *I am dying.*

VIII. *Interrogation III:* the experimenter again interrogates the dying and hypnotized M. Valdemar (*do you still sleep?*); the latter answers by linking the first two answers he has already made: *still asleep—dying.*

IX.  *Interrogation IV*: P. attempts to interrogate M. Valdemar a
fourth time; he renews his question (M. Valdemar will answer
starting with lexia 105, cf. below).

We then come to the point of the narrative where we shall resume
the textual analysis, lexia by lexia. Between *Interrogation III* and
the beginning of the following analysis intervenes an important
term of the sequence *"medical death"*: this is the mortification of
M. Valdemar (101–102). M. Valdemar, under hypnosis, is henceforth *dead*, medically speaking. We know that recently, on the
occasion of organ transplants, the diagnosis of death has been called
into question: today the testimony of electroencephalography is
required. In order to attest the death of M. Valdemar, P. collects
(in 101 and 102) all the clinical signs which scientifically attested
the death of a patient in his period: eyes revulsed, cadaverous skin,
extinction of hectic spots, loosening of the jaw, black tongue,
general hideousness which compels the retreat of those present away
from the bed (once again we may take note of the braiding of the
codes: all these medical signs are also elements of horror; or rather,
horror is always given under the alibi of science: the scientific code
and the symbolic code are actualized at the same time, in an undecidable fashion).

Once M. Valdemar is medically dead, the narrative must conclude: the death of the hero (except in the case of religious resurrection) ends the story. The revival of the anecdote (starting with
lexia 103) therefore appears at once as a narrative *necessity* (for the
text to continue) and a logical *scandal*. This scandal is that of the
*supplement*: for there to be a supplement of the narrative, there
must be a supplement of life: once again, the narrative is *equivalent
to* life.

## TEXTUAL ANALYSIS OF LEXIAS 103 TO 110

**(103)**  *I now feel that I have reached a point of this narrative at which every reader will be startled into positive disbelief. It is my business, however, simply to proceed.*

*a.*   We know that the announcement of a discourse to come is a term of the rhetorical code (and of the metalinguistic code); we also know the "aperitive" value of this connotation.

*b.*   *Business* to proceed with the facts, without concern for the unpleasantness of the circumstance, belongs to the code of scientific deontology.

*c.*   The promise of an incredible "reality" belongs to the field of the narrative considered as a commodity; this raises the "price" of the narrative; hence we have here, in the general code of communication, a subcode, that of exchange, of which every narrative is a term, cf. (5) *b.*

**(104)**  *There was no longer the faintest sign of vitality in M. Valdemar; and concluding him to be dead, we were considering him to the charge of the nurses,*

In the long sequence of "Medical death" we have pointed out, mortification was noted in (101): it is here *confirmed*; in (101), M. Valdemar's state of death was described (throughout a range of indications); it is here asserted by means of a metalanguage.

**(105)**  *when a strong vibratory motion was observable in the tongue. This continued for perhaps a minute. At the expiration of this period,*

*a.*   The chronologic code ("a minute") sustains two effects: an effect of reality-precision—cf. (7) *a.*—and a dramatic effect: the laborious raising of the voice, the birth of the cry recalls the combat of life and death: life tries to release itself from the snares of death, it struggles (or rather here it is death which cannot manage to release itself from life: let us not forget that M. Valdemar *is dead:* he does not have to retain life, but to retain death).

*b.*   Shortly before the moment we have reached, P. has interrogated (for the fourth time) M. Valdemar; and before he answers,
he is clinically dead. Yet the sequence *Interrogation IV* is not closed
(it is here that the *supplement* we mentioned intervenes): the movement of the tongue indicates that M. Valdemar *is going to speak.*
Hence we must construct the sequence thus: *question* (100)/(*medical
death*)/*effort to answer* (the sequence will continue).

*c.*   There is apparently a symbolism of the tongue. The tongue
is speech (to sever the tongue is to mutilate language, as we see in
the symbolic ceremony of the punishment of blasphemers); further,
the tongue has something visceral (internal) about it, and at the
same time something phallic. This general symbolism is here reinforced by the fact that the tongue in motion is in (paradigmatic)
opposition to the tongue black and swollen by medical death (101).
Hence it is visceral life which is identified with speech, and speech
itself is fetishized in the form of a phallic organ that begins vibrating,
in a sort of pre-orgasm: the vibration continuing for perhaps a
minute is the desire for orgasm and the desire for speech: it is the
movement of Desire *to come to something.*

(106)   *there issued from the distended and motionless jaws a voice—*

*a.*   The sequence *Interrogation IV* gradually continues, with extended elaboration of the general term "Answer." Of course the
delays in answering are familiar to the grammar of Narrative; but
they generally have a psychological value; here, the delay (and the
detail it involves) is purely physiological: it is the rising of the
voice, filmed and recorded in slow motion.

*b.*   The voice comes from the tongue (105), the jaws are merely
gates; it does not come from the teeth: the voice preparing itself is
not dental, external, civilized (the emphatic dentalism of a pronunciation is a sign of "distinction"), but internal, visceral, muscular. Culture valorizes the distinct, the bony, the clear (the teeth);
the dead man's voice arises from the sticky, from the internal muscular magma, from the *depths.* Structurally, we have here a term
of the symbolic code.

(107)  *such as it would be madness in me to attempt describing. There
are, indeed, two or three epithets which might be considered as applicable
to it in part; I might say, for example, that the sound was harsh, and
broken, and hollow; but the hideous whole is indescribable, for the
simple reason that no similar sounds have ever jarred upon the ear of
humanity.*

a.  The metalinguistic code is present here, as a discourse on
the difficulty of conducting a discourse; whence the use of frankly
metalinguistic terms: *epithets, indescribable.*

b.  The symbolism of the Voice unfolds: it has two characteristics: the internal (*hollow*) and the discontinuous (*harsh, broken*):
this prepares a logical contradiction (guarantee of the supernatural):
the contrast between the *broken* and the *glutinous* (108), though
the internal accredits a sensation of distance (108).

(108)  *There were two particulars, nevertheless, which I thought then,
and still think, might fairly be stated as characteristic of the intonation—
as well adapted to convey some idea of its unearthly peculiarity. In the
first place, the voice seemed to reach our ears—at least mine—from a
vast distance, or from some deep cavern within the earth. In the second
place, it impressed me (I fear, indeed, that it will be impossible to make
myself comprehended) as gelatinous or glutinous matters impress the sense
of touch.*

*I have spoken both of "sound" and of "voice." I mean to say that
the sound was one of distinct—of even wonderfully, thrillingly distinct—
syllabification.*

a.  We have here several terms of the metalinguistic (rhetorical)
code: the announcement (*two characteristics*), the résumé (*I have
spoken*) and the oratorical precaution (*I fear that it will be impossible
to make myself comprehended*).

b.  The symbolic field of the Voice extends, by the repetition
of the *approximations* of lexia (107): 1. the *distant* (absolute distance): the voice is distant *because/so that* the distance between
Death and Life is (might be) total (the *because* implies a motive
which belongs to reality, to what is "behind" the paper; the *so that*

refers to the demand of the discourse which seeks to continue, to survive as discourse; by noting *because/so that*, we accept the alternation of the two instances, that of reality and that of discourse, we attest the structural duplicity of all writing). The distance (between Life and Death) is affirmed *the better to be denied*: it permits the transgression, the "encroachment" whose description is the very object of the tale; 2. the *subterranean*: the thematics of the Voice is generally double, contradictory: sometimes it is the light thing, the bird-thing which flies away with life, sometimes it is the heavy, cavernous thing which comes from below: this is the voice attached and anchored like a stone; this is an old mythic theme: the chthonic voice, the voice from beyond the grave (as is the case here); 3. the discontinuous establishes language; hence there is a supernatural effect in hearing a gelatinous, glutinous language; the notation has a double value: on the one hand, it underlines the *strangeness* of this language which is contrary to the very structure of language; and on the other, it lists the difficulties, the dysphorias: the broken and the sticky (cf. the suppuration of the eyelids at the moment the dead man is aroused from the hypnotic trance, *i.e.* as he enters into actual death (133); 4. the *distinct syllabification* constitutes the imminent speech of the dead man as a full, complete, adult language, as an essence of language, and not as a stammered, approximative language, a minor language clogged by non-language; whence the terror and the effect of dread: there is a gaping contradiction between Death and Language; the contrary of Life here is not Death (which is a stereotype), it is Language: it is undecidable if M. Valdemar is living or dead; what is certain is that he is speaking, without our being able to relate his speech to Death or to Life.

c. We may note one artifice which belongs to the chronological code: *I thought then and still think*: here we have a copresence of three temporalities: the time of history, of diegesis (*I thought then*), the time of writing (*I still think*), the time of reading (swept on by the present tense of the writing, we think so ourselves at the moment we read). The whole produces an *effet de réel*.

**(109)** M. Valdemar spoke—*obviously in reply to the question I had propounded to him a few minutes before. I had asked him, it will be remembered, if he still slept.*

　　*a.* Interrogation IV is still under way: the question is here recalled (cf. 100), the answer is announced.

　　*b.* The speech of the hypnotized dead man is the very answer to Problem III, posed in (14): *to what extent or for how long can hypnosis halt death?* The answer is here given to this problem: *to the point of language.*

**(110)** *He now said: "Yes; —no; —I have been sleeping—and now— now—I am dead."*

From the structural point of view, this lexia is simple: it is the term "answer" ("I am dead") of *Interrogation IV*. Yet, outside of the diegetic structure (presence of the lexia in an actional sequence), the connotation of the phrase (*I am dead*) is of an inexhaustible richness. Of course there exist any number of mythic narratives in which the dead speak; but it is to say: "I am alive." There is here a true *hapax* of narrative grammar, a staging of *speech impossible as speech: I am dead.* Let us attempt to unfold a few of these conno-tations:

　　1.　We have already determined the theme of *encroachment* (of Life upon Death); encroachment is a paradigmatic disturbance, a disturbance of meaning; in the paradigm *Life/Death*, the slash is normally read "against" (*versus*); it would suffice to read it as "upon" for the encroachment to appear and the paradigm to be destroyed; this is what happens here; there is an undue erosion of one space by another. What is interesting is that the encroachment occurs here on the level of language. The notion that the dead man can continue to act once he is dead is commonplace enough; it is what is expressed by the folk saying: "the dead takes the living"; it is what the great myths of remorse or posthumous vengeance express; it is what is comically expressed by Forneret's crack: "Death teaches the incorrigible how to live"; but here the dead man's action is a pure action of language and, to top it off, this language is of no purpose, it does not come with a view to an action on the living, it says nothing but itself, it designates itself tautologically; before saying "I am dead," the voice simply says "I am speaking"; it is something like an example of grammar which refers to nothing but to language; the uselessness of the utterance is part of the scandal: it is a matter of affirming an essence which *is not in its place* (the *displaced* is the very form of the symbolic).

2.   Another scandal of utterance is the return of the metaphor to its literal status. In fact it is banal enough to utter the sentence "I'm dead!"—this is what the woman who has spent the afternoon shopping says to her hairdresser, etc. The reversal of the metaphor to its literal version is impossible, *precisely in the case of this metaphor*: the utterance "I am dead," literally, is foreclosed (whereas "I am sleeping" remained literally possible in the field of hypnotic sleep).

3.   We are also concerned with a scandal of language (and no longer of discourse or utterance). In the ideal total of all the possible utterances of the language, the juxtaposition of the first person (*I*) and of the attribute *"dead"* is precisely the one which is radically impossible: it is the blank, the blind spot of language, which the tale comes to occupy. What is said is nothing but this impossibility: the sentence is not descriptive, not constative: it affords no other message than that of its own utterance: one might say in a sense that it is a performative, but such as neither Austin nor Benveniste had foreseen in their analyses (let us recall that the performative is that mode of utterance according to which the statement refers only to its being made: *I declare war*; performatives are always, perforce, in the first person, otherwise they would slip into the constative; *he declares war*); here, the unwarranted sentence performs an impossibility.

4.   From the strictly semantic point of view, the sentence "I am dead" asserts two contraries at once (Life, Death): it is an enan-

tioseme, but, once again, itself a unique one: the signifier expresses a signified (Death) which is contradictory to its utterance. And yet, we must go still further: this is not a matter of a simple denial, in the psychoanalytic sense, "I am dead" then meaning "I am not dead," but rather of an affirmation-negation: "I am dead and not dead"; this is the paroxysm of transgression, the invention of an unheard-of category: the *true-false*, the *yes-no*; the *death-life* is conceived as an indivisible, incombinable, non-dialectic *whole*, for the antithesis implies no third term; it is not a two-sided entity, but a single and new term.

5.   On "I am dead," a psychoanalytic reflection is still possible. We have said that the sentence achieved a scandalous return to the literal. This means that Death, as a primordial repressed, erupts directly into language; this return is radically traumatic, as is shown later on by the image of explosion (147: *"ejaculations of 'dead! dead!' absolutely* bursting *from the tongue and not from the lips of the sufferer* . . ."): the phrase "I am dead" is an exploded taboo. Now, if the symbolic is the field of neurosis, the return of the literal, which implies the foreclosure of the symbol, opens the space of psychosis: at this point in the story, every symbol ceases, and every neurosis as well; it is psychosis which enters into the text, by the spectacular foreclosure of the signifier: Poe's *extraordinary* is indeed that of madness.

Other commentaries are possible, notably that of Jacques Derrida.[3] I have limited myself to those which can be derived from a structural analysis, attempting to show that the unheard-of sentence "I am dead" is not at all the incredible statement [*énoncé*], but much more radically, the *impossible utterance of that statement* [*énonciation*].

Before proceeding to our methodological conclusions, I shall recall, on a purely anecdotal level, the story's end: Valdemar remains dead under hypnosis for seven months; with the agreement of the doctors, P. then decides to waken him; the passes succeed,

---

[3] *La Voix et le Phénomène*, Paris: PUF, 1983, pp. 60–61.

and a little color returns to Valdemar's cheeks; but, while P. tries to activate the subject's awakening by intensifying the passes, the ejaculations of "Dead! Dead!" explode on his tongue, and all at once his whole body caves in, crumbles away, rots beneath the experimenter's hands, leaving no more than a *"nearly liquid mass of loathsome—of detestable putridity."*

## METHODOLOGICAL CONCLUSIONS

The remarks which will serve as a conclusion to these analytical fragments will not necessarily be "theoretical"; theory is not abstract, speculative: the analysis itself, although bearing on a contingent text, was already theoretical, in the sense that it observed (which was its purpose) a language in the process of formation. Which is to say—or recall—that we have not conducted an explication of the text: we have simply tried to grasp the narrative as it was being constructed (which implies at once structure and movement, system and infinity). Our structuration does not proceed beyond that spontaneously achieved by reading. Hence there is no question, to conclude, of producing the "structure" of Poe's tale, still less that of all narratives, but only of returning, in a freer, less attached way, to the gradual unfolding of the text, to the main codes we have identified.

The word *code* itself should not be understood here in the rigorous, scientific sense of the term. The codes are simply associative fields, a supratextual organization of notations which impose a certain notion of structure; the instance of the code, for us, is essentially cultural: the codes are certain types of already-seen, of already-read, of already-done: the code is the form this *already* takes, constitutive of the writing of the world.

Though all the codes are in fact cultural, there is one, among those we have encountered, which we shall privilege by calling it the *cultural code*: this is the code of knowledge, or rather of human knowledges, of public opinion, of culture as it is transmitted by the book, by teaching and, more generally, by the whole of sociality; this code has for its reference knowledge as the body of rules elaborated by society. We have encouraged several of these cultural codes (or several subcodes of the general cultural code): the scientific code which is supported (in our tale) both on the precepts of experimentation and on the principles of medical deontology; the rhetorical code, which collects all the social rules of *speaking*: encoded forms of narrative, encoded forms of discourse (announcement, résumé, etc.): the metalinguistic utterance (the discourse speaks of itself) belongs to this code; the chronological code: assigning a date, which seems to us quite natural, even objective today, is in fact a very cultural practice—which is to be expected since it implies a certain ideology of time ("historical" time is not the same as "mythic" time): the total of chronological references therefore constitutes a strong cultural code (a historical way of segmenting time for purposes of dramatization, of scientific reliability, for an *effet de réel*); the socio-historical code permits mobilizing within the utterance all the infused knowledge we have of our time, of our society, of our country (the fact of saying M. Valdemar—and not Valdemar—it will be recalled, takes its place here). We must not be troubled by the fact that we can constitute as a code some extremely commonplace notations: on the contrary it is their banality, their apparent insignificance which predispose them to being a code, as we have defined it: a body of rules so worn down that we take them for natural features; but, if the narrative were to depart from them, it would very quickly become *unreadable*.

The code of communication might also be called a code of destination. *Communication* should be understood in a limited sense; it does not cover all the *signification* which is in a text, still less its *signifying process*; it merely designates any relation which, in the text, is uttered as a form of *address* (this is the case of the "phatic" code, responsible for emphasizing the relation between narrator and reader), or as *exchange* (narrative is exchanged for truth, for life). In short, communication should be understood here in an economic sense (communication, circulation of commodities).

The *symbolic* field ("field" here is a looser term than "code") is to be sure very wide; especially since we are here taking the word "symbol" in the most general sense possible, without troubling ourselves over any of its habitual connotations; the meaning to which we are referring is close to that of psychoanalysis: the symbol is, in short, that feature of language which *displaces* the body and affords a "glimpse" of another scene than that of the utterance, as we suppose we are reading it; the symbolic armature, in Poe's tale, is obviously the transgression of the taboo of Death, the disturbance of classification; what Baudelaire has (very well) translated by the *empiétement* (encroachment) of Life upon Death (and not, banally, of Death upon Life); the tale's subtlety derives in part from the fact that the utterance seems to proceed from an *asymbolic* narrator, who has assumed the role of the objective scientist, attached to facts alone, alien to the symbol (which does not fail to return in force within the tale).

What we have called the code of *actions* sustains the anecdotal armature of the narrative; the actions, or the utterances which denote them, are organized into sequences; the sequence has an *approximate* identity (we cannot determine its contour rigorously nor irrefutably); it is justified in two fashions: because we are spontaneously led to give it a generic name (for instance a certain number of notations, poor health, deterioration, agony, mortification of the body, its liquefaction naturally group themselves under a stereotyped notion, that of "Medical Death"), and then because the terms of the actional sequence are linked together among themselves (from one to the next, since they follow each other through the narrative) by an appearance of logic; we mean by this that the logic which institutes the actional sequence is, from a scientific point of view, very impure; it is merely an appearance of logic, which proceeds not from the laws of formal reasoning, but from out habits of reasoning, of observing: it is an endoxal, cultural logic (it appears "logical" to us that a severe diagnosis should follow the determination "bad health"); further, this logic is identified with chronology: what comes *after* seems to us *caused by*. Temporality and causality, although, in the narrative, they are never pure, seem to us to establish a sort of *naturalness*, of intelligibility, of anecdotal legibility: they allow us, for example, to *summarize* the anecdote (as what the ancients called the *argument*, a word at once logical and narrative).

A last code has (from the start) traversed our tale: that of the *Enigma*. We have not had occasion to see it at work, because we have not analyzed more than a very small part of Poe's tale. The code of the Enigma collects the terms by whose linkage (as in a narrative *sentence*) we posit an enigma, and after a few "delays" which constitute the very spice of the narrative, the solution is disclosed. The terms of the enigmatic (or hermeneutic) code are well differentiated; we must distinguish for example the *positing* of the enigma (any notation whose meaning is "there is an enigma") from the *formulation* of the enigma (the question is exposed in its contingency); in our tale, the enigma is posited in the very title (the "truth" is announced, but we do not yet know about what question), formulated from the start (it is the scientific account of the problems linked to the projected experiment), and even, from the start, delayed: every narrative obviously has an interest in de-laying the solution of the enigma it poses, since this solution will signal its own death as a narrative: we have seen that the narrator takes a whole paragraph to delay the exposition of the case, under the pretext of scientific precautions. As for the solution of the enigma, it is not, here, of a mathematical order; it is in short the whole narrative which answers the question raised at the beginning, the question of truth (yet this truth can be condensed into two points: the utterance of "I am dead" and the sudden liquefaction of the corpse at the moment of its awakening from hypnosis); truth here is not the object of a *revelation*, but of a *revulsion*.

Such are the codes which have traversed the fragments we have analyzed. It is quite deliberately that we have not structured them further, that we are not trying to distribute the terms, within each code, according to a logical or semiological schema; this is because, for us, the codes are merely *déjà-lu departures*, initiations of intertexuality: the *frayed* character of the codes is not what contradicts structure (as, apparently, life, imagination, intuition, disorder contradict system, rationality), but is on the contrary (this is the fundamental affirmation of textual analysis) *an integral part of structuration*. It is this *fraying* of the text which distinguishes structure—object of structural analysis proper—from structuration—object of the textual analysis we have attempted to perform here.

The textile metaphor we have just used is not accidental. Textual analysis actually needs to represent the text as a *tissue* (moreover this is its etymological meaning), as a braid of different voices, of many codes, at once interlaced and incomplete. A narrative is not a tabular space, a plane structure, it is a volume, a stereophony (Eisenstein repeatedly insisted on the *counterpoint* of his direction, thus suggesting an identity of film and text): there is a *field of listening* of the written narrative; meaning's mode of presence (except perhaps for the actional sequences) is not a development, but an *explosion*: calls for contact and communication, positing of contracts, exchanges, outbursts of references, gleams of knowledge, dimmer, more penetrating impulses from "the other scene," that of the symbolic, the discontinuity of actions attached to the same sequence, but in a loose manner, ceaselessly interrupted.

All this "volume" is drawn forward (toward the end of the narrative), thereby provoking an impatience of reading, under the effect of two structural arrangements: *a. distortion*: the terms of a sequence or of a code are separated, braided with heterogeneous elements; a sequence seems to be abandoned (for example, the deterioration of Valdemar's health), but it is *continued* later on, sometimes much later on; there is the creation of an expectation; we can even, now, define the sequence: that floating microstructure which constructs not a logical object but an expectation and its resolution; *b. irreversibility*: despite the floating character of structuration, in the classical, readerly narrative (such as Poe's tale), there are two codes which maintain a vectorized order, the actional code (based on a logico-temporal order) and the code of the Enigma (the question is crowned by its solution); an irreversibility of narrative is thereby created. It is obviously on this point that modern subversion will come to bear: the *avant-garde* (to retain a convenient expression) seeks to render the text thoroughly reversible, to expel the logico-temporal residue, to attack *empiricism* (logic of behavior, actional code) and *truth* (code of the Enigma).

Yet we must not exaggerate the distance separating the modern text from the classical narrative. As we have seen, in Poe's tale one and the same sentence frequently refers to two simultaneous codes, without our being able to choose which one is "true" (for example, the scientific code and the symbolic code): the characteristic of narrative, once it achieves the quality of a *text*, is to constrain us to the *undecidability* of the codes. In whose name might we decide? In the author's? But the narrative gives us only a speaker, a performer who is caught up in his own production. Of this school of criticism, or that? All are challengeable, swept away by history (which does not mean that they are useless: each school participates, *but only for one voice*, in the volume of the text). Undecidability is not a weakness, but a structural condition of narration: there is no univocal determination of the utterance: in a statement, several codes, several voices *are there*, without preeminence. Writing is precisely that loss of origin, that loss of "motives" to the gain of a volume of indeterminations (or of overdeterminations): this volume is precisely the *signifying process*. Writing occurs at just the moment when speech ceases, *i.e.*, starting from the moment when we can no longer identify *who is speaking* and when we can establish only that *speaking has begun*.

In *Sémiotique narrative et textuelle* (Larousse), 1973